UNDERSTANDING POLITICS
An A level course companion

Moyra Grant

Stanley Thornes (Publishers) Ltd

First published in 1992 by:
Stanley Thornes (Publishers) Ltd
Old Station Drive
Leckhampton
CHELTENHAM GL53 0DN
England

British Library Cataloguing in Publication Data
Grant, Moyra E.
    Understanding politics: A course companion.
    I. Title
    321.00941

    ISBN 0–7487–1178–3

Typeset by Tech-Set, Gateshead, Tyne & Wear
Printed and bound in Great Britain at Scotprint Ltd, Musselburgh.

Contents

Acknowledgements

The author is grateful to the following organisations for permission to reproduce material:

Guardian News Service Ltd (pp. 50, 67, 118, 121, 153)
Times Newspapers Ltd (p. 80)
The Independent (pp. 81, 102, 161)
The Observer (pp. 156–7)
The Press Council of Great Britain (p. 154)
The Conservative Central Office (p. 122)
The Labour Party (p. 123)
Pan Macmillan (p. 137).

Examination Boards:

University of Cambridge Local Examinations Syndicate
Oxford and Cambridge Schools Examination Board
The Associated Examining Board
University of Oxford Local Examinations Syndicate
Joint Matriculation Board
London Examination Board.

Picture Credits:

The Cabinet Office (p. 106)
Mary Evans Picture Library (p. 119)
Peter Newark's Historical Pictures (pp. 64, 86)
Press Association (p. 64)
Syndication International (p. 136)
Universal Pictorial Press (pp. 39, 151)
United Feature Syndicate, Inc. (p. 190).

1 Studying A Level Politics

> ## KEY POINTS
>
> ▶ The right – and wrong – approaches
>
> ▶ Study skills
> Note-taking
> Hints on factual learning
> Hints on essay and exam techniques
>
> ▶ You and the examiner
>
> ▶ What *not* to do

—— THE RIGHT APPROACH

Take the practical approach: you are not aiming to learn everything there is to know about politics; you are aiming for a good A Level grade. The first is a matter of weighty learning and deep thought; the second is simply a matter of technique. As the examiners say repeatedly, it is seldom lack of knowledge which fails students, but poor application of good knowledge. What you should not be doing is passive reading, parrot-learning and irrelevant regurgitation of facts; the key to success is **active study** which focuses as much on technique as on content.

Study skills

Focus on the exam from start to finish. Read your syllabus carefully and break it down into a list of topics; ensure that your course is covering them fully, and tick them off as you go.

Obtain as many past exam papers as you can – order them directly from the exam board if your teacher cannot supply them. Make sure that you are thoroughly familiar with the *current* 'rubric', i.e. the total time allowed for each paper, the number of sections on each paper, the type and number of questions which you must do etc.

The types of questions may include **essays**, **stimulus response** (questions on and around a passage or piece of data) or **short answers**. Each requires a different technique and different timing; they may be worth different marks and feature in different sections of the exam, and your work schedule should allow for this. The different techniques and timing are simply a matter of frequent practice, but it is clearly not enough just to 'learn a topic'.

If your teacher is not already doing this for you, go through every past paper after each topic that you do, and list every past question on that topic. Go through the list carefully and critically; look at the 'angle' of each question. You will find that there are only four or five angles on every topic.

P. M. and Cabinet

(London Board: A Level Government and Political Studies, Paper 1)

Jan. '87 To what degree has Mrs Thatcher's exercise of Prime Ministerial authority been a break with tradition?

June '87 To what extent is British government becoming presidential?

Jan. '88 'The role of the Prime Minister is what he or she makes of it.' Discuss.

June '88 Which is the better description of the British system of government – 'Cabinet government' or 'Prime Ministerial government'?

Jan. '89 To what extent does Britain still have a system of Cabinet government?

June '89 'Full Cabinet meetings are becoming a mere rubber stamp for decisions made elsewhere.' How far is this true, and why?

Jan. '90 Discuss the view that the Prime Minister is only as powerful as colleagues allow.

Jan.'91 What factors determine the nature of the relationship between the Prime Minister and the Cabinet?

June '91 (a) What are the factors determining the relationship between the Prime Minister and the Cabinet?
(b) To what extent can these factors be controlled by the Prime Minister?

When you come to revise each topic, look for relevant points on key angles as you re-read your material, and re-note that topic under the key headings. This will help to ensure relevance in your essay answers, rather than writing 'all you know about …'.

RELEVANCE IS ALL

Examiners' comments from subject reports

◀ **London 1988**

GOOD, honest competence characterised the quality of work submitted for this paper, with few really weak candidates but also a limited number of outstanding answers. Many candidates displayed up-to-date political knowledge but too many candidates were dependent on 'current affairs' information, offering too little depth in their answers. As usual, the main weaknesses were a failure to read and accurately interpret the questions, and time wasted on irrelevancies and repetition. Too many candidates still seem unable to integrate political concepts with political institutions. The principal regional differences of Scotland, Wales and Northern Ireland is an area of the syllabus which appears to cause some difficulty, as also is order and disorder. The overall standard of candidates' approaches to the questions improved significantly again this year, although the importance of including examples to gain extra credit in Question 1 still needs to be stressed.

THIS year's candidates excelled in the quality of their performance with the proportions of those passing and those gaining a high grade increasing substantially. Examiners were pleased to see contemporary examples integrated into critical discussions which answered the questions set in a comprehensive and effective manner.

Those whose performance fell below this high level should note the following points:

(a) The rubric must be obeyed. Questions divided into two parts must be answered in two parts which are clearly identifiable. The instruction on the paper says two questions are to be attempted from a section, therefore candidates will penalise themselves if they attempt one or three!

(b) Restrict answers to the precise demands of the question and show how the points in the answer provide an effective response to the question set. (For example, Paper 1, Question 10 was seeking the limitations on Prime Ministerial power, not a detailed recitation of the powers themselves.)

(c) Candidates do not gain marks it examiners cannot read their answers. Very small handwriting or very untidy answers written in pale blue may mean that candidates are penalising themselves. The wise candidates are those who write clearly and as neatly as possible, who use black ink and who leave one or two lines between each paragraph.

It is very pleasing to report that this year's candi[...]
They were obviously making good use of [...]
well briefed on current affairs and especially on [...]
provided by the Politics Association, had [...]
Studies Review and The Economist [...]
newspapers such as The Observer [...]

◀ **AEB 1988**

Oxford and Cambridge 1985 ▶

THE overall impression of this year's entry is a favourable one. If anything the general standard was higher than in previous years and the recent improvement in answers to questions in Section A was sustained. Common and traditional faults, however were again frequently in evidence and prevented many candidates from deploying their often considerable knowledge of the subject to maximum effect.

It is frequently the case that, in answering questions, candidates take too much for granted. Answers to Q.2, for example, were sometimes seriously weakened by a failure to define an interest group. Similarly, it is difficult to argue rigorously and coherently about the role of an M.P. (Q.6) without explicit consideration of the distinction between a delegate and a representative. Again a full and critical discussion of Q.9(b) on the democratic credentials of the concept of democracy. Its meaning ought not to be assumed, since so much hinges on it. An argument, for example, which is informed by a concept of totalitarian democracy will be very different from one which is informed by a concept of liberal or constitutional democracy.

One very obvious and wholly predictable fault is the failure of candidates to focus clearly and consistently on the specific issue raised by a question. Ideally that issue should structure the argument from beginning to end. Often candidates either raise the issue immediately only to lose sight of it within the first page of the answer or greatly delay its introduction. In either case the argument inevitably loses much of its impact. This fault was evident, for example, in many answers to Q.11(a) on the relation between the Bourgeoisie and Proletariat. A general summary of Marx's thought, however competently [...] could not be regarded as an adequate response to the question. [...] [...] well informed answers to Q.9(b) allowed the specific issue of [...] [...]come submerged in a general discussion of the problem of [...] [...]e neglect of the question is partial rather than total, as [...]wers to Q.11(b) on the state as capitalist machine [...]g phrase 'no matter what its form'.

Cambridge 1987 ◀

THERE were some outstanding answers on this paper. However, more often than in previous years, many candidates seemed to be relying on question-spotting and prepared answers. This was reflected in lower marks on some questions where good but irrelevant material was included and little, if any attempt, made to adapt material to the question as asked. This was particularly clear in answers to three questions: on Cabinet government; on the two/three/multi-party system in Britain; and on local government. Conversely, two questions which required thought elicited some interesting and thoughtful answers: those concerned, firstly, the relative powers of resistance to central government enjoyed by local government and Parliament and, secondly, the contribution of civil servants, backbenchers, and judges to the law-making process. Overall the standard was pleasing and this was also reflected in some good performances by S-level candidates. The fact that the examination took place on the day of the election did not seem to have unduly influenced candidates – with the exception of those who had presumably made a case study of the campaign and wished to employ this material even when it was irrelevant.

Note-taking

Do take **brill** notes throughout your course, from your reading and class discussions. Brill notes are:

Brief;
Relevant;
Itemised and well-organised;
Laid-out clearly;
Legible.

> Do not note as you read.
> Read a whole section first;
> re-read and mark key points;
> then note them in 'potted' form.

Organise your notes in ringbinder files with section dividers.

Bad notes

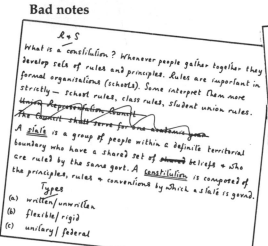

Good notes

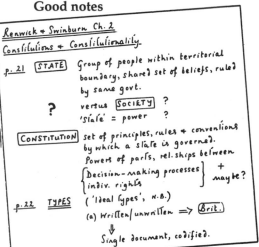

Ten hints on factual learning

1) Write your own revision 'quizzes' on key definitions, events, dates, issues, examples, quotes and names.
2) Write lists – quotes on the left and names on the right, or events on the left and dates on the right etc. – so that you can cover one side with a sheet of paper and reveal the answer once you have tested yourself.
3) Write lists and stick them on mirrors.
4) Photocopy sheets of information with blanked out sections for self-testing on names, dates and examples.

5) Keep a box file of small index cards with key concepts and definitions to revise on the bus or in the bath (don't drop them!).
6) Draw picture diagrams showing 'factors influencing …' (e.g. policy-making) or 'methods used by …' (e.g. pressure groups).
7) Work with a friend doing the same subject and test each other.
8) Make up sentences using the initials of key names as the first letter of each word (the more silly or rude the sentence, the more memorable).
9) Tape key facts and play them back to yourself on your portable stereo Walkperson.
10) Try putting them to music!

Keep a current events diary

- Use a good sized notebook.
- On a daily basis, take brief notes from TV or radio news and documentaries, and from the quality press. Always note the source and date.
- You may want to organise it under topic headings for easy revision: PM/pressure groups/Parliament etc.
- Concentrate on relevant events and issues; if your exam is purely on British politics, skip the foreign news items.
- Include not only key facts, but arguments and opinions, with names and sources.
- Feel free to add your own comments and opinions on events and arguments; it helps you to remember them, it makes your diary more interesting to re-read during revision, and it clarifies your own ideas for essay writing.
- If you include newspaper cuttings, highlight the key points in the margin for easy re-reading and revision; do not just stick them in unmarked (or unread!).
- Do not save all the newspapers up for a week before going through them – it can ruin your Sundays!

24 Jan

- Agric. Min. John MacGregor collapses in Brussels. Will miss big Commons debate (Duodenal ulcer).
- Thousands of miners to be offered shares in privately run pithead power stations in return for no strike agreements.
- IRA disarms & disbands cross-border unit after controversial killings of civilians.
- Freedom Assoc. lost in court action seeking to prevent International Cricket Conf. from imposing bans (up to 5 years) – on players who go to S. Africa.
- Dali dead ☹
- Govt. to guillotine Prev. of Terr. Bill – provides for detention of suspects without trial for up to 7 days. After Eur. Court ruling 4 days max. Hurd announced intention to derogate, allowing Brit. to opt out of court ruling. Still investigating poss. of judicial control instead of derogation.
- Home Office shelves pol. sensitive proposals for reform of parole system, including early release, & shorter sentences.

THE Security Service Bill puts MI5 on a statutory basis for the first time. It gives power to the Home Secretary to issue warrants for 'entry on, or interference with, property' to obtain substantial information for the protection of national security. The Bill also allows for the revues of such warrants by a commissioner and investigation of public complaints by a tribunal.

— YOU AND THE EXAMINER

Writing politics essays

ANSWER THE TITLE, NOT JUST THE TOPIC

The essay question

- <u>Answer the question, the whole question and nothing but the question</u>. This is the most common source of failure among students. Read the question, slowly and carefully, three times. Underline or circle all key words and phrases, e.g.:

To what extent does Britain still
have a <u>system</u> of Cabinet government?

- This question does not ask, 'Write down everything you know about Cabinet'. Unasked-for information will gain no extra marks, however accurate it may be.
- Do not parrot-learn 'model answers', or you may answer the question you wanted to get rather than the one you were asked.
- Practise writing timed essays as much as possible before the exam.
- Learn to assess your own strengths and weaknesses, and make a concentrated effort to eliminate those weaknesses one by one.

The essay plan

- Writing an essay plan may feel unduly time-consuming, but, second only to reading the question carefully, it is the most important part of the whole process.
- Divide the essay up into appropriate sections; this helps to plan the timing of the essay as well as the content. It is especially necessary if the essay title is divided into parts (a) and (b) because the answer *must* be similarly divided. If total marks are shown for each part of a question, obviously use them as a guide to the relative timing and length of each section.
- Write a very brief skeleton outline of the main headings and subheadings for each section; then if necessary rearrange them in logical order – **structure** is as important as **content**.
- Leave spaces to add to the plan as new points come to mind.
- Feel free to question the question – e.g. to point out and discuss ambiguities in the wording or examine critically any assumptions made in the title. If there is more than one possible interpretation of the title, plan to answer all angles.
- If you consult the plan frequently and tick off each point as you go it will help you in writing the essay; and it will also enable the examiner to see what you intended to say if your actual essay is unfinished or goes astray.
- Be sure that you have a clear and explicit conclusion before you start the essay, and structure the essay accordingly. Always put your own case last.
- Head it 'Essay Plan' or 'Rough Work' and put one diagonal line through it when the answer has been completed (it is thus clearly differentiated from the essay, but still legible to the examiner).

Sample essay plan

To what extent does Britain still have a system of Cabinet government?

Intro. ⟶ Cab. govt. – def.... coll. resp....

Hist. ⟶ 'Still' – implies did have: Bagehot.

Case for ⟶ Still now – Jones, St John Stevas; constraints on PM: party, hire/fire (Macmillan), econ., personality, internat. insts., events, need for authority ...

Case agst. ⟶ 'PM govt.': Crossman (changed mind), Mackintosh, Benn, Heseltine ...
Cab. comms (Hennessy 'engine room ...') – '89 transport strikes.
Ad hoc groups ('79 exchange controls).
No. 10 office ... C.S. ... Westland ...
Falklands, GCHQ, Libyan bombing, poll tax, GLC ...

Hist. trend ⟶ { BUT also pre-Thatcher – Attlee quote ... Callaghan/Wilson 'nukes' ...

Not pure Cab. govt. since WW1 (Crossman 3 reasons ... ⇒ 1916/1919).

Even less so in eleven years of 'Thatcherism' ...
BUT resignation 1990; Major – different experience, character ...

Conc. ⟶ Not pure PM govt.: Cab. ⇒ rent controls, no school vouchers.
Depends on PM, circumstances, economy, majority, war/peace ...
'Central exec. territory' – Madgwick. Not dem./accountable ...
Reforms: PM powers in law (Benn), more min. advisers (Kinnock).

The essay

- Waffly introductions are pointless, literally, and give the examiner a bad first impression. A useful way to introduce the essay is to define key terms so learn the precise definitions of political terms and concepts. A 'constitution' is not 'the law of a country'. Imprecise definitions are usually plain wrong; at best they will lose marks, and at worst they will put you off course for the whole essay. Where necessary, give your interpretation(s) of the title in the introduction. It is not logical to give your conclusion in the introduction – reserve it for the end.

Before answering this title we must first consider what is meant by the key concepts in the title, such as Cabinet government, and who actually says we do still have Cabinet government, and who says we don't and why. I would agree with critics that we have Prime Ministerial government.

Cabinet government means policy-making and responsibility by all senior ministers as a collective body, with the Prime Minister *primus inter pares*. The word 'still' in the title implies that Britain used to have Cabinet government, but this is debatable, as we shall see.

- Every paragraph in the essay should refer explicitly to (some part of) the title, using the wording of the title.

- Use structure and language (paragraphs and wording) so that each point is clearly made.

- Think out each sentence before you write it to avoid messy errors or ambiguities.

- Make your point once, clearly, then move on to the next. Avoid repetition which gains no extra marks and wastes valuable time – both yours and the examiner's. A good short answer will gain more marks than a long rambling one.

- Use the correct terminology – 'constitutional monarchy' rather than 'a Queen who can't actually do much', etc. Show that you know your subject.

- Use concrete evidence and examples to illustrate every general point made, so that the examiner knows that you understand what you are saying and have not just parrot-learnt a list of notes. Mere assertion, without factual evidence, gains no marks. Whenever possible, make your examples topical rather than out-dated or hypothetical: this obviously means keeping abreast of current political events.

- Avoid slang, colloquialism and an over-personal approach. (Write 'Public opinion polls indicate that the monarchy is a popular institution' rather than 'I think the Queen is great'.) Style should be **ABCD** – **A**ccurate, **B**rief, **C**lear and **D**irect.

- Consult your essay plan frequently and review your time periodically throughout the essay. Devote an appropriate amount of time to each section of the essay to give a balanced answer. You should always put your own case last and do not leave less time for it than the case you have rejected.

- Write legibly and neatly. The examiner cannot give you credit for something [s]he cannot read, and will not appreciate having to struggle to understand your work (which may be script number 149 on the pile).

- Spell political terms and names correctly. If you are unsure of any, drill them until you are sure. Any student of politics who cannot spell such words as sovereignty, independence, committee, bureaucracy or biased evidently has not done enough reading and does not know the subject.

Spellcheck

acquisition	criticism	Hoskyns
allege	Crosland	ideological
amendment	Crossman	influential
arbitrary	deferential	irrelevant
argument	deterrent	Macmillan
Attlee	dissension	manifesto
Bagehot	eligible	practice (noun)
bankruptcy	Falklands	practise (verb)
Brittan	fulfil	precedent
bourgeois	Gaitskell	privilege
by-election	Gilmour	separation
coercion	Denis Healey	toe the line
consensus	hierarchy	vox populi

- Re-read the title before you write your concluding paragraph. The conclusion must explicitly answer *every part* of the title, using the precise wording of the title, and it should follow logically and predictably from the structure of the essay.

- If you run out of time, give a skeleton answer, i.e. a full and detailed answer, with evidence and conclusion, in note form. Do not write three paragraphs and 'Sorry, ran out of time'; you will probably get three marks. Never omit any questions – remember that no answer at all means no marks at all. A further point to realise is that first marks are easier to earn than last marks, i.e. it is harder to increase the value of an answer from, say, 12 to 15 marks than to earn the first five marks on the next question.

- Finally, always try to allow time to read over your work – often a painful process, but worthwhile. Careless errors like omitting a 'not' can be crucial. And if, in the exam, you do finish early, do not sit staring into space and do not leave early. Instead, use any spare time to re-read your answers.

Common essay formats

'Quote – discuss'

'In recent years real doubts have grown about the adequacy of the British political system to adapt itself to social and economic change.' Discuss.

(JMB, June 1984, P. II.)

'In theory monarchy is indefensible in modern government; in practice no-one has invented a better system.' Discuss.

(Oxford, Summer 1986, P. 1.)

These kind of questions are asking: 'Do you agree with this contentious statement wholly, partially or not at all? Weigh up the arguments and evidence for each side of the case(s), and say in the conclusion which view(s) you support and why'. Evaluation of every part of the title statement, based on sound reasoning and evidence, is required. Note that you can agree with one part of the statement and disagree with another part. If it is a famous quotation, the first sentence of the essay should say who said it. Otherwise it may express a clear political or philosophical viewpoint – e.g. socialist, conservative, anti-PM government, etc. in which case point this out. If the statement is ambiguous, draw attention to this explicitly and say in the introduction, 'I shall consider each interpretation in turn'.

'Should ... ?'

Should party leaders respond more to their parties or to the voters who might support them?

(Oxford, Summer 1989, P. 1.)

Should the courts have greater control over legislation?

(London, January 1989, P. 1.)

This category requires balanced evaluation of both sides of the argument, based on topical evidence, coming down explicitly on one side in the conclusion – yes or no.

'Compare and contrast'

Compare and contrast the roles of chief officers in local government and permanent secretaries in central government.

(AEB, June 1987, P. 1.)

Compare and contrast the contributions of the Commons and Lords to the operation of parliamentary government.

(Cambridge, June 1989, P. 1.)

This category requires direct and explicit comparison of similarities and contrasting of differences throughout the whole essay. Every paragraph (or two paragraphs) should link both items. If you write half of the essay on one, and half of the essay on the other, with no linkage, you will *not* have answered the question, and you will fail outright (no matter how accurate the factual content). The conclusion should say whether, on balance, there are more similarities or contrasts.

'State a case for and a case against'

Some people believe that parliamentary government actually restrains democracy. State the cases for and against this view.

(London, February 1976, P. 1.)

Make a case for the activities of pressure groups, and a case against them.

(London, January 1981, P. 1.)

Answers to this kind of question require **empathy**: the ability to argue either side of a case persuasively. They must be balanced and can be done either point-for-point, for and against in successive paragraphs or all points for, then all points against (or vice-versa) in two separate halves. The conclusion should say whether, on balance, the case for or against is stronger and why. Put your own case last throughout the essay, whichever format you adopt.

'Is Z X or Y?'

Is it the function of the media to reflect public opinion or to form it?

(Oxford and Cambridge, July 1984, P. 0.)

Are senior civil servants too powerful, or are they too pliable?

(London, June 1984, P. 1.)

There are four possible answers:

Z is only X;
Z is only Y;
Z is both X and Y;
Z is neither X nor Y.

You must reach one of these four conclusions. You could point out in the introduction that the title implies either/or, but that this is not necessarily so, i.e. it could be both or neither.

Structure: first, is it X, yes or no … ; then, is it Y, yes or no … ; conclusion.

'Does A lead to B?'

Does nationalism lead to racialism?

(London, June 1978, P. 3.)

Examine the view that freedom consists in the silence of the law.

(Oxford and Cambridge, July 1980, P. 1.)

Consider: A → B; B → A; A alone (leading to factors other than B); B alone (stemming from factors other than A). Conclusion is usually 'Sometimes – not always'.

'If ... then ... ?'/'Since ... then ...'

If the quality of work of departmental select committees is maintained, their influence is bound to increase. Is it?

(Oxford, Summer 1989, P. 1.)

Since one of its consequences is to weaken the link between the *government* and the electorate, a system of proportional representation is less rather than more democratic. Discuss.

(Oxford and Cambridge, July 1986, P. 1.)

Both parts of the title require critical scrutiny.
Structure: first part of the title: case for/against (or vice versa) – conclusion, true or not. Second part: case for/against, and does it follow from first part or not – conclusion, yes or no. In final paragraph, explicitly conclude on both parts of the question, and say whether one does or does not always follow from the other.

'To what extent/how far/how true is it to say ... ?'

'Cabinet meetings are little more than a ritual. Power has moved. The major decisions are now taken elsewhere.' How far is this a fair comment on the modern executive?

(AEB, November 1990, P. 1.)

How true is it to say that voting behaviour in Britain is becoming more volatile?

(JMB, June 1984, P. 1.)

The answer is invariably 'To some extent ...'
Structure: first, outline how far it is the case and why, with evidence ... then, how far it is not the case and why, with evidence ...
Summary conclusion: 'It is true to the extent that ... but not to the extent that ...' Be explicit and concrete.

Keywords in essay titles

In essence, some key words in essay titles seek mere description; others require critical evaluation.

Descriptive	Evaluative
Define	Discuss
Outline	Examine
Describe	Comment on
Explain	Evaluate
Give an account of	Account for
Compare	Compare and contrast
Illustrate	Explore
Enumerate	Analyse
List	Assess
State	Criticise
Summarise	Interpret
	Justify
	Relate
	Review

- Obviously, A Level questions usually seek evaluation rather than mere description; but often they are combined: 'Describe and account for ...', 'Define and discuss ...', 'Explain and comment on ...'
- If you are short of time for your final question in the exam, it might be a good idea to seek out a descriptive title; they tend to be shorter or at least simpler than evaluative titles.
- If you are short of time on any evaluative question, do *not* waste time on a lengthy descriptive introduction. Go straight to the core of the question – arguments and evidence for and against – and give an explicit conclusion to the title asked.
- Some evaluation in answer to a descriptive question will always gain extra credit; mere description in answer to an evaluative question will probably fail.

Examiners are human too

Put yourself in the place of the examiners: try marking your own (or friends') scripts, pretending that you have already marked a couple of hundred, that it is hot and sunny outside, that you still have shopping to do or next term's teaching to prepare and that you are only human! Marks will be awarded if:

- the script is legible;
- it is clear what section of what question you are answering;
- the answer bears some relation to the examiners' marking scheme ('In checking the marking scheme care is taken to ensure that the anticipated answers match the questions and that account has been taken of acceptable different answers. Marks are not allocated to answers which are not relevant to, or required by, a question.' AEB);
- the structure is logical;
- arguments are backed up with evidence;
- facts are relevant and accurate;
- wording is clear and concise;
- the title is explicitly addressed throughout;
- the conclusion answers the question asked.

—— WHAT *NOT* TO DO

Do not:

- Overwork;
- Underwork;
- Parrot-learn;
- Try 'topic-spotting' or 'question-spotting';
- Cheat at patience, e.g. announcing loudly to the family, 'Well, I'm off to do some work now', then retreating to your room to read Jeffrey Archer;
- Try last-minute cramming, or think 'It'll be all right on the day' – it will not, without some help from you.

2 Basic Principles of British Government and Politics

```
┌─────────────────────────────────────────────────────────────┐
│                                                             │
│    KEY ISSUES                                               │
│                                                             │
│    ▶  The concept of 'democracy'                            │
│       'Power' and 'authority'                               │
│       What is 'liberal democracy'?                          │
│       The nature and extent of democracy in Britain         │
│       Pluralist, elitist and Marxist theories               │
│                                                             │
│    ▶  The British constitution: principles and practice     │
│       'Unconstitutional' and 'anti-constitutional' activity │
│       British parliamentary government                       │
│       Parliamentary sovereignty and its limits              │
│       The power of the executive – 'elective dictatorship'? │
│                                                             │
└─────────────────────────────────────────────────────────────┘
```

—— TOPIC NOTES

Key facts and concepts

A **state** is an independent entity with ultimate political power – **sovereignty** – over all the individuals and groups within its territorial boundaries. It is made up of all the formal institutions of political power such as the Crown, legislature, executive, judiciary, army and sometimes the Church. It has a legal monopoly on the use of violence, but will often use **consensus** (agreement) as well as **coercion** (force) to keep order.

The **government** is the agent of the state; it enforces the rulings of the state and acts under its authority. Whereas elements of the state are said to make up a permanent, abstract entity (e.g. the Crown), the people and the institutions of government come and go (e.g. the monarch).

Society is the body of people within and under the power of the state – both individuals and informal power bodies such as pressure groups.

A **nation** is a group of people who share a sense of common culture, based on common ties of, for example, language, religion, race, territory and/or history. One state may embrace many nations (e.g. the Scots, Irish, Welsh and English in the United Kingdom all have a distinct sense of nationhood), or one nation may be spread across many states (e.g. the Jews were a nation without a state until the creation of Israel in 1948).

Like most countries, Britain claims to be a democracy. **Democracy**, from the Greek *demos kratos*, literally means 'people power', or self-government of the people, by the people, for the people. Britain is not, therefore, a **direct democracy** in the full sense of the term. Britain claims to be an **indirect** or **representative democracy**. This involves the election by qualified citizens of representatives who govern over, and on behalf of, the people. All representative democracy therefore entails **oligarchy** or **elitism**: rule by the few.

Nevertheless, all modern states, whatever their type of economic or political system, have some valid claim to call themselves democratic if they contain elements of one or more of the following.

1) **People-power**: e.g. referenda, effective pressure groups, trade unions etc.
2) **Participation**: e.g. through voting, standing for political office, political meetings, demonstrations, etc.
3) **Representation**: This can mean different things:
   (a) The political power holders may carry out the views and *wishes* of the voters. If they act as instructed by the voters they are called **delegates**. This view of representation is associated with the radical French philosopher **Jean-Jacques Rousseau** (1712–78), and applies within many trade unions. It does not apply to British MPs.
   (b) The political power holders may act in what they see as the best *interests* of the voters. This weaker view of representation is associated with the British conservative **Edmund Burke** (1729–97). It may apply to British MPs, but they are also closely tied to their parties.
4) **Consent**: Most modern states – even some dictatorships and military juntas – rest on the general agreement of the people that the governors have the right to govern (even if many people do not agree with what they are doing).

A system of government without this minimum criterion of consent rests solely on **power**: the ability to make people do things by the threat or use of punishment, force or violence. Such a system cannot claim to be democratic. Most political systems, however, rest on a substantial degree of **authority**: the ability to make people do things because they think the power holders have the right. Authority involves legitimate power based on consent, respect and support. It is the basis of any democracy. It may derive from election, but also from tradition, personal popularity (charisma), efficiency, or other sources.

Representative democracies take many forms: one-, two- or multi-party systems etc. Britain, like the United States and most European countries, claims to be a **liberal democracy**. This is a representative system embodying the concepts of diversity, choice and individual rights and freedoms (as opposed to collective equality or mass participation). It involves the following principles.

1) **Pluralism**: Diverse centres of economic and political power; thus private ownership in the economy and two or more parties in the political system, together with many pressure groups. This should generate competition and hence freedom of choice and effective representation of different views and interests.
2) **Limited government**: Checks and constraints on the power of government (e.g. by the courts and pressure groups) to safeguard individual liberties.
3) **Open government**: Non-secretive government, to ensure that government is representative and accountable to the people.
4) **Independent judiciary**: A fair and impartial legal system.

Supporters of Western liberal democracy, such as **Schumpeter** and **Dahl**, argue that any other system is undemocratic. However, many essay questions ask how far the above principles apply in the practice of British government and politics. Critics of the system would point, for example, to:

- The high concentrations of wealth, income and economic power;
- The election of strong, single-party governments with a minority of votes cast;
- The lack of effective opportunities for minority parties and independents in the British electoral system;
- The lack of effective power of many pressure groups, and most individuals, in politics, work, education etc.;
- The lack of balanced debate and discussion about alternative political ideas, e.g. communism, fascism, anarchism;
- The lack of separation of powers in Britain between legislature, executive and judiciary;
- The centralisation of government, and relative weakness of Parliament, Opposition, the courts and local government;
- The exceptional secrecy of British government;

- Alleged injustices in the legal system, ranging from expense of litigation for ordinary citizens to social and political bias;
- The lack of guaranteed civil liberties in law, together with legal constraints on free speech, movement, assembly, protest, etc.;
- The concentration of media ownership and control;
- International constraints and controls – EC, NATO, IMF etc.

The strongest critics of British 'liberal democracy' fall into three main camps.

1) **Radical liberals**, e.g. **Bottomore** and **Hain**, who argue that the system needs substantial reform to make it more liberal and democratic. They advocate for example a written constitution, Bill of Rights, devolution, freedom of information, and the reform of legislation on secrecy, terrorism and police powers.
2) **Classical** or **single elitists**, e.g. **Pareto** and **Mosca** in the 1920s and **Guttsman** today. They argue that all effective political power is concentrated in the hands of a single self-serving elite, comprising: the leaders of the main political parties, the government, MPs and peers, top civil servants, judges, police, church and military leaders, businessmen, academics and scientists and a few key pressure group leaders. Guttsman estimates that the British political elite totals around 11,000 people, all of whom, regardless of party label, share a common interest in

preserving the existing power structure. Single elitists are pessimistic about the prospects for change.

3) **Radical socialists** and **Marxists** such as **Miliband**. They argue that the present power structure and political system serve and protect the interests of a dominant economic class (as opposed to a political elite), while depriving the majority of effective economic or political power. They also apply their critique to all of the major political parties. They believe, however, that fundamental economic and political change will happen, and that minor reforms to the system merely prop it up temporarily.

Short answer questions are a compulsory part of some examinations – for example, on the London Board – and they are a useful revision exercise even if they are not a feature of your particular examination. On the London Board they require around ten minutes' worth of concise, precise, relevant, factual definition, detail and example. They should not be miniature essays. Aim for maximum information in the minimum space; avoid waffle, repetition or messy errors. Think before you write; quality is more important than quantity. Note form is acceptable if it is absolutely clear and comprehensible; but do not use any short forms which you would not find in a book (such as gov., pol., soc., auth.).

Short answers are a valuable aid to essay revision because they help you to learn precise terms, definitions and facts, and to express them briefly and clearly.

Example

Distinguish between *two* different types of democracy.

(London, June 1989, Paper 3, part (a) of qu. (x))

Good answer
In a direct democracy, political decisions are made by all qualified citizens, as in the ancient Greek city-states. However, even there, women and slaves were not allowed to participate; and it is often argued that this system is not feasible in large modern states. Therefore most societies today have a system of indirect or representative democracy, where representatives are elected to govern on behalf of voters. This may be pluralist (e.g. Britain) or single-party (e.g. former USSR), but is inevitably oligarchic or elitist.

Bad answer
Direct democracy is where people do it themselves, whereas with indirect democracy other people do it for them, which isn't really democratic at all.

Bad answer
In direct democracy, everyone votes for everything, like in ancient Greece, though actually women and slaves didn't, so it wasn't really very democratic, and anyway it's not possible in big, complicated societies, whereas in Greece it was only in small cities, so it doesn't really happen now except in some African tribes, and referenda like on the EC in 1975 are a bit like direct democracy. Instead voters vote for representatives to represent them, i.e. indirect, usually in a party system like Britain's two-party system which is called pluralist, or Russia's one-party system which isn't democratic anyway, but anyway only a few people are doing the ruling, which is oligarchy.

---

1. Say why the above examples are good or bad. If you were the examiner, how many marks (out of ten) would you give to each?

Examples of short answers

1) (a) Distinguish between 'power' and 'authority'.

Power is the ability to dictate others' behaviour through sanctions or coercion. Authority is the ability to shape others' behaviour through consent, respect and support, i.e. authority is rightful, legitimate power, and a feature of representative democracy. The German sociologist Max Weber distinguished three types of authority: traditional (e.g. House of Lords), charismatic (e.g. Churchill) and legal/rational (e.g. MPs). Power may exist without authority (tyranny), or authority without much power (e.g. the British monarch). Authority tends to generate power, but power may generate authority through indoctrination. Conversely, misjudgement or misuse of power may lose authority, e.g. Thatcher's downfall in 1990.

(b) What is meant by 'pluralism'?

A pluralist society is one with a diffusion of power among many divergent groups. Political pluralism implies a multi-party system and competing pressure groups, and economic pluralism implies competing centres of ownership and control. Genuine pluralism requires a wide distribution of property and wealth, a distinction between the roles of government, society and individual, and checks and balances between the different sources of power. Many writers, especially Marxists (e.g. Miliband) question the extent to which power in 'liberal democracies' like Britain is really diffused.

---

2. Write short answers to the following questions (simulated examples).

1) (a) Distinguish between 'the state' and 'the government'.
   (b) What is the 'organic' theory of the state?

2) (a) Define the concept of 'a political elite'.
   (b) Explain the theory of single elitism.

3) (a) Distinguish between a delegate and a representative.
   (b) How far may British MPs be described as 'representative'?

4) What is meant by 'pluralist democracy'?

5) (a) What is meant by 'sovereignty'?
   (b) How far can Parliament be said to be sovereign?

The British constitution

A **constitution** is the set of rules and principles by which a state is governed. If a constitution is outlined in a single document it is described as **written**, e.g. the US constitution. The British constitution is described as **unwritten**, because it derives from many different sources.

(a) **Common law**: Ancient, unwritten law, e.g. the powers of the Crown.
(b) **Acts of Parliament (statute law)**: e.g. the Criminal Justice Act 1991.
(c) **Case law (judge-made law)**: Judicial interpretations of common and statute law, e.g. the 'Spycatcher' case 1987.
(d) **EC law** (since 1973): Takes precedence over domestic law.
(e) **Conventions**: Unwritten customs which are traditionally regarded as binding, but which have no legal force, e.g. the practice that the Queen chooses as Prime Minister the leader of the majority party in the House of Commons.

(f) **Historical documents** and **constitutional writings**: e.g. Magna Carta (1215), **Walter Bagehot's** *The English Constitution* (1867) which were not legally binding but merely interpretive.

The British constitution is **flexible**, i.e. it requires no special procedures for amendment, but can be changed by an ordinary Act of Parliament. Thus there is no distinct body of constitutional law. This does not necessarily mean that the constitution is quick or easy to change; some critics (e.g. **Ponton** and **Gill**) argue that the British political system is too static and outdated in many respects. A **rigid** constitution, by contrast, requires a special process for change: e.g. the USA requires two-thirds of Senate and House of Representative votes, plus three-quarters of the state legislatures; and the Australian constitution requires a referendum for major change. A constitution may be written but flexible, e.g. New Zealand.

An action is **unconstitutional** if it breaks any part of the constitution. For example, in 1909 the House of Lords broke the convention that they should not try to change 'money bills'; and in 1983 Thatcher broke a 20-year practice by creating two new hereditary peerages. Whether 20 years was long enough to establish a constitutional constitutional 'convention' is, however, debatable. It is therefore often hard to know what is 'unconstitutional'. Similarly, a rule of the constitution may itself break the 'spirit', if not the letter, of the constitution; e.g. Lord Denning described the Local Government Finance Act 1987 as 'unconstitutional' because it contained clauses preventing the government's policy being challenged in the courts – an apparent breach of 'the rule of law'. The British constitution is, in many ways, uncertain and even unknowable. For this reason, **Alexis de Tocqueville** in the nineteenth century said that Britain had no constitution.

An action is **anti-constitutional** if it aims to destroy the whole constitution, whether to replace it or not. Anarchists would not replace it, whereas the IRA would set up a united, independent Ireland, the neo-Nazi National Front would create a one-party state and the Trotskyist Socialist Workers Party (SWP) would seek a socialist republic. The action itself may be illegal and violent (e.g. IRA bombs), or legal and peaceful (e.g. an SWP meeting). It is the aim – the ultimate overthrow of the whole system – which makes it 'anti-constitutional'.

It might be argued that the Liberal Democrats are anti-constitutional because they seek major reforms: a written constitution and supreme court, a Bill of Rights, devolution, a reformed House of Lords etc.; but they pursue them by constitutional means, such as the ballot box. As they are seeking to improve rather than to overthrow the existing constitution, it would not be accurate to call them anti-constitutional.

Any system of government has three branches:

1) A **legislature**, which makes the laws;
2) An **executive**, which implements the laws and policies;
3) A **judiciary**, which interprets and enforces the laws.

The British System of Government

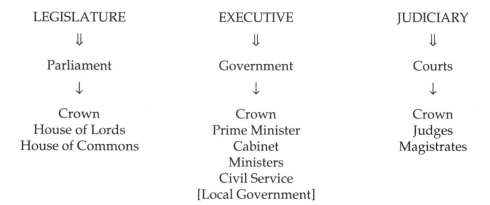

LEGISLATURE	EXECUTIVE	JUDICIARY
⇓	⇓	⇓
Parliament	Government	Courts
↓	↓	↓
Crown	Crown	Crown
House of Lords	Prime Minister	Judges
House of Commons	Cabinet	Magistrates
	Ministers	
	Civil Service	
	[Local Government]	

If the three branches of government are completely united, the system may be a tyranny. Liberal democratic theory advocates the **separation of powers**, to ensure checks and balances between the different parts of the system and hence freedom for the citizen. The United States has a substantial degree of separation between the Congress, the President and the judiciary. Britain, however, does not practise extensive separation of powers.

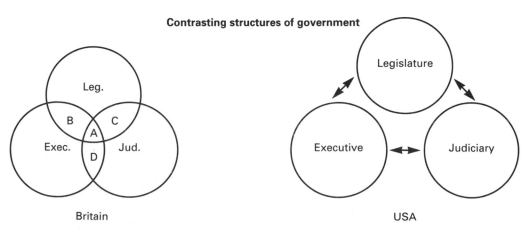

Contrasting structures of government

Britain

USA

3. List the institutions and individuals which are located in the overlapping areas A, B, C and D (above left).

The main overlap in the British system is between the legislature and the executive. The term '**parliamentary government**' refers to this overlap between Parliament and government: the executive is chosen from within the legislature (MPs and peers), and is, in theory, subordinate to the legislature. For example, an important convention of the constitution is that, if a government is defeated in a vote of censure by the House of Commons, it should resign. Government is also **responsible** (i.e. accountable) to Parliament through Question Time in the Commons, debates, votes, committees, and financial security. Thus, through its link with Parliament, and especially with the elected House of Commons, Britain is said to have both **representative** and **responsible government**. Many essay questions ask about these key concepts, and their limits in practice.

The United States and many other countries, by contrast, have a **presidential system**. This does not refer to the fact that they have a President and Britain does not: it means that the executive is separately elected from the legislature, is outside of the legislature and is, in theory, equal to the legislature.

Parliamentary government in Britain

There are said to be two pillars of the British constitution; but both are questionable. One is the **legal sovereignty** or **supremacy of Parliament**. This suggests that Parliament is the supreme law-making body, and that no institution in the country can override its laws. Thus no Parliament can bind its successors – i.e. a future Parliament may amend or repeal any previous statute. Also, Parliament is not bound by its own statutes, but instead by a special body of law known as **parliamentary privilege**. This exempts MPs from much ordinary law, for instance, they cannot be sued for slander for words spoken in Parliament.

However, parliamentary sovereignty is limited in practice by international law and courts, such as the EC Parliament and Court of Justice and the European Court of Human Rights, which may oblige it to change the law; e.g. the Equal Pay Act (EC) and Telecommunications Act (Court of Human Rights). Parliament is also constrained by pressure groups, the City and other economic power bodies, the media, and ultimately by the **political sovereignty of the electorate**, who choose the MPs in the Commons.

Internally, Parliament tends to be dominated by a majority government which, with party discipline and backbench support, can usually ensure that its legislative proposals are passed by Parliament. No majority government has been forced to resign by a vote of no confidence in the House of Commons since 1880.

The exceptions to this balance of power within Parliament are:

(a) A backbench revolt: e.g. the Shops Bill 1986;
(b) Defeat by the House of Lords: e.g. War Crimes Bill 1990;
(c) A minority government: e.g. Labour 1976–9.

The exceptions are quite rare; therefore in his 1976 Dimbleby Lecture, **Lord Hailsham** used the term **'elective dictatorship'** to suggest that a majority government in control of a sovereign Parliament, with a flexible constitution, could effectively change the constitution at will. Critics say that this does not take sufficient account of the practical constraints on parliamentary sovereignty, and hence on a government within Parliament.

The second pillar of the British constitution according to **Dicey** in 1885 – is **'the rule of law'**. Again, this is an ideal principle which is often breached in practice (see page 23).

Short answers

What is meant by sovereignty?

Sovereignty resides in that body which has supreme decision-making power. It also implies authority, i.e. consent and legitimacy. The state has sovereignty over all individuals and groups within its boundaries. In Britain, Parliament is said to have legal sovereignty, i.e. it can pass, amend or repeal any law without challenge. In practice it is subject to constraints, e.g. EC, pressure groups, media and the electorate who have ultimate political sovereignty. Thus sovereignty is divided between state (exercised by the executive), Parliament and electorate; it is therefore debatable where, or whether, it exists at all.

What is meant by calling British government 'parliamentary government?

In British parliamentary government the executive is chosen from the majority party in the legislature, and is therefore dependent on its support and hence in theory subordinate to it (unlike the US presidential system, where the executive is separately elected and in theory equal to the legislature, and the principle of separation of powers is generally followed). In practice in Britain, the executive tends to dominate the legislature because the party and electoral systems usually produce a strong majority government; Lord Hailsham has described this as 'elective dictatorship'.

Define the word 'control' in the phrase 'parliamentary control of government'

In 'parliamentary government', the executive is chosen from the legislature and is, in theory, subordinate and accountable or responsible to it. Parliament is therefore supposed to examine, debate, criticise and check the activities of government, publicise executive actions, convey public opinion to government, and authorise the raising and spending of money by government, through, for example, debates, Question Time, committees and votes. However, some see parliamentary control as inadequate – 'elective dictatorship' (Hailsham).

Distinguish between Conservative and Liberal Democrat views on the constitution

The Conservatives strongly uphold the existing constitution, because of their stress on tradition, parliamentary sovereignty, strong government, gradual 'organic' evolution and the status quo. Thus they defend the monarchy, House of Lords and 'rule of law'. The Liberal Democrats, however, advocate a written, federal constitution and a Bill of Rights, together with devolution, PR, reform of the Lords and greater protection of individual rights and liberties. They fear the concentration of power which can result from a flexible constitution and ('the myth of') parliamentary sovereignty.

What is meant by 'the rule of law'?

The 'rule of law' (Dicey, 1885) is a principle of the constitution which seeks to equate law and justice: everyone should be equally subject to the same laws although some bodies and individuals – e.g. the Crown, diplomats, MPs etc. – are not. There should be a clear statement of people's legal rights and duties, fair and consistent trial and sentencing, and no arbitrary law or government. Justice should be an end in itself and always impartial. However, all of these principles are breached in practice by ambiguous law, 'sus' laws, remand, inconsistent sentencing, high legal costs and judicial 'bias' (J. A. G. Griffith).

---

4. Say what is wrong with each of the following statements, and why.

1) The legislature – Parliament – is elected by the people.

2) The two elements in parliamentary government are the House of Commons and the House of Lords.

3) In parliamentary government the executive is elected from the majority party in the legislature.

4) In parliamentary government the Cabinet and ministers are taken from the House of Commons.

5) The legislature is often, in theory, subordinate to the executive.

6) The British constitution is unwritten, therefore flexible.

7) The British constitution is flexible, therefore Britain has no constitutional laws.

8) A minority government has a minority of the votes but a majority of the seats.

9) A coalition government is where two or more parties have merged to form a single governing party.

10) A manifesto is what the government proposes to do, and the mandate is what they actually do when they get in.

—— ESSAYS

- **Note** Most of the essay titles relevant to this chapter are wide-ranging questions on the British constitution and British democracy, which require material covered in later chapters. See Chapter 11 for a more detailed summary of the broad themes commonly raised in essay questions, including:

  (a) Representative and responsible government;
  (b) Secrecy in British government;
  (c) Calls for a written constitution.

1) *Theme* **'Elective dictatorship' of the executive**

Q? Has the executive's dominance of the legislature weakened during the last twenty years, and if so why?

(Oxford and Cambridge, July 1986, P. 3.)

A✓ **Short plan for guidance**

- **Note** This is not, of course, the sort of plan which students should write (compare p. 7). Instead, use it to write a full essay; or, alternatively, write another plan for an essay on the same title which arrives at a different conclusion.

1) 'Parliamentary government' – define.
2) Aims: representative and responsible government – define both.
3) Methods of parliamentary control of executive – brief list, including key conventions.
4) With weakening of parliamentary control in this century, rise of 'Westminster model' of British parliamentary government, which sees Parliament's tasks as the scrutiny and legitimising of the executive, rather than control.
5) 'Executive dominance of legislature': party system, electoral system, parliamentary procedures, weak House of Lords, executive secrecy, delegated legislation and retrospective law, control of civil service → 'elective dictatorship' (Hailsham). Topical examples …
6) Changes in last 20 years which may have weakened executive dominance (rise of Parliament – **Norton** etc.).
   (a) Minority governments in 1970s. But they were not necessarily weak, e.g. nationalisation of shipbuilding 1977; and they were exceptional; large majority governments in 1980s and 1990s.
   (b) Backbench revolts increasing (Norton): Nationality Act 1982, Shops Bill 1986. But not treated as issues of confidence.
   (c) Specialist select committees 1979, e.g. British Aerospace/Rover inquiries. But they are relatively weak, and often ignored by government, e.g. 1985 Employment Committee report on miners' strike. Civil service and ministerial responsibility limited, e.g. Osmotherly memorandum 1980 (listing many issues and areas where civil servants should not answer questions); Westland 1986.
   (d) Other Parliamentary reforms: Ombudsman (since 1966) – lacks power and publicity; Special Standing committees – rare; Estimates and Opposition Days – few; Public Accounts Committee and National Audit Office – useful.

(e)   Less secrecy: Green Papers etc. But still: Ponting 1984; Westland 1985–6; Zircon 1987, sale of Rover to British Aerospace 1990 – information withheld from Parliament.

(f)   House of Lords defeats of government, e.g. GLC abolition 'Paving Bill' 1984, Statutory Sick Pay Bill 1991; but still weak (justifiably, since non-elected).

(g)   Lords select committees; useful, but often neglected.

(h)   Influence of pressure groups on Parliament and government: e.g. trade unions forced withdrawal of Industrial Relations Bill 1969 and National Industrial Relations Court 1974. But trade unions in 1980s and 1990s weak – recession, unemployment, new laws, Thatcher government was anti-corporatist.

7)   **Conclusion:** The executive's dominance of the legislature has weakened only slightly during the last 20 years. Parliamentary reforms have improved Parliament's scrutiny of the executive, and changing attitudes among back-benchers have increased parliamentary control to some extent. However, writers like **Johnson** argue that the changes are only marginal. Further reforms are needed for more representative and responsible government: for example, PR (to lessen the likelihood of one-party government); an elected second chamber which could then be given more powers of control; freedom of information legislation; and more powerful select committees (along the lines of the US congressional committees).

2)   *Theme*   **Pluralism and elitism in the British power structure**

Q?   Some people believe that parliamentary government actually restrains democracy. State the cases for and against this view.

(London, February 1976, P. 1.)

A✓   **Examiners' comments**

'The simplest and barest pass answer will be in terms of popular direct democracy versus parliamentary indirect democracy. The better answer will add to the arguments for and against the Revolutionary Socialist, or sometimes the Radical Liberal, view that the working of the two party system and the conventions of Parliamentary procedure stifle extreme and allegedly popular solutions. Some empathy should be displayed for this viewpoint, but a formal rebuttal in the form of either "it is so that the present system restrains, but it should be so" or "it is not so, the present system could be used for revolutionary policies if anyone wanted them" would be acceptable.'

Additional essay tips

Keywords
'Some people': i.e. who? Give political viewpoints/groups/names.
'Parliamentary government': define and discuss theory versus practice of representative and responsible government in and through Parliament.
'Democracy': define and discuss broad and narrow interpretations, from people-power to consent, including the extent to which Britain lives up to the principles of its own 'liberal democratic' theory.
'State the cases for and against': this format requires *balanced* argument for a pass grade. However, even where they sound merely descriptive, A Level essay questions *always* (as the examiners' comments indicate) require your own informed, reasoned arguments, critical analysis and conclusions.

Possible angles
This is a very broad-ranging title; your answer could include discussion of, for example:

- The effective degree of popular participation in the system, beyond mere vote casting;
- The party system, and the extent to which the parties in Parliament, especially the governing party, reflect public opinion (choice of parties and candidates, manifestos, the doctrine of the mandate, differences between England, Scotland, Wales and Northern Ireland etc.);
- The electoral system, and the extent to which it reflects public opinion, including the disproportions between votes and seats, regional imbalances, and the range of power bodies which are not elected;
- The degree of executive accountability to Parliament and the people – power and influence of backbench MPs, committees, Ombudsman etc., 'elective dictatorship', secrecy, collective and individual ministerial responsibility etc.;
- Contrasts with presidential system: pros and cons of US separation of powers and direct election of executive;
- The degree of centralisation of the British parliamentary system – lack of devolution etc.;
- The Marxist and/or single elitist arguments that the parliamentary system protects the economic and political power of a small ruling class or dominant elite;
- Arguments against 'democracy': that people may be ill-informed, selfish, fickle, inconsistent; that a more 'democratic' system may be inefficient, bureaucratic etc.

---

5. Write at least one of the following essays.
   Always write a brief plan first.

   1) Should a government which appears to be losing electoral support trim its policies accordingly or maintain its course?
      (Oxford and Cambridge, July 1986, P. 2.)

   2) What are the respective merits and demerits of the Marxist and pluralist theories of politics? Have the actions of British governments since 1974 provided any evidence for or against these theories?
      (Cambridge, June 1986, P. 1.)

   3) To what extent is it accurate to describe the British political system as a 'representative democracy'?
      (AEB, November 1982, P. 1.)

   4) Has the British system of government become an 'elective dictatorship'?
      (London, June 1990, P. 1.)

   5) Can sovereignty be divided?
      (Oxford, Summer 1990, P. 4.)

—— GUIDE TO EXERCISES

Page 17

1. Note that the 'bad' short answers are not factually wrong. The first is much too short and skimpy; it would be lucky to get one mark. The second is long-winded, repetitive, clumsy and colloquial in style, without adequate definition of terms, and contains unsubstantiated value-judgements. However, it could gain five to six marks for factual detail.

Page 18

2. 1) (a) Distinguish between 'the state' and 'the government'.

        The state is an independent, territorial entity with ultimate sovereignty over all individuals and groups within its boundaries. It is a permanent and abstract institution with power to use consensus where possible and coercion where necessary – it has a legal monopoly on the use of violence. The government is the executive agent of the state which enforces its rulings and acts under its authority. It is a finite and regularly changing institution.

    (b) What is the 'organic' theory of the state?

        This theory likens state and society to a living organism (rather than to a machine). Like any living organism, it has different components, each with a different and specific place and role (brain versus hand, rulers versus ruled), and all must work together in a harmonious and co-ordinated way; therefore the whole entity is more than the sum of its parts, and the society as a whole is more important than the individual within it. There is a natural and desirable inequality within the organic state. Often this theory stresses tradition and resists radical change on the grounds that society cannot be severed from its roots if it is to survive; e.g. the theory of political conservatism.

    2) (a) Define the concept of 'a political elite'.

        A political elite is a small, privileged group who dominate the decision-making processes in society. Any representative democracy generates political elitism or 'oligarchy'. Classical elite theorists (Pareto, Mosca and Michels) say that elite rule is inevitable and desirable; so does Toryism (political conservatism). Plural elitists or democratic elitists (e.g. Dahl) see diverse and competing elites as good; they disagree with Marxists (e.g. Miliband) who perceive a single ruling class in Britain and the USA, and with radical elite theorists (e.g. Guttsman) who perceive a single self-serving power elite.

    (b) Explain the theory of single elitism.

        The theory of classical or single elitism was first advanced by Pareto, Mosca and Michels in the 1920s. They argued that apparently diverse and competitive power holders in fact share common origins, aims and interests, above all the aim of preserving their own political and economic power. Together they form a single self-serving elite. Guttsman identifies an elite of around 11,000 in Britain, e.g. top businessmen, academics, ministers, MPs, civil servants, judges, church and military leaders. This elite does not represent the people, but dupes them by the façade of elections etc. into believing that the country is a democracy.

3) (a) Distinguish between a delegate and a representative.

A 'representative', once elected, exercises his/her own judgement, supposedly in accordance with the best interests of the electors as the representative sees them; whereas a 'delegate' acts on particular issues according to the specific wishes of the electors. Rousseau advocated a system of delegates; Burke argued in 1774 that MPs should be representatives rather than delegates. A trade union leader at a conference is often a delegate with a specific 'mandate' from the members. A representative may also be 'typical' of the voters in terms of social background.

(b) How far may British MPs be described as 'representative'?

MPs are not representative of the voters in the sense of 'typicality' of social background: they are predominantly middle class (over 50% professionals and under 10% manual workers); university educated (60% compared with 5% of the adult population); white and male. Only 6% of MPs are women and only four MPs are black (1991). Nor are MPs delegates of their voters (and it would be very hard in practice for them to refer back to their constituents on every issue). They sometimes exercise independent judgement in the Burkean sense, notably in free votes and backbench revolts in the Commons; but more often they toe the party line and are sometimes perceived as mere 'lobby fodder'.

4) What is meant by 'pluralist democracy'?

Pluralism advocates a diffusion of political and economic power, in order to prevent tyranny and to enhance individual freedom, choice, representation and power. In the economic sphere this means diverse, independent and competing centres of economic power and influence, implying private property and a competitive market economy with a wide distribution of ownership and wealth. In the political sphere it means a choice of political parties (formalised in Britain in Her Majesty's Opposition) and pressure groups, with checks and balances between the different parts of state and society, including active local government. In this way, all diverse views and interests should be represented, and the system is thus 'democratic'. A one-party system from this viewpoint, is by definition not democratic.

A modified version of pluralist theory is 'plural elitism' or 'democratic elitism' (e.g. Schumpeter, Dahl). This accepts that power is not equally dispersed from top to bottom in society; indeed, it argues that full pluralism would be inefficient, and is therefore not desirable. Instead it accepts that power is concentrated at the top, but is divided among competing elites – parties, pressure groups and economic power bodies. These effectively represent the diverse interests and views of the rest of society, and the system therefore provides the ideal combination of representative democracy and efficiency.

5) (a) What is meant by 'sovereignty'?

Sovereignty means ultimate power – the capacity to decide, to do, or make others do what you wish through threat or use of sanctions such as rewards, punishment, force or violence. It also implies authority, i.e. consent and legitimacy. A state has sovereignty over all groups and individuals within its boundaries. In Britain, Parliament is said to have legal sovereignty (Dicey 1885). In practice it is subject to constraints, e.g. EC, pressure groups and the 'political sovereignty' of the electorate. The nominal Sovereign – the monarch – now has little *de facto* power. Thus sovereignty is divided between state (exercised by the executive under the royal prerogative), Parliament and electorate: it is therefore debatable as to where, or whether, sovereignty exists at all. Pluralist theory says this is as it should be.

(b) How far can Parliament be said to be sovereign?

'Sovereignty' means ultimate or supreme power and authority. In Britain, Parliament (legislature – Commons, Lords and Crown) has legal sovereignty, i.e. in theory it can pass, amend or repeal any law without limit or challenge from any domestic body, unlike e.g. the USA and Supreme Court. Thus Parliament itself cannot be ruled illegal or unconstitutional. It can 'legalise illegality' through retrospective law, often passed in support of the executive – e.g. Ridley versus GLC 1985 over funding of London Regional Transport. Ascherson and others therefore argue that 'absolutism' has shifted from the Crown to the Crown-in-Parliament. In practice there are constraints: the EC as long as Parliament chooses to remain a member; pressure groups; international bodies such as NATO and IMF; the media; and the 'political sovereignty' of the electorate (Dicey) as long as the Commons submits to periodic elections and ultimately reflects the political will of the voters.

Page 20

3. A   Crown, Lord Chancellor, Home Secretary, Attorney General and Solicitor General.
   B   PM, Cabinet and other ministers; some local councillors who are also MPs.
   C   Law Lords.
   D   Judges who are appointed to chair executive inquiries; magistrates who are also councillors; executive functions of judges and magistrates (e.g. pub licensing).

Page 23

4. 1) Only the House of Commons is elected; not the Lords or Crown.
   2) The two elements in parliamentary government are the legislature and the executive.
   3) The executive is not elected: it is selected by the Crown.
   4) Ministers may be taken from the Lords as well as from the Commons.
   5) The legislature is often, in practice, subordinate to the executive; but always sovereign in theory.
   6) There is no necessary connection between an unwritten and a flexible constitution.
   7) Britain does have constitutional laws, though they are enacted in the same way as other laws.
   8) A minority government has under 50% of the seats in the House of Commons; its percentage vote is irrelevant.
   9) A coalition government consists of two or more parties (either in a 'hung' Parliament or in a crisis, e.g. war).

10) A manifesto is the list of policy proposals issued by any party prior to a general election. A 'mandate', strictly, is the assent and authority, or even duty, given to the government by the electors to govern along the policy lines indicated in the manifesto. However, voters often do not read manifestos, and cannot choose between specific policies; while governments usually win under 50% of the votes cast, and often do not adhere to their manifestos. They may claim a 'Doctor's Mandate' to do as they see fit in changing circumstances. The 'doctrine of the mandate' is therefore said to be a myth (Marshall).

—— REFERENCES

Neal Ascherson, *Games with Shadows* (Radius, 1988).

Walter Bagehot, *The English Constitution* (1967) (Fontana, 1963).

T. B. Bottomore, *Elites and Society* (Watts, 1964).

Edmund Burke, Letter to his Bristol Constituents (1774).

R. A. Dahl, *Modern Political Analysis* (Prentice-Hall, 1963).

Alexis de Tocqueville, *Democracy in America* (1840) (Mentor, 1956).

A. V. Dicey, *Introduction to the Law of the Constitution* (1885) (Macmillan, 1961).

J. A. G. Griffith, *The Politics of the Judiciary* (Fontana, 1985).

W. L. Guttsman, *The British Political Elite* (MacGibbon and Kee, 1964).

Lord Hailsham, 'Elective Dictatorship. The Dimbleby Lecture' in *The Listener* 21.10.76.

Peter Hain, *The Democratic Alternative* (Penguin, 1983).

Nevil Johnson, *In Search of the Constitution* (Methuen, 1980).

G. W. Marshall, *Constitutional Theory* (Oxford University Press, 1971).

Robert Michels, *Political Parties* (Free Press, 1915: first published in German, 1911).

G. Mosca, *Histoire des doctrines politiques* (Payot, 1936).

Ralph Miliband, *The State in Capitalist Society* (Quartet, 1969).

Philip Norton, *The Constitution in Flux* (Basil Blackwell, 1982).

V. Pareto (ed. S. E. Finer), *Sociological Writings* (Pall Mall, 1966).

G. Ponton and P. Gill, *Introduction to Politics* (Blackwell, 1982).

J. J. Rousseau, *The Social Contract* (1762) (Penguin, 1968).

J. A. Schumpeter, *Capitalism, Socialism and Democracy* (Allen & Unwin, 1977).

3 Voters and Elections

KEY ISSUES

▶ Merits and demerits of: 'first-past-the-post'; various types of PR; other 'democratic' reforms

▶ Implications of each for
  • Political equality: one person, one vote, one value
  • The doctrine of the mandate
  • Parliamentary government
  • Representative and responsible MPs/government

▶ Constitutional consequences of different reforms

▶ Factors influencing voting behaviour
  Declining influence of class on voting behaviour
  Changing national/regional patterns of voting behaviour
  Reasons why people may abstain from voting

—— TOPIC NOTES

Key facts and concepts

The **extension of the franchise (the right to vote)** dates from the **1832 Reform Act**. Only half a million of the male middle-class population were given the vote, but the principle of electoral sovereignty was established, then later extended.

1867   Representation of the People Act: reduced property qualification to £5 → two million male voters.

1872   Ballot Act: introduced the secret ballot and made intimidation of voters illegal.

1884   Representation of the People Act: extended the franchise to all male householders → five million.

1918   Representation of the People Act: extended the franchise to all men over 21 and all women over 30 → 21 million.

1928   Representation of the People Act: extended franchise to all women over 21 → 'universal adult suffrage'.

1948   Plural voting abolished (previously holders of business premises and Oxbridge degrees had two votes).

1969   Voting age reduced to 18. Electorate now around 42 million.

Voting is not compulsory in Britain as it is in, for example, Australia. To be eligible to vote, a person must be on the register of electors, and resident in the constituency on the qualifying date (though there is provision for postal voting). Those not allowed to vote are peers, non-British citizens, under 18s, certified mental patients, prisoners under sentence, and people disqualified for corrupt electoral practices (e.g. bribery).

There are 650 single-member parliamentary constituencies: England 523, Scotland 72, Wales 38 and Northern Ireland 17. A **general election**, involving all constituencies, must be held when Parliament has run its full five-year term (under the Parliament Act 1911) or is dissolved. A **by-election** is held in a single constituency if the MP dies, retires, is expelled or disqualified by accepting a peerage or paid Crown office.

Electoral systems

'First-past-the-post'

Britain has a single-vote, '**first-past-the-post**' electoral system: one vote per person; and the one candidate with the most votes wins the constituency, with or without an absolute majority (i.e. more than 50% of votes cast).

Advantages

1) The 'first-past-the-post' system is **simple**, **quick** and **cheap**.
2) One person, one vote is a basic form of **political equality**.
3) It is said to favour the two-party system with single-party, majority government and one strong Opposition party in the House of Commons: hence **strong** and **stable** government which is clearly accountable to the voters. However, this must be qualified: the system produced minority governments in the 1970s; and a two-party system has both advantages and disadvantages – the latter including lack of choice and diversity (especially in safe seats), unfair representation of minority parties and voters, and a majority government with a minority of votes cast. The rise of the Liberals in the 1970s and the new centre parties in the 1980s for a time undermined the two-party system; as have the marked regional differences in party support e.g. in Scotland and Northern versus Southern England – producing a clear north–south, Labour–Conservative political divide and, critics say, two Britains.

The 1987 General Election results

	Votes	% Votes	% Electorate	Seats	% Seats
Cons	13,760,525	42.3	32.0	376	59.4
Lab	10,029,994	30.8	23.0	229	36.1
Alliance	7,341,152	22.6	17.0	22*	3.5
SNP	416,873	1.3	1.0	3	0.5
Plaid Cymru	123,589	0.4	0.3	3	0.5
Green	89,753	0.3	0.2	0	0.0
Other	37,576	0.1	0.1	0	0.0
N. Ireland parties	730,152	2.2	1.7	17	2.6
TOTAL	32,529,564	100.0	75.3	650	100.0

Electorate:	43,199,952	*17 Liberal & 5 SDP MPs	
Turnout:	75.3%	[41 women MPs]	
Majority:	102	[4 black MPs]	
Seats under PR:	Cons: 274, Lab: 200, Alliance: 146, SNP: 8, Green: 2, Plaid Cymru: 3		

4) It is also sometimes said (e.g. by **Duverger**) that the two-party system created by 'first-past-the-post' electoral systems reflects a 'natural' political divide between conservatism and radicalism. However, the substantial third-party vote in the 1970s and 1980s belied this argument.

5) Finally, it is said that contact between MP and constituents is closer than in large, multi-member constituencies. In principle there is a **one-to-one relationship**; but in practice MPs need not even live in their constituencies and contact is often negligible, especially in 'safe seats' (though these are now declining as voters become more volatile).

Disadvantages

1) Many MPs have **fewer than 50% of the votes cast** in their constituencies. More seriously, no government since 1935 has had an absolute majority of votes cast, though most have had an absolute majority of seats in the Commons. This usually produces a powerful government which the majority of people voted *against* – arguably an 'elective dictatorship' of an unrepresentative kind. Opinion polls suggest that around 60% of voters now favour a system of proportional representation (PR).

2) Occasionally, a government may have **more seats** but **fewer votes** than the 'losing' party: e.g. the Conservatives in 1951 and Labour in February 1974 (because of unequal constituency sizes and winning margins).

3) Since any vote for a losing candidate is 'wasted', i.e. not directly represented at all in the Commons, **all votes do not carry equal weight**; i.e. the system does not grant one person, one vote, *one value*, and political equality is denied. Voters may therefore be discouraged from voting for minority parties, or from voting at all.

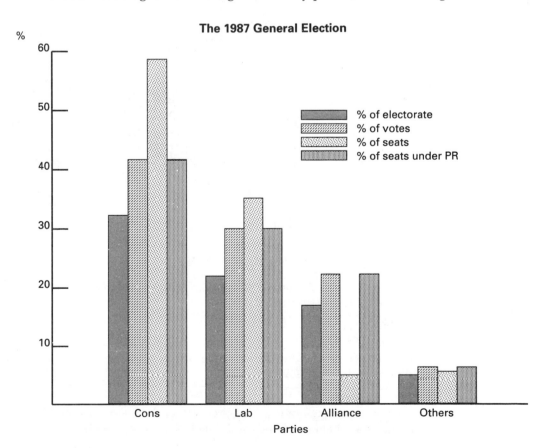

The 1987 General Election

4) The two main parties are consistently over-represented in the Commons, while **all other parties** are **consistently under-represented**. Independent candidates have very little chance of success; in Britain, none has been elected to the Commons since Dick Taverne in 1974. This may exclude diversity and quality from the system.

5) Finally, in the period of economic boom, from the 1950s to mid-70s, the two-party system was based on '**consensus politics**', when the two main parties shared very similar, centrist policies in support of the mixed economy, welfare state and nuclear defence. This was praised by some for producing moderation and stability, but criticised by others for its lack of innovation and choice. Conversely, the 1980s' recession was said to have produced '**adversary politics**', with a more right-wing style of Conservative government and a more influential left-wing in the Labour Party. The opposite pros and cons were advanced – more diversity and choice, but also more risk of a 'pendulum swing', i.e. sharp policy reversals between different governing parties. With the shift to the right of the Labour Party in the late 1980s and 1990s, together with the fall of Thatcher and the appointment of a less 'radical right' Prime Minister in 1990, a new and more consensual phase began to emerge once again.

Non-proportional voting systems

Alternatives to 'first-past-the-post' are many and varied; they need not involve proportional representation.

The alternative vote
Voters list candidates in order of preference; the last candidate(s) are struck out and their votes are redistributed among the second choices marked on their ballot papers until one candidate has an absolute majority (over 50%) of the votes (e.g. Australia).

The second ballot
Voters list candidates in order of preference; the last candidate(s) are struck out and new ballots are held until one candidate has an absolute majority (e.g. France).

A preferential ballot paper

		Mark order of preference in space below
DALEY, James	Lib. Dems	3
FOSTER, Mark	Labour	
LEEDS, Mary	Labour	
PAUL, John	Green Party	
POWELL, Jim	Conservative	1
RADCLIFFE, Susan	Lib. Dems	4
THOMPSON, Simon	Conservative	2

Proportional representation

This label covers a wide variety of electoral systems where **votes** are more or less proportional to **seats**. Each system has different pros and cons; beware of generalising in essay answers. PR is advocated not only by the Liberal Democrats, but also by some Conservatives (e.g. Douglas Hurd) and Labour MPs (e.g. Austin Mitchell).

The single transferable vote (STV)
Based on multi-member constituencies. Voters list candidates in order of preference. Any candidate obtaining the necessary quota (a simple majority) of first preference votes is elected. Any surplus votes are redistributed among the other candidates in proportion to the second choices on the winning candidate's ballot papers, and so on until all seats are filled. If too few candidates achieve the quota, the last candidate(s) are dropped and their votes redistributed proportionately. (e.g. used in Ireland; advocated by the Liberal Democrats.)

The party list system
This is the most common form of PR. The elector votes for a particular party list of candidates, and seats are allocated to each party in proportion to votes received. They are then allocated to specific candidates (e.g. USA, Switzerland, Israel).

There are two main varieties:

1) **Bound list**: The elector simply votes for a party label and the party then chooses the candidates to fill the seats;
2) **Free list**: The elector may have several votes, and may vote for specific candidates on one list or across different party lists. Seats are then given to the candidates with the most personal votes.

Party list systems

Place a cross in one box only		You may cast up to five votes for different candidates			
Conservative Party........	[X]	**LIBERAL DEMOCRATS**	**CONSERVATIVE**	**GREEN**	**LABOUR**
Green Party	[ ]	Ben Osbourne..	Matt Gee...........	Janet Young...........	Marni Singh .....
Labour Party.................	[ ]	Bob Pawson .X.	Andrew Hunt....	Calum Thomson	Vince Meate .X..
Liberal Democratic Party	[ ]	Meg Nelson......	Brian Leeds	Sally Green ...X......	Mike Pettavel .X.
National Front	[ ]		David Lewis......	Peter Myer..............	Carol Reld ..X...
Workers' Party...............	[ ]		Lucy Johns.......		Sue Smith ....

Bound list   Free list

Additional member system (AMS)

Sometimes referred to as the **mixed proportional system**, this combines 'first-past-the-post' and PR. The ballot paper has two parts, and the elector has two votes. One vote is cast for a candidate, who wins a seat in a single-member, 'first-past-the-post' constituency. The second vote is cast for a party label; and the remaining seats in the legislature (perhaps 50%) are filled by non-constituency candidates, 'additional members' chosen through the 'bound' party list system in proportion to the votes cast for each party. This provides 'top-up' proportionality for parties which would otherwise be under-represented by 'first-past-the-post' alone (e.g. West Germany).

Place a cross in one box only	
Jane Dean (Cons)....................................	[X]
Michael Taylor (Lab).............................	[ ]
Raj Rajah (Lib Dem)	[ ]
Max King (Green)....................................	[ ]
Place a cross in one box only	
Conservative Party..................................	[X]
Labour Party...	[ ]
Liberal Democratic Party.......................	[ ]
Green Party...	[ ]

● **Note**   The examiners do not want to see detailed descriptions in essays of every type of electoral system; they *do* want to see an informed assessment of the advantages and disadvantages of the various systems, without sweeping and simplistic generalisations.

1. Make a list of the potential merits and demerits of each of the six systems outlined above; then answer the questions below.

   1) Which system seems to give most power to the parties in choosing candidates?

   2) Which system seems to produce the closest proportion of seats to votes?

   3) Which system does not have single-member constituencies? List three advantages and three disadvantages of multi-member constituencies.

   4) Which system(s) produce one winning candidate with more than 50% of the votes cast?

   5) Which system produces two types of MPs, one with a local constituency and one without? Suggest two advantages and two disadvantages of this arrangement.

   6) Which system requires the electorate to turn out to vote more than once? Give one advantage and one disadvantage of such a system.

   7) Which system(s) allow for cross-voting between parties and/or candidates? Give two possible advantages and two disadvantages of cross-voting.

   8) Which system(s) are likely to give more accurate representation to minority parties? Give two advantages and two disadvantages of such systems.

   9) Suggest one reason why STV is not purely proportional.

   10) List four *alternative* reforms to the present 'first-past-the-post' system which may make it more 'democratic'.

Some factors influencing voting behaviour

Social class and occupation

These have long been the most important influences in Britain. Broadly, the wealthier upper and middle classes are more likely to vote Conservative, and the working class is more likely to vote Labour; while centrist parties such as the Liberal Democrats have suffered from their lack of class identity. However, there have always been exceptions. Lower-income Conservative voters used to be classified by sociologists either as 'deferential' voters (regarding the Conservatives as superior governors) or as 'secular' or 'instrumental' voters (seeking personal advantages such as tax cuts (**McKenzie and Silver**)).

This analysis is now regarded as too simplistic. Since the 1970s voters have become more volatile and quicker to change sides, and the old class allegiances are weakening, a process known as **class** or **partisan dealignment**. There are several suggested reasons for this process.

(a)   The traditional manual working class has declined in size with structural changes in the economy and rising unemployment. Trade union membership has also fallen for the same reasons, and with it some of the traditional working-class values of collectivism, solidarity and Labour support. Rising living standards for those in work, increasing home and share ownership, geographical mobility (often due to the break-up of traditional working-class communities e.g. after pit closures), population shifts to the south, privatised and non-unionised work have also weakened traditional working-class values and voting patterns.

(b)   Many workers looked to the Conservatives in the 1980s' elections for promised tax cuts and council house sales. Other key policy issues, e.g. defence, law and order and local government, also caused problems for Labour.

(c)   As the Conservative and Labour parties were seen to be polarising, growing support for the centre parties increased the distortions of the 'first-past-the-post' system, giving the Conservatives 59% of the seats in 1987 on their lowest winning proportion of the vote since the war.

(d)   Constituency boundary changes (reflecting population shifts from the inner-cities to the suburbs) before the 1983 election also disadvantaged the Labour Party by over 20 seats.

The 1987 general election voting by class

	Cons.	Lab.	Alliance
Prof./managerial	59	14	27
Office/clerical	52	22	26
Skilled manual	43	34	24
Semi/unskilled	31	50	19
Unemployed	32	51	17

Source: BBC Gallup Survey of G.B., June 10/11 1987.

Therefore, to quote election analyst **Ivor Crewe**, 'The Labour vote remains largely working class; but the working class has ceased to be largely Labour'. Note, however, that definitions of 'class' vary; and different classifications produce different results. For example, if foremen and supervisers are separated out from the 'skilled manual' category, the resulting voting pattern is predominantly Labour rather than Conservative.

Other important factors also cut across class divisions.

Regional variations
Labour is stronger in inner-city areas and in Scotland (with 50 out of 72 Scottish seats in the 1987 election, against ten for the Conservatives). The Conservatives are stronger in rural areas and in Southern England. These patterns are linked to both class and local culture. The Liberal Democrats have pockets of support in Wales, south-west England and the Scottish Isles and borders.

Sex, age and race
Women tend to vote Conservative more than Labour: 44% in 1987, versus 31% for Labour and 25% for the Alliance (BBC/Gallup). However, 44% of men also voted Conservative, versus 33% Labour and 22% Alliance. It used to be the case that more young people tended to vote Labour; but in 1987, 45% of first-time voters voted Conservative, as opposed to 34% for Labour and 21% for the Alliance (BBC/Gallup).

Surveys of ethnic minorities consistently showed around 70% support for Labour, 25% for the Conservatives and 5% for the Alliance.

Religion
Roman Catholics and non-conformists tend to be less conservative than Anglicans; but this influence is declining and, again, may be linked to class.

Mass media
TV and newspapers both create and reflect public opinion, and can highlight a particular political issue (e.g. inflation, unemployment), party images and personalities as a basis for voting. The national press in Britain is largely Conservative.

'Image boosting' by the media – Margaret Thatcher's authoritative/aggressive style of leadership contrasts with John Major's more consensual/weak image.

Personal experience
Family, friends and work associates can help to form political opinion; parental influence is particularly strong (and linked to social class).

Party image and party policy
Because of the 'first-past-the-post' and parliamentary systems – when we vote for a single MP, we are indirectly voting for a government – electors tend to vote for a party

more than for an individual candidate. Some voters look at the parties' past records and present policies; many vote on the basis of a broad party image (united or divided, pro-spending or cutting, pro- or anti-welfare, helping the poor or the wealthy etc.), although this may not correspond to the parties' actual policies when in power.

Qualified voters may abstain from voting for many reasons: lack of information about, or interest in, the election (especially in local council elections, by-elections and European elections, and also in safe seats where campaigning may be minimal); dislike of all available candidates or lack of effective choice (again, especially in safe seats); difficulty in getting to the polling station (though the local parties may provide transport for some voters) – i.e. apathy, disillusionment, protest or practical difficulties. The young, the poor and the unemployed are most likely to abstain, which tends to hit the Labour vote hardest.

---

2. True or false?

    (a) Candidates lose their deposits if they win under 12.5% of votes cast.

    (b) A 'safe seat' is one which a particular candidate is virtually certain to win.

    (c) The Boundary Commissioners usually report every ten to fifteen years.

    (d) Once elected, MPs may not resign.

    (e) The party which wins the most votes always wins the general election.

—— ESSAYS

1) *Theme* **Electoral systems**

Q?   (a) Assess the advantages and disadvantages of an electoral system based upon proportional representation.   (12 marks)
       (b) Why has such a system not yet been introduced throughout the United Kingdom?   (13 marks)
                                                                        (AEB, June 1982, P. 1.)

A✓   **Examiners' comments**

'In part (a) poor candidates were uncertain which electoral systems are based on proportional representation and which are not; this led to some candidates describing the alternative vote and second ballot systems. Even when the correct systems were referred to, some candidates felt obliged to give a meticulous and over-elaborate description of the mechanics of the systems. Some description was required, but not as full as some candidates offered. The majority of candidates were able to list some of the advantages, such as the close relationship between votes cast and seats won, and the reduction in the number of "wasted" votes. Most answers also listed the major disadvantages such as the complexity of the various PR systems, the blurring of representation in multi-member constituencies and the alleged tendency of PR to produce "weak" coalition governments. Good candidates looked at the operation of PR elsewhere and at the strength and stability of coalition governments, and saw that such governments are not necessarily weak.

'In part (b) even weak candidates were able to note the reluctance of the major parties to introduce electoral reform, but were unable to explain the persistence of the present electoral system in any other terms. The lack of widespread public demand for reform, and the limited pressures for reform in the back-benches of the major parties was noted in good answers. Good candidates referred to the attempts of the Liberal party in the 1970s to "trade" their support in a coalition for reform, and some speculated on the possibility of reform if the SDP/Liberal Alliance holds the balance of power in the next Parliament.'

3.   Examine the table and answer the question below.

General election results 1970–87

Date	Party	Votes	% Votes	Seats	% Seats
1970	*Cons	13,145	46.4	330	52.4
	Lab	12,179	42.9	287	45.6
	Lib	2,118	7.5	6	1.0
	Others	903	2.2	7	1.1
1974	Cons	11,869	37.9	297	46.8
(Feb)	*Lab	11,639	37.1	301	47.4
	Lib	6,063	19.3	14	2.2
	Others	1,762	5.6	23	3.6
1974	Cons	10,465	35.8	277	43.6
(Oct)	*Lab	11,457	39.2	319	50.2
	Lib	5,347	18.3	13	2.1
	Others	1,920	6.6	26	4.2
1979	*Cons	13,698	43.9	339	53.4
	Lab	11,510	36.9	268	42.2
	Lib	4,314	13.8	11	1.7
	Others	1,700	5.5	17	2.7
1983	*Cons	13,103	42.4	397	61.0
	Lab	8,462	27.6	209	32.2
	Lib/SDP	7,776	25.3	23	3.6
	Others	1,420	4.6	21	3.2
1987	*Cons	13,760	42.3	376	59.4
	Lab	10,030	30.8	229	36.1
	Lib/SDP	7,341	22.6	22	3.5
	Others	1,398	4.3	23	3.5

*governing party

Explain the reasons for the variation in the % of votes and the % of seats won by the various parties, and consider the consequences of this for the principle of majority rule in British politics. (AEB, June 1986, P. 1: 1987 figures added.)

● **Note**   Unless an essay question on electoral reform specifies PR, do not confine your answer to PR. Read the following examiners' comments carefully.

Q?   Would a more democratic electoral system be compatible with strong and stable cabinet government?

(London, February 1976, P. 1.)

A✓   Examiners' comments

'Firstly, there must be a clear discussion of what "more democratic" could mean. Merely to plunge into Proportional Representation would be a poor beginning. Credit could be gained by anyone who sees that initiative, recall, referenda and fixed-term elections have also been called "more democratic". An **A grade** can only be awarded if the discussion ranges more widely than Proportional Representation, but this alone if *very well* done could be awarded a **grade B**. Either conclusion can (and must) be reached. If both conclusions are reached then, for a candidate to progress beyond **grades D and C**, the difficulties must be faced. For example, the likely result is minority government or coalition, but these are not necessarily weak or unstable as this would depend on the circumstances, e.g. wartime crises, and other countries. If conclusions are not reached, the candidate is unlikely to score beyond a **D or C grade**, particularly if he cannot see that simple majority government is not always strong. An **A grade** candidate will realise that "strong" and "stable" can work against each other.'

Additional essay tips

Keywords
'Initiative': where a new law (or repeal of an existing law) can be proposed directly by voters through a petition, and then put to a referendum, e.g. USA, Switzerland.
'Recall': where a representative can be removed from office between ordinary elections by a vote of the people, e.g. former USSR.

Note that, e.g., in 1987, PR (party list system) in Portugal produced a single-party majority (Social Democratic) government with over 50% of both votes and seats. Coalition governments produced by PR may be stable and strong, e.g. Sweden, Germany. Some would argue that PR may produce a near-permanent, centrist coalition which could be too static. Equally, some would argue that a majority government may be too strong, in effect an 'elective dictatorship', especially if it rests on a minority of votes.

However, a majority government with a minority of votes may be deemed weak in terms of popular support (former MP **Roy Jenkins'** argument); or relative to extra-parliamentary interests such as pressure groups, or financial and international power bodies. Alternatively, it may only be stable within 'safe' policy limits, beyond which its own backbenchers may defeat it. Finally, 'stable' may mean different things: a secure majority, consistent policy and/or stable ministerial team, etc.

Q?   Discuss the proposition that electoral systems are meant to shape political attitudes rather than reflect them.

(London, June 1985, P. 1.)

● **Note**   This title has very little to do with 'first-past-the-post' versus PR, and any answer which did not recognise that would fare badly.

A✓   Short plan for guidance

1) (a)   The orthodox argument is that elections are intended to choose

representatives in accordance with the wishes of the people. Hence, in Britain, the convention that the Queen chooses the leader of the *majority* party as PM; or in PR, the principle that seats match votes ...

(b) *But*: electoral results are rarely an arithmetical reflection of votes – not in 'first-past-the-post', alternative vote, second ballot, *nor* sometimes in PR (e.g. Spain, 1982: Socialists won 57% of seats on 46% of votes).

Problem with PR: no one votes for a coalition. Nor, in most electoral systems, can people usually vote for specific policies.

Even votes themselves may not wholly reflect political attitudes, either at election, e.g. tactical voting, or after it. Fringe candidates and small parties are often deliberately excluded: e.g. by £500 deposit in Britain; and 5% minimum threshold of votes required to gain seats in Germany, which was ruled illegal by the German courts in 1990.

2) The British electoral system is clearly not meant to mirror political attitudes; it is meant to produce a workable government from within Parliament – the constitutional emphasis is more on 'responsible government' than on 'representative democracy'. Radical critics of Western electoral systems, e.g. single elitists and Marxists, would argue that a limited vote casting system was introduced in order to *prevent* a more radical degree of people-power or stronger representation of people's views.

3) 'Electoral systems are meant to shape political attitudes', e.g. through electoral campaigns, use of media, posters etc. Key function of all political parties: education, propaganda, organising/shaping political opinion into cohesive blocks. Some parties produce their own opinion polls (or use others') to manipulate opinion, not merely to measure it.

Dismissive treatment (e.g. by media and main parties) of minority parties during elections probably reduces their support; may be meant to do so.

4) Also, all electoral systems shape political attitudes in the wider sense by *legitimising* government at home and abroad: 'rigged' elections e.g. Marcos in the Philippines; Britain's 'mythical' mandate (**Marshall**); elections in 'totalitarian' systems, e.g. Nazi Germany.

But, once political attitudes are shaped, they may then be reflected by an electoral system.

5) 'Rather than': implies either/or. Title implies the very strong and cynical view that all electoral systems are deliberately intended to indoctrinate rather than to represent the voters. More accurate to say that all electoral systems *both* shape and reflect political attitudes to varying degrees; some are meant to do one more than the other.

2) *Theme* **Voting behaviour**

Q? How true is it to say that voting behaviour in Britain is becoming more volatile?

(JMB, June 1984, P. 1.)

---

4. Write an essay on the title above, using your own notes, the contents of this chapter, and the points below, which are *not* in any logical order. Note carefully the examiners' comments below. Write a brief plan first.

- Influence of opinion polls ...
- 'Deferential' versus 'secular' voting – outdated theory?

- 46% of Labour and Conservative voters expressed 'very strong' allegiance in 1964, versus 33% in 1983.
- Changes in voting population ...
- Changes in relative class sizes: increasing public service sector and white collar workers etc. ...
- 1945–55, governments lost only one seat in a by-election; 1970–80, they lost 12.
- Images of party leaders (e.g. 1983 Thatcher versus Foot).
- In 1983, for the first time, less than half of the voters – one-third of the electorate – voted for their 'natural' class party, compared with two-thirds in 1966 (47% versus 66%).
- Special factors, e.g. the miners' strike 1974, the 'Falklands factor' in 1982.
- Rise of third party – cause or consequence of class dealignment?
- Increasing fragmentation rather than volatility of electorate?
- Previously safe seats have changed hands: e.g. Eastbourne (Cons. → Lib. Dems., 1990).
- Influence of media on voting attitudes...
- 'Consensus politics' → 'adversary politics' → 'consensus politics'...
- % of middle-class voting Cons. has fallen from over 60% in 1945 to under 55% in 1987.

A✓   **Examiners' comments on above question**

'This most popular question very effectively discriminated the abilities of candidates. Answers varied from the poor and imprecise recital of theories now dated and no longer relevant to contemporary British politics to those that applied the recent work of Crewe and Rose. These better answers offered evidence from recent elections to show that there has been considerable class and partisan de-alignment, and that also there has been the development of more distinct regional voting patterns.'

---

5. Write at least one of the following essays.
    Always write a brief plan first.

    1) 'Since one of its consequences is to weaken the link between the government and the electorate, a system of proportional representation is less rather than more democratic.' Discuss.
        (Oxford and Cambridge, July 1986, P. 1.)

    2) If there were electoral reform, what other constitutional changes do you think would have to follow?
        (London, June 1978, P. 1.)

    3) Are 'democracy' and 'majority rule' the same thing?
        (Oxford, Summer 1985, P. 4.)

    4) Was the 1983 General Election a turning point in voting behaviour?
        (London, June 1988, P. 2.)

5) (a) To what extent and for what reasons do voters abstain in local government and Parliamentary elections? (12 marks)
   (b) Assess the significance of abstention for results of elections.

(13 marks)

(AEB, June 1987, P. 2.)

—— GUIDE TO EXERCISES

Page 37

1. 1) The 'bound' party list system.
   2) The party list system (both types).
   3) STV; and the party list system may be based on multi-member constituencies, or may treat the whole country as a single constituency (e.g. Israel).
   Advantages of multi-member constituencies:
   (a) Voters have a choice of MPs to represent them.
   (b) Competing MPs may work harder for their constituents.
   (c) Different shades of thinking in one party can be represented by different MPs in one constituency.
   Disadvantages of multi-member constituencies:
   (a) Constituencies would probably be larger, less homogeneous and less easy to represent.
   (b) Blurring of accountability between different MPs.
   (c) MPs may work *less* hard if others are there to do the work.
   4) The alternative vote and the second ballot.
   5) AMS.
   Advantages:
   (a) Non-constituency MPs can concentrate on 'national' issues and on parliamentary versus constituency work (e.g. committees).
   (b) Maintains one-to-one relationship between constituency MPs and voters, whilst also giving a greater degree of proportionality.
   Disadvantages:
   (a) Non-constituency MPs are not elected by voters.
   (b) Bound party list element gives greater power to party machines.
   6) The second ballot.
   Advantage:
   Produces one winner with absolute majority of votes, while also allowing sophisticated recasting of votes, or second thoughts.
   Disadvantage:
   Prone to apathy and low turnout on second ballot.
   7) Alternative vote, second ballot, STV, 'free' party list and AMS.
   Advantages:
   (a) More choice for voter.
   (b) Allows electorate to vote for personalities as well as parties – may improve quality of representatives.
   Disadvantages:
   (a) Complexity.
   (b) Undermines 'the doctrine of the mandate' – theory that link between voters and policies is party.

8) STV, party list and AMS.
   Advantages:
   (a) Fairer and more representative.
   (b) More 'pluralist'.
   Disadvantages:
   (a) May produce coalitions where small parties have disproportionate power.
   (b) May produce fragmented and inefficient legislature.
9) Second and third preference votes are given the same weight as first preference votes.
10) Initiative, recall, referenda, fixed-term elections, primaries, votes for 16 to 18-year-olds, a presidential system, an elected second chamber, lower (or no) deposit, devolution ... and many others.

Page 40

2. (a) False – now 5%.
   (b) False – it is one which a particular *party* is virtually certain to win, regardless of candidate.
   (c) True.
   (d) True – they must disqualify themselves e.g. by taking a paid Crown office.
   (e) False – e.g. 1951 and Feb. 1974.

—— REFERENCES

Ivor Crewe (ed.), *Electoral Change in Western Democracies: Patterns and Sources of Electoral Volatility* (Croom Helm, 1985).

I. Crewe and M. Harrop (eds), *Political Communications: The General Election Campaign of 1987* (Cambridge University Press, 1989).

Maurice Duverger, *Political Parties* (Methuen, 1964).

G. W. Marshall, *Constitutional Theory* (Oxford University Press, 1971).

R. T. McKenzie and A. Silver, *Angels in Marble* (Heinemann, 1968).

Richard Rose, *Understanding the United Kingdom* (Longman, 1982).

4 Members of Parliament and Political Parties

KEY ISSUES

▶ Representative and responsible MPs; definitions and degrees
Diverse and conflicting roles and loyalties of MPs
Government versus Opposition/Conservative versus Labour MPs
Power/influence of backbenchers: forms and constraints

▶ Merits and demerits of a party system
Extent, merits and demerits of a two-party system: Implications for
● Representation
● Pluralism
● Elective dictatorship'

▶ Principles and policies of the major parties
Organisation and financing of the major parties
Different degrees of internal party democracy

—— TOPIC NOTES

Key facts and concepts

Parliamentary candidates and MPs are not 'representative' of the electorate in their social background; as some essay questions put it, they are predominantly white, middle class and male. This is partly because of discrimination in the process of **selection of candidates** (the controversy over the selection of the black candidate John Taylor in the Cheltenham Conservative Constituency Party in 1990 serves as a good example); and partly because working-class people, women and ethnic minorities are slower to come forward as candidates (because of pressure of work, financial constraints, lack of political background, contacts or self-confidence). Whether MPs must be 'typical' of voters in order to 'represent' them adequately is, however, debatable.

1. Complete the following passage.

Parliamentary candidates are chosen by their local constituency parties (unless they are standing as _____). In 1987 the _____ Party conference agreed on a new method of selection based on 'one _____ one vote', with an electoral college for the votes of _____ _____. This is similar to the American system of _____ elections for political candidates. British MPs must be British subjects, over _____ years of age, and must deposit £____ with the _____ _____ which is forfeited if they obtain under 5% of the votes cast in the constituency. Those disqualified from membership of the Commons include those disqualified from _____, plus undischarged bankrupts, clergy of the established churches, judges, civil servants and other Crown officials, heads of nationalised industries and directors of the Bank of _____.

In the Conservative Party, candidates are selected by local constituency associations. The Labour Party in 1979 introduced a system of **mandatory re-selection** of Labour MPs: i.e. compulsory review of each MP's record of work between general elections. Unsatisfactory MPs could be **de-selected**, and a new candidate chosen to stand at the next election. The 'mandatory' element of the re-selection process was removed in 1990.

Case for mandatory re-selection

(a)   Increased intra-party democracy.

(b)   Constituency parties select the candidates and provide the resources and support for the election campaign; MPs should therefore be accountable primarily to them, rather than to the national or parliamentary party.

(c)   It may encourage MPs to work harder in their constituencies and perhaps to represent their constituents' interests better.

Case against mandatory re-selection

(a)   Technically, MPs cannot be sacked by the parties, because liberal democratic theory suggests that only the voter should have the power to select or reject an MP (though none of the parties allows the voters to select parliamentary *candidates*).

(b)   Local party activists may not be representative of the voters and may de-select a popular MP (e.g. Frank Field in 1990).

(c)   MPs may be forced to neglect 'national' issues and interests, or to rebel against their parliamentary whips.
       In practice, only six Labour MPs (out of 210) were de-selected before the 1987 election (e.g. former chief whip Michael Cocks, who was subsequently given a life peerage).

Many essay questions ask about the **diverse roles** and **conflicting loyalties** of MPs; the key concepts of '**representation**' and '**responsibility**' should be addressed in essay answers. Who, or what, should MPs represent? How feasible or valuable are different theories of representation? To whom should MPs be accountable? Thus, in a parliamentary system, what is, or should be, the theory and practice of 'representative' and 'responsible' government in Britain? (Bear in mind that the question of what should be raises issues of both principle and practicality.)

Diverse roles of an MP

Legislator

MPs are elected to a national legislative assembly. They debate and vote on parliamentary bills in the House and in standing committees. They are constrained by party discipline from speaking or voting against the party line on a two- or three-line whip, on pain of suspension from the party. However, backbenchers may assert themselves by rebelling collectively against a bill. This usually happens where MPs see the bill as contrary to the basic principles of their party. **Norton** argues that backbenchers have been more ready to revolt since the 1970s, and that this increases both the power and the authority of the House of Commons.

---

2.   Read the paragraph above, then do the following exercises.

   1)   Find and list *three* important examples of backbench revolts.

   2)   Were any of these 'contrary to the basic principles of the party' and, if so, how?

   3)   From Norton or elsewhere, find figures to support, or to refute, Norton's argument.

   4)   Explain why backbench revolts may increase (a) the power, and (b) the authority of the Commons. What is the difference between the two?

Backbenchers may initiate legislation in the form of private members' bills: e.g. Conservative MP Richard Shepherd's Protection of Official Information Bill 1987, which was defeated because the government imposed an unprecedented three-line whip against it. The frontbenchers of the main parties, especially the government, tend to monopolise the time available in the House. Also, private members' bills are easily defeated (especially those introduced after Question Time under the Ten Minute Rule). Therefore few are passed (though good publicity may be won for the issue): on average, over 100 are introduced in each parliamentary session but only around 20 are passed.

Controller of executive

According to the theory of parliamentary government, MPs, regardless of party, are supposed to scrutinise, check and publicise the activities of the government, through debate, Question Time, standing and select committees, voting on bills, adjournment motions, the Ombudsman and control of government finance as well as the media etc. Some MPs have made their mark in this role (e.g. Tam Dalyell (Labour) on the sinking of the General Belgrano during the 1982 Falklands conflict). They are, however, constrained in this role by:

(a)   The power of a majority government to command party loyalty (e.g. the unanimous vote of confidence in the government by Conservative backbenchers over the Westland affair on 27 January 1986);

(b)   Lack of time available to backbenchers in the Commons;

(c)   Lack of information granted to Parliament by government in Britain's highly secretive system (e.g. the withholding of information about the sinking of the Belgrano during the Falklands conflict (1982); the Zircon satellite project (1987); and the arrangements for the sale of Rover to British Aerospace (1988));

(d)   Lack of office, research and secretarial facilities available to MPs.

Labour MP Austin Mitchell once wrote that trying to control the executive was 'as useful as heckling a steamroller'. However, although only a backbench rebellion has the real *power* to defeat a majority government, MPs of all parties may have *influence* on government, by publicising embarrassing information or by conveying public opinion to government.

To this end, they use 'early day motions' and 'points of order' with growing frequency; and the 1922 Committee of Conservative back-benchers was largely responsible for pressurising Trade and Industry Secretary Leon Brittan into resigning over the Westland affair in 1986.

> THIRTEEN Labour MPs have tabled a parliamentary motion to embarrass Mrs Thatcher over the Westland affair by citing Mr Rodney Tyler's book, *Campaign*, the Conservative account of the general election, as further evidence that the Prime Minister's office was aware of the leaking of the law officer's letter to discredit the former Cabinet minister, Mr Michael Heseltine.
>
> *The Guardian*, 5 November 1987

Trainee minister

All ministers are selected from either the Commons or the Lords. Parliamentary work – in debate, in committee, and in the constituency – may provide some useful training for future executive office. However, since ambitious MPs may hesitate to offend their party leaders, MPs who see themselves as 'trainee ministers' may do little to control their own governing party. The parliamentary system thus creates 'role conflict' for some backbenchers.

Diverse responsibilities of an MP

MPs have wide-ranging, and sometimes conflicting, loyalties. To whom MPs are, or should be, responsible is a matter of debate; the answer depends on political ideology, party structure, and personal inclination. The demands on an MP's loyalty include the following.

The parliamentary party

Disraeli said 'Damn your principles! Stick to your party'. The 'doctrine of the mandate' suggests that electors vote for a package of party policies as outlined in a manifesto, and therefore MPs are most effectively representing the voters' wishes if they 'toe the party line'. The Conservative Party, especially, has a strong philosophical emphasis on party unity and loyalty to the leadership.

Party conference

Whereas the Conservative conference is not a policy-making body, the Labour conference in theory is. Democratic socialists such as Tony Benn argue that Labour MPs should pursue conference policy, even if that means defying the whips. They argue that the conference is a more broadly democratic forum than is the party leadership; though right-wing critics would point out that the conference, unlike the party leadership, tends to support radical, democratic socialist, 'Bennite' policies. The Labour leadership has therefore increasingly ignored radical conference policies, e.g. on cuts in nuclear defence (1991).

Constituency party

The local party selects the MP and provides the electoral campaign back-up; rank-and file activists may also have a good understanding of constituency needs. Many MPs therefore pay special heed to the local party. In the Labour Party especially, mandatory re-selection obliged MPs to pay close, if sometimes reluctant, attention to the wishes of their local party, even where this may have jeopardised their standing with the national leadership.

Constituents

Total subservience to the national party would negate the role of constituency MPs; and the strict theory of liberal democracy does not recognise the party at all – it perceives a one-to-one relationship between the individual MP and voter. Thus, for example, an MP who leaves one party and joins another need not stand for re-election. The Liberal Democrats, especially, stress this 'individualist' interpretation of the role of an MP; Cyril Smith was a notable constituency MP. This may cause difficulties where special constituency interests conflict with the 'national interest' (if there is such a thing) or with national party policy. It may also be difficult to serve diverse local interests: e.g. farmers versus farm-workers; and it is hard for an MP to gauge the views of constituents as a whole.

Interest groups

Many MPs have special personal interests (e.g. Jack Ashley MP campaigns on behalf of the handicapped). They are often **sponsored** or **lobbied** by pressure groups and private companies to act on their behalf. About one-third of Labour MPs are sponsored by trade unions (e.g. Dennis Skinner by the National Union of Mineworkers); here, the trade union pays some of the candidate's campaign costs in return for a voice in Parliament where possible. Many other MPs, especially Conservatives, are paid *personal* fees (ranging from £1,000 to £20,000 per year) as consultants or directors by pressure groups and private companies seeking to promote their own interests: e.g. Conservative MP Michael Grylls in 1990 listed 22 interests in the Register of Members' Interests, in fields as diverse as transport, drugs, energy, property and finance. MPs look to pressure groups for specialist information, and they may introduce a private member's bill, table an early day motion or ask parliamentary questions in support of a private company's interests or a pressure group's aims. Such links between MPs and outside interest groups may pose problems: Michael Mates, in 1990 chair of the Select Committee on defence, severed his link with SGL (Defence) Ltd. because of the controversy it was causing. These special interests may not coincide with constituency or national interests; and MPs are not obliged to declare details or payments.

National interest

Burke argued in 1774 that an MP was a member of 'a deliberate assembly of one nation with one interest, that of the whole', and that MPs should pursue the 'general good' according to their personal judgement. The concept of a 'national interest' is central to political conservatism, but is denied by liberals (who perceive diverse individual interests) and socialists (who perceive conflicting class interests).

Conscience

This is the second feature of Burke's theory of the role of an MP: 'Your representative owes you not his industry only, but his judgement; and he betrays instead of serving you, if he sacrifices it to your opinion'. Private conscience is given expression particularly in free votes in the Commons (e.g. on capital punishment) and in private members' bills. It may obviously conflict with party, constituency and other interests outlined above.

Political Parties

A **party system** implies political decision-making and representation on the basis of formal, organised groups of (more or less) like-minded people who stand as candidates for election on a common policy programme. This may be a one-, two- or multi-party system. A party system of any type has merits and demerits as compared with, for instance, representation and political decision-making by independent individuals. This is the subject of many essay questions: e.g. 'Could Britain be well-governed without a party system?' (London, June 1978, P. 1.). The issues involved include representative and responsible government, 'elective dictatorship' and pluralism.

1987 General Election

Key to the parties

C – Conservative; **Lab** – Labour; **Lab Co-op** – Labour and Co-operative; **L** – Liberal; **SDP** – Social Democratic Party; **SNP** – Scottish National Party; **Comm** – Communist; **OUP** – Official Unionist Party; **DUP** – Democratic Unionist Party; **Pop U** – Popular Unionist; **SDLP** – Social Democratic and Labour Party; **SF** – Sinn Fein; **WP** – Workers' Party; **Ind** – Independent; **Loony Socy** – Loony Official Monster Raving Party; **FP** – Feudal Party.

BT – Blancmange Thrower; **CPRP** – Capital Punishment Referendum Party; **CC** – Independent Community Campaigner, East Oxford People; **Dem** – Independent Democrat; **Falkland** – Right of Falkland Islands to Elect Westminster MP; **OFP** – Official Fidgeyitous Party; **OSM** – Orkney and Shetland Movements; **OOBPC** – Only Official Best Party Candidate; **RF** – Red Front; **RRPRC** – Revolutionary Reform Party Representative of Christ; **SE** – Spare the Earth; **Workers' Rev** – Workers' Revolutionary Party.

FDP – Fancy Dress Party; **ML** – Moderate Labour Party; **NFFG** – National Front Flag Group; **Prot U** – Protestant Unionist; **PRP** – Protestant Reformation Party; **RABIES** – Rainbow Alliance Brixton Insane Extremist Section; **CSOSMG** – Christian Socialist Opposing Secret Masonic Government; **CPWSML** – Capital Punishment Will Save More Lives; **Ex Lab Mod** – Ex Labour Moderate; **GP** – Gold Party; **HP** – Human Party.

ICN – Independent Christian Nationalist; **LAPP** – Let's Have Another Party Party; **LO** – Law and Order; **NPR** – National People's Rally; **PIP** – Public Independent Plaintiff; **Real U** – Real Unionist; **RCP** – Return Capital Punishment; **SPGB** – Socialist Party of Great Britain.

Advantages of a party system

- Parties provide the basis for a coherent and comprehensive body of policies for government.
- Parties organise and crystallise public opinion into coherent blocks.
- Parties educate public opinion via their activities in Parliament, the media etc. (though they may also try to manipulate and mislead public opinion for party advantage).
- Parties provide effective organisation, financing and campaigning for parliamentary candidates.
- According to the 'doctrine of the mandate', an elected government is authorised, or even obliged, to implement the policy proposals contained in its party manifesto; the party system is therefore essential for representative government.
- The convention of collective responsibility, whereby government is accountable to Parliament and hence to the electorate, assumes an executive united around a common body of policy. The party system is therefore essential for responsible government.
- The party system provides stability and consistency of government.

Disadvantages of a party system

- A single-party, majority government based on strong party discipline may amount to 'elective dictatorship'.
- Parties may encourage partisan conflict for its own sake, undermining effective government.
- Voters have no choice between the policies of any one party.
- Voters have no say in the parties' candidates (though 'open primaries' could be introduced, as in the USA).
- The party system discourages close, personal contact between MPs and voters.
- The party system undermines MPs' independence and individualism.
- The national or local party machines may have excessive power (e.g. over MPs) at the expense of the voters.
- The party system may permanently exclude some minority views, or may neglect important issues which cut across orthodox party lines (e.g. moral issues such as abortion or capital punishment).
- The party system excludes able independents.

Britain is often also described as a *two*-**party system**.

---

3. 1) Define a 'two-party system'.

    2) Give three reasons *for*, and three reasons *against*, describing Britain as a two-party system. On balance, do you think Britain is a two-party system or not?

    3) Suggest three likely advantages, and three likely disadvantages, of a two-party system.

Principles and policies of the major parties

The **Conservative Party** under Margaret Thatcher was led by **economic conservatives** who emphasise private property, the free market, individual enterprise and self-help, reducing inflation, public spending and taxation (at the expense of employment, if necessary). Paradoxically, the stress on 'rolling back the frontiers of state' in the economy was combined with growing political centralisation and state control e.g. of education and local government. There is also, however, an older school of **traditional political conservatives** in the party (e.g. Lord Whitelaw) who emphasise social stability and consensus, traditional institutions (e.g. monarchy, Church and Lords), the nuclear family, Christian morality and public duty. The 'wets' (a derogatory label coined by Mrs Thatcher) combine traditional Toryism with a Keynesian approach to economic policy, favouring some state intervention, a mixed economy, public spending and welfare. All Conservatives advocate private property, hierarchy, strong defence and law and order.

The **Labour Party** is similarly divided between a more right-wing, **social democratic** leadership which favours market socialism – freedom, fairness and fraternity in a mixed, mainly private enterprise, economy – combined with state control and planning, welfare and multilateral nuclear disarmament within international bodies such as NATO and the EC; and the more radical **democratic socialists** (e.g. Tony Benn), who seek extensive collective ownership, workers' democracy, welfare, social equality, greater political participation and political reform (e.g. abolition of the House of Lords), unilateral nuclear disarmament and withdrawal from NATO and the EC.

The **Liberal Democrats** emerged out of the break-up of the SDP/Liberal Alliance after the 1987 election and the merger of most of its members under the leadership of Paddy Ashdown. They are much the same, philosophically, as the old Liberal Party. They favour a private enterprise economy but with positive state intervention to promote positive individual freedom through, for example, the provision of welfare and legislation to promote freedoms such as access to official information and the prevention of discrimination. They are the party most enthusiastic about civil rights and liberties, and issues of constitutional reform, notably a written constitution and Bill of Rights, proportional representation, devolution and a reformed second chamber.

Organisation and financing of the major parties

The structure of the major parties reflects their different philosophies and principles. For example, traditional conservative ideology stresses political hierarchy, 'natural governors' and loyalty to leadership; the Conservative leader – elected by Conservative MPs only since 1966 – is therefore responsible for policy-making, party headquarters and internal appointments (e.g. the chairman and Shadow Cabinet). The conference is not a policy-making body, but a political rally intended to demonstrate unity and loyalty to the leader. A Conservative faction called the Charter Movement is pressing for more internal party democracy, pointing, for example, to its own party's legislation on the election of trade union leaders by members.

The Labour Party's philosophy, by contrast, demands greater intra-party democracy: the Shadow Cabinet is elected by the MPs; any policy passed by two-thirds of conference votes should go into the manifesto; and the National Executive Committee, elected by conference, directs policy and controls the party machine. The leader has much less formal power.

The Conservative Party is financed largely by private firms, whereas the Labour Party is financed largely by trade unions. The Liberal Democrats are disadvantaged in this respect, having to rely mainly on membership fees and donations, and limited funding from pressure groups and firms such as the British School of Motoring. However, all three parties are helped by state financing, free party political broadcasts and electoral post, as well as by membership fees and fundraising events staged by the local parties.

Controversial issues, requiring balanced discussion (i.e. case for and case against) in relevant essays, include:

(a) The rise and fall of 'Thatcherism': was the 'New Right' merely old wine in new bottles, and can it survive the loss of Thatcher herself?

(b) The close correlation between company donations to the Conservative Party and awards of honours to company directors by Conservative Prime Ministers: should such patronage be abolished?

(c) The trade unions' block votes at Labour Party conferences for policy decisions and leadership elections: should their voice in party affairs be further reduced or reformed?

(d) The need for members of affiliated trade unions to 'contract out' if they do not want to pay a levy to the Labour Party; should they instead be able to 'contract in'; or, indeed, should individual company shareholders be able to 'contract out' of paying a donation to the Conservative Party?

(e) The relative power of Labour and Conservative leaders, in and out of office: does the power and authority of Prime Ministerial office outweigh formal party differences?

(f) Intra-party democracy in theory and practice: does it necessarily decline when a party is in office?

(g) The growth of factionalism within the parties, and the divergence between the parties, since the 1970s: why did it happen; is 'adversary politics' rhetoric or reality; is it good or bad; why and how much is it declining in the 1990s?

---

4. Write short answers to the following questions.

1) (a) What is a sponsored MP?
   (b) Does sponsorship pose any potential problems for MPs?

2) (a) Distinguish between a political party and a political faction.
   (b) Describe any *one* current political faction.

3) Distinguish between 'representative' and 'responsible' government.

ESSAYS

1) *Theme* **Role of MPs**

Q? State a case for and a case against backbench MPs more frequently initiating legislation in the House of Commons across party lines.

(London, June 1978, P. 1.)

A✓ **Short plan for guidance**

Introduction: descriptive outline of 'parliamentary government', the party system and private members' bills.

Case for

1) To represent special interests of constituents in accordance with liberal democratic theory of MPs' role; or to promote sponsors' interests.
2) To gain publicity for an issue, or for the MP, even if the bill is not passed. (Bills introduced under the Ten Minute Rule are most relevant here.)

3) Thus to increase support for MP/party.
4) To enhance parties' awareness of constituency needs and of MPs' opinions.
5) Burkean concept of role of MP: to use independent judgement and conscience.
6) Thus to make up for the loss of independents in the party system.
7) To give more power to MPs and Parliament, versus executive, in accordance with the theory of parliamentary sovereignty.
8) To reduce the danger of 'elective dictatorship' of single-party, majority government based on strong party discipline.
9) To pursue important issues neglected by the parties (e.g. moral issues, minority interests, or those where an MP has special expertise).
10) To produce more active MPs.
11) To enhance the Commons' role as a deliberative chamber.

Case against

1) Need for strong party system to produce effective government in Parliament.
2) 'Doctrine of the mandate': MPs are elected and expected by voters to support party manifesto policies.
3) Government should be allowed to govern; trivial, obstructive or unsuccessful private members' bills may simply waste valuable Commons' time (and money).
4) MPs depend on party for election, and owe loyalty to party, besides their natural sense of loyalty and support for party.
5) Focus on narrow sectional or local interests may undermine national interest which national party is pursuing.
6) May produce conflicting body of statute law.
7) MPs' power to abstain or rebel against government legislation is adequate.
8) May antagonise party and jeopardise MPs' promotion prospects within it.
9) Practical difficulties of drafting bill etc. may deflect MP from more important and productive tasks – e.g. select committee work, constituency surgeries etc.

Additional essay tips

- The format 'state a case for and a case against ...' requires *balanced* argument, but also a reasoned conclusion; the above structure leads to the conclusion that, on balance, the 'case against' is stronger; if you favour the 'case for', *put it last*.
- Consider whether the *number* of points in a plan is the crucial factor in deciding how to conclude, or whether some points have more *weight* than others (e.g. do constitutional principles matter more than practical pros and cons?).
- Note also that the phrase 'initiating legislation' does not imply that the private members' bills are necessarily passed.
- Finally, as an optional extra, if your syllabus includes coverage of other countries (e.g. the USA and the role of members of Congress) you can use that information to make comparisons in this essay.

5. What other arguments, and topical examples, can you add to the above plan? For example, does it make any difference whether the MP is a government or Opposition backbencher, or to which party the MP belongs?

2)   *Theme*   **The party system and 'elective dictatorship'**

Q?   'When a government enjoys a large parliamentary majority, effective opposition comes only from within the ranks of its own party.' To what extent has this been the experience of governments since 1945?

(AEB, June 1986, P. 1.)

A✓   **Examiners' comments**

'Most candidates understood the reasons why the Opposition is relatively power-less when the government has a large parliamentary majority, and made reference to the nature of party discipline and the government's control of parliamentary time. There was a less good understanding of the full range of opportunities available to the government minister or MP to challenge and influence the government. Many candidates quoted the recent opposition of Pym, Walker and the "Wets" but few could distinguish the various techniques and methods that they had used; even fewer examined the events of the recent Westland issue. There were good answers which noted that effective opposition can come from elsewhere in the system and referred to the work of the House of Lords and select committees.'

---

6.   List *ten* opportunities, techniques and methods available to government opponents to challenge or influence the government; give *one* effective, and *one* ineffective, example of the use of each (ensure that your examples are topical). Consider, as you do this exercise, what you take to mean by 'effective'.

---

3)   *Theme*   **Parties, power and pluralism**

Q?   Does the alternation of parties in government make any real difference to economic and political life in Britain?

(Cambridge, June 1985, P. 1.)

---

7.   First, write brief notes on how you would answer this essay question; then read the notes below; then write a concise but comprehensive plan incorporating both sets of notes.

A✓   **Notes for guidance**

This title is open to broad and diverse interpretations.

(a)   **Single elitist or Marxist theory:** The arguments that all major parties serve the interests of a single dominant elite or ruling class, and therefore a change of party makes no significant difference to the economic or political power structure.

(b)   **Consensus politics:** The narrower argument that the two main parties in Britain share similar, centrist policies, despite their rhetoric of opposition. This argument was popular during the boom years, but from the late 1970s to early 1990s the opposite thesis of adversary politics was more often advanced.

(c)   **Limits to the power of government:** Arguments contrary to the thesis of 'elective dictatorship', suggesting that even a radical government is constrained by Parliament, opposition parties, civil service, pressure groups, the international economic climate and international bodies such as the IMF, EC, NATO and USA etc. A comprehensive answer would include the cases for *and* against *all* of these arguments, with persuasive evidence about [lack of] changes in economic and political life in Britain at least since the war, and some attempt at value-judgement – is [lack of] change good or bad?

Q?   'In a successful system of Parliamentary government, the parties should agree on fundamentals and differ only over details.' Discuss, with reference to the present state of British Parliamentary government.

(London, June 1984, P. 1.)

A✓   **Examiners' comments**

'Candidates who answered this question largely ignored the words "successful", "fundamentals" and "details" that appeared in the quotation. Many candidates concentrated on differences in policy between the Conservative and Labour Parties, but few discussed whether the alleged post-war consensus was itself successful or a condition of success. Other fundamentals, which might include agreement about the basic rules underlying the political system, went largely unnoticed.'

Additional essay tips

- The core of this question is the problem that too little choice and diversity between parties undermines the freedom of electoral choice which is central to the pluralist theory of liberal democracy; while too much divergence and polarisation may produce deadlock, weak government, excessive conflict or even breakdown of the system. A balanced approach is necessary here.
- The points must be related to the theory and practice of 'parliamentary government' (as opposed to separation of legislature and executive).
- Go beyond discussion of consensus and adversary politics to consider all of the parliamentary parties, major and minor, including the Irish, Scottish and Welsh parties.
- Bear in mind that the Thatcher government was often described as 'Radical Right': how true was this description, and is there any risk of extremist government or opposition ever threatening British parliamentary democracy itself?

---

8.   Write at least one of the following essays.
     Always write a brief plan first.

1)   Should a backbench MP try to follow his or her party, the wishes of his or her constituents, or his or her own judgement?

(Oxford, Summer 1986, P. 1.)

2)   How far and in what sense does Britain currently have a two-party system?

(AEB, November 1981, P. 1.)

3)   Internal constitutional issues have caused many difficulties in the Labour Party in recent years. Why should this have been so?

(Cambridge, June 1986, P. 1.)

4) Is participation through political parties a necessary condition of representative government?

(London, January 1991, P. 1.)

5) 'Predictably, the Alliance of Liberal and Social Democrat Parties failed to achieve its objective of altering the fundamental balance of British politics.' Discuss.

(Oxford and Cambridge, June 1989, P. 2.)

—— GUIDE TO EXERCISES

Page 48

1. Independents; Labour; member; trade unions; primary; twenty-one; £500; Returning Officer; voting; England.

Page 49

2. 1) Nationality Bill 1982; proposed increase in parental contributions to student grants 1983; Shops Bill 1986.
   2) The Nationality Bill proposed relaxation of immigration laws; the increase in parental contributions to student grants would have hit middle-class Conservative voters hardest; the Shops Bill neglected the traditional conservative stress on Christian morality and family unity.
   3) 'The 7-year period from April 1972 to April 1979 witnessed a total of 65 Government defeats on the floor of the House of Commons. To find a similar number in a 7-year period one has to go back to the 1860s.... This new attitude was not confined to the 1974–9 Parliament. It carried over into the current Parliament' (Norton, p. 112).
   4) Backbench revolts may force government to abandon a proposal – power; and may increase respect for MPs who are seen to be performing their constitutional functions effectively – authority.

Page 53

3. 1) A system in which two major parties dominate the political scene, and no other single party is able to win executive power.
   2) **For**
   Balance of seats in Commons (give current figures).
   Labour/Conservative single-party governments since 1945.
   'Her Majesty's Government' and 'Her Majesty's Opposition', plus salary for Opposition leader and Chief Whip, Commons procedures such as Opposition Days, etc.
   Against
   Balance of votes in country (give current figures).
   Regional factors, e.g. Northern Ireland parties.
   All parties are coalitions, e.g. factions within the Conservative Party (the Tory Reform Group, the Bow Group, the Monday Club) and within the Labour Party (the Fabian Society, the Tribune Group, the Militant Tendency).
   3) **Advantages**
   (a) Effective and accountable government and Opposition.

(b) Clear choice for voters in system of parliamentary government.
(c) Reflects natural divide in population between conservatism and radicalism (**Duverger**).

Disadvantages

(a) Strong, single-party government may mean elective dictatorship.
(b) Narrow choice for voters, contrary to pluralist theory.

Tends either to consensus politics – lack of choice and innovation; or to adversary politics – excessive polarisation and 'swing of the pendulum' between policies of different governments.

Page 55

4. 1) (a) What is a sponsored MP?

Pressure groups 'sponsor' an MP by paying some of his/her local party's campaign costs in return for a voice in Parliament where possible in debate, Question Time, committees, private members' bills, etc. Over one-third of Labour MPs are sponsored by trade unions and co-operatives, e.g. Dennis Skinner by the NUM and Neil Kinnock by the TGWU. This does not, however, make MPs delegates of those pressure groups. Sponsorship should be distinguished from political lobbying, whereby many MPs become paid consultants and advisers of interest groups, private firms etc., e.g. John Browne MP (Cons.) who was suspended from the Commons for 20 days in 1990 for failing to register a payment of $88,000 from the Saudi government.

(b) Does sponsorship pose any potential problems for MPs?

Sponsorship may create some conflict of interest for MPs, e.g. between the pressure group's aims and those of the party leadership or constituency. Sponsors should not pressurise MPs too hard or expect them simply to be mouthpieces and agents of the pressure group. In 1991 the NUM sought to withdraw its sponsorship from Kevin Barron MP (Lab.) because he criticised NUM leader Arthur Scargill, and the MP therefore charged the NUM with breach of the privileges of the Commons.

2) (a) Distinguish between a political party and a political faction.

A political party is a formal organisation of people who share similar views, and stand candidates for election on a common political programme. A faction is a group within a party which favours and seeks to promote a particular part of the party's broad ideology: e.g. the left-wing Militant Tendency and right-wing Solidarity Group in the Labour Party; and the 'wet' Tory Reform Group and right-wing Monday Club in the Conservative Party. All main parties are therefore broad, and often conflicting, churches: e.g. the Labour Party expelled Dave Nellist and Terry Fields of the Militant Tendency in 1991.

(b) Describe any *one* current political faction.

The Campaign Group in the Labour Party is a radical left, democratic socialist faction led by Tony Benn, which broke away from the 'soft left' Tribune Group to pursue more left-wing policies such as extensive collective ownership and welfare, equality for black people and women, and unilateral disarmament. It also seeks constitutional reforms such as withdrawal from the EC, abolition of the House of Lords, fixed four-year terms for Parliament, the abolition of Crown prerogatives and curbs on the powers of the Prime Minister, including the transfer of powers of patronage to the House of Commons. It is frequently in conflict with the party leadership, which is much less radical, especially in the 1990s.

3)   Distinguish between 'representative' and 'responsible' government.

'Representative' government implies government *of* the people: elected or accredited by them; typical of them in social background; reflecting their views as a delegate, or their interests. 'Responsible' government implies government *for* the people: being responsive and ultimately accountable to them; governing wisely and sensibly but perhaps not popularly; or governing in the interests of the electors as perceived by the governors (**Burke**). In Britain the Labour Party stresses representative government, while the Conservative Party stresses responsible government. The constitutional arrangement of parliamentary government involves both: by convention, the executive is appointed from the majority party in the Commons in order to make it representative.

The doctrines of collective and individual ministerial responsibility are intended to make ministers answerable to Parliament and the people for government policy and for departmental and individual errors. Ultimately Parliament can dismiss government on a vote of no confidence, as it did in 1979. The 'doctrine of the mandate' seeks to link party, policy and people, and thus make government representative of the views of the voters. However, in practice there are flaws: the electoral system usually means that a majority government in fact has a minority of votes cast. The strict doctrine of the mandate cannot apply when voters do not read manifestos or do not support all of the policies in them. The doctrines of collective and individual responsibility are not always applied, e.g. Chancellor Nigel Lawson did not resign over the Johnson Matthey Bank scandal in 1986. Critics therefore seek reforms such as PR and devolution to enhance representative and responsible government in the UK.

Page 56

5.   'Effective opposition' may come from ministers themselves, backbenchers, the House of Lords, select committees, the civil service, the courts, pressure groups, media and international bodies. Methods may include: Commons' debates and votes, early day and adjournment motions, Opposition Days, cross-party criticism by the select committees, votes of censure, lobbying, the Ombudsman, ministerial speeches, leaks to the media or resignation, backbench committees, press or TV criticism, civil service obstruction, domestic or overseas courts ruling the government *ultra vires* etc. Find and list topical examples of each.

—— REFERENCES

M. Duverger, *Political Parties* (Methuen, 1964).
Austin Mitchell, 'The Seven Roles of an MP – a Personal View' in *Social Studies Review* May 1986.
Philip Norton, *The Constitution in Flux* (Blackwell, 1982).

5 Parliament: House of Lords and House of Commons

KEY ISSUES

► Functions, [in]effectiveness and reform of Parliament

► Lords
  - Power and authority
  - Criticisms and reform/abolition
  - Reasons for lack of reform

► Commons
  - Procedural issues, e.g. timetable, Question Time, facilities for MPs, televising debates and committees
  - Substantive issues: e.g. representativeness: electoral system, two-party system, role of the opposition, parliamentary privilege, devolution
  - 'Elective dictatorship': delegated legislation, devolution, MPs' control of finance, access to information
  - Assessment of past reforms, e.g. departmental committees

── TOPIC NOTES

Key facts and concepts

Essay questions on Parliament cover the Commons, Lords and monarchy (legislative functions only, e.g. royal assent).

Functions of Parliament

- Making the law
- Controlling the executive
- Representing the people

Subsidiary functions
- Debate and deliberation
- Controlling government finance
- Channel of communication between government and electorate

These could provide a useful framework for general essay questions such as 'In what sense, or senses, do we still have an effective Parliament in Britain?' (London, January 1981, P. 1.) Such broad essay questions on the role of Parliament cover the electoral system, party system and practice of parliamentary government – all of which, critics say, combine to limit Parliament's effectiveness in carrying out its functions today. Essay answers should be very broad-ranging, concise and topical.

House of Lords

1. The House of Lords usefully illustrates the difference between the key political concepts of 'power' and 'authority'. Complete the passage below, using either 'power' or 'authority' as appropriate.

   Under the Parliament Acts of 1911 and 1949, the _____ of the Lords to delay legislation was limited to one year. It has no _____ over money bills; but it has the _____ of absolute veto over (a) any bill seeking to extend the life of Parliament, (b) private bills and (c) delegated legislation. However, the Lords derive _____ from tradition, expertise and responsible use of their legal _____. Television broadcasting of their proceedings may also have enhanced their _____.

Essay questions on the House of Lords usually centre on one of the following themes:

(a) How useful is it?
(b) Should it be reformed and, if so, how?
(c) Why has it not been substantially reformed since 1911?

Note the following points.

1) Arguments in support of *a* second chamber do not necessarily justify *this* second chamber: i.e. it is not enough to say 'there must be a check on the Commons'; an essay in defence of the House of Lords must defend a non-elected chamber, the hereditary principle, Prime Ministerial patronage, the permanent Conservative majority, the legislative role of senior judges and Church of England bishops and the low rate of attendance (a product of other factors listed above).

2) A defence of the hereditary principle (and hence non-election) is available from Conservative MP **John Stokes**: 'They are trained for the job from youth onwards and they are truly independent, being answerable to no constituents' (speech in House of Commons, 10 April 1981).

3) Although Conservatives have a numerical majority in the second chamber, it is no longer true to say that the Lords only seek to obstruct or amend Labour legislation. By the 1987 election they had blocked one hundred items of Conservative legislation, including the restrictive Protection of Official Information Bill 1979; the 1984 'Paving Bill' – i.e. the Local Government (Interim Provisions) Bill, paving the way for abolition of the Metropolitan councils by replacing them with nominated bodies; the sale of council houses built for the elderly (1984 and 1986); and the retention of corporal punishment in state schools (1986) against the spirit of a European Court ruling. Within four hours of its first post-election sitting in 1987, the Lords forced the withdrawal and amendment of new extradition proposals contained in the Criminal Justice Bill. This may be because Conservative peers tend to be old-style, traditional Tories; and also because they perceive a duty to provide

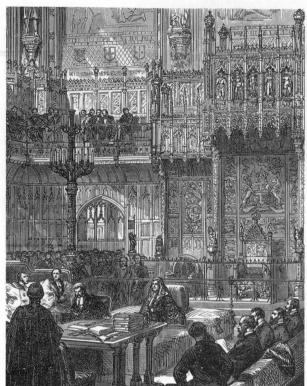

The House of Lords 'then and now': scenes from the Chamber in the 1860s and the 1980s.

effective opposition to strong government when the balance of power in the Commons 'really amounts to a one-party state' (**Norman St John Stevas** – now **Baron St John of Fawsley** – on Channel 4 TV News 17 November 1987). Also, Conservative peers tend to follow the principle that, if a bill was not in the government's manifesto, it does not have a mandate (the so-called 'Salisbury Doctrine'). Many, especially hereditary Conservative 'backwoodsmen', rarely attend at all. Finally, the 250 or so crossbenchers, including Law Lords and bishops, provide a relatively independent element which is absent from the Commons (though most, in practice, usually vote with the Conservative whip).

4) The Lords can help the government and Commons by giving detailed consideration to bills which the Commons, with its crowded timetable, may skimp. For example, the government itself introduced 500 amendments to the Financial Services Act 1986 while it was going through the Lords. Many non-controversial bills, and some controversial ones, are introduced first in the House of Lords, e.g. the Shops (Sunday Trading) Bill 1986. This delays scrutiny by the 'democratic' chamber, and can be an unpopular tactic with the Opposition. The Lords also relieve the Commons of much detailed work especially on delegated legislation, private bills and EC law.

5) Textbooks sometimes cite, as advantageous, the fact that 'the Lords is a place where the Prime Minister can honourably dispose of unwanted MPs', and that 'peers do not have to look to constituency opinion'. Is there also a case against these points?

6) Expertise is often cited as a merit of the Lords; ensure that you can give topical examples in essays, from press and TV coverage of Lords' debates (e.g. Lord Hives is an expert on beekeeping, and contributed usefully to the Bees Act 1980). This point can be related particularly to the Lords' select committees, e.g. on finance, science and technology. Remember, however, that the Commons also contains

experts in many diverse fields, i.e. election does not preclude expertise, though it may render it less permanent.

7) *The views of the parties*

    The **Conservatives** have no official policy on reform of the Lords (traditional Tories support it) though Margaret Thatcher considered introducing the guillotine (time limit on examination of bills) because of the many defeats inflicted by the Lords. This would undermine the usefulness of the Lords, and would have been resisted strongly.

    The **Labour Party** advocated complete abolition of the Lords in its 1983 manifesto, together with reform of the Commons to make it more efficient. However, the more moderate 1987 manifesto did not mention the Lords at all. Then in its 1989 policy review Labour advocated a Charter of Rights: i.e. a number of specific statutes (rather than a Bill of Rights) legally guaranteeing freedom of information, a right to privacy, freedom from discrimination, devolution and stronger controls on the executive and security services. These would be protected by an elected second chamber, replacing the House of Lords, which would have the power to delay for the lifetime of a full Parliament any legislation which seemed to contradict the Charter. The method of election, said Roy Hattersley, was 'unlikely' to be first-past-the-post.

8) Finally, the judicial function of the Lords – as the highest UK court of appeal – should not be included in discussion of the 'parliamentary' (legislative) role of the Lords.

---

2. True or False?

    1) The Lords can veto legislation curbing their own powers.

    2) There is no party discipline in the House of Lords.

    3) Tony Benn was the first peer to renounce his title.

    4) Women cannot inherit peerages.

    5) The Law Lords do not take part in debates on legislation.

Reform of the Lords

Past proposals include:

- 'Functional representation' of pressure and interest groups, rather than a party system (suggested by **Mackintosh**);
- Phasing out of hereditary peers (Labour, 1969 – defeated by a combination of left-wing Labour and right-wing Conservative MPs for whom it was too little and too much, respectively);
- Complete abolition (Labour, 1983);
- Indirect election of representatives from regional bodies (Alliance, 1987 manifesto);
- A directly elected second chamber based on proportional representation (**Lord Hailsham** in his 1976 lecture 'Elective Dictatorship').

---

3. (a) Select any *three* of the above, and write two paragraphs on each: a case for, and a case against.

    (b) Now, decide whether you would advocate reform of the Lords in an essay and, if so, how. Think about its functions, powers and composition, and be as specific and detailed as possible. Remember that the kind of second chamber you want (if any) depends on what you want it to do (if anything).

(c)   Consider any possible problems arising from your proposal; how would you counter or overcome them?

(d)   If you reject reform or abolition of the Lords, write a reasoned and persuasive defence of the present second chamber.

House of Commons

This section attempts to provide only a selective outline of some current controversies, under the headings of Parliament's three key functions listed on page 62.

Making the law

- The **timetable** of the **House of Commons** – 2.30 p.m. to 10.30 p.m., with frequent late and all-night sittings – is often said to be inefficient. Morning sittings, however, were abandoned after a six-month experiment in 1967 and are opposed by most MPs, especially those with jobs outside Westminster. MPs also need time for committee work, and ministers need time for departmental work. A survey by the All Party Reform Group of MPs in 1985 did find strong support among MPs for a fixed 10.00 p.m. adjournment and a fixed parliamentary year; both would make life easier for MPs and more difficult for the government, which often manipulates the timetable to suit itself.

- It is a matter of debate whether Parliament today actually 'makes the law' or merely endorses laws created by the executive. The latter view, the Westminster model of parliamentary government, perhaps understates the legislative function of both Lords and Commons in amending and even defeating government proposals and initiating other types of bills.

  There are **two** main types of bills

  1) **Public bills** – concern the general public interest:
      (a)   Government bills;
      (b)   Money bills (a special type of government bill, which cannot be amended by the Lords);
      (c)   Private members' bills (usually public bills).

  2) **Private bills** – concern individual or group interests: these breach the 'rule of law' and the principle of legal equality; they are therefore subject to special procedures and scrutiny, e.g. the Felixstowe Dock and Railway Bill 1987, extending the harbour area (over which Labour MPs staged a 'filibuster', trying to talk the bill out in an all-night sitting).

  'Hybrid bills' concern both public and private interests: e.g. the Channel Tunnel Act 1987. The Speaker decides classification of bills.

  Public bills lapse if they have not completed all stages at the end of a parliamentary session; this forces the government to organise its legislative programme carefully, and allows a re-think of controversial bills, but it may also waste time.

- In the **committee stage** of bills, if discussion is protracted the government may introduce the 'guillotine': a time limit. Early clauses may therefore be debated at length, and later clauses not considered at all. Ministers blame Opposition MPs for time-wasting; the Opposition argue that the guillotine negates the parliamentary process. Timetabling of all bills in committee, from the start, was recommended by the Select Committee on Procedure but defeated by the House in 1986; it would have strengthened the executive's hand, since time is one of the few weapons available to the Opposition against a majority government.

Kinnock slates guillotine 'outrage'

GLC BILL

By Colin Brown

THE LABOUR leader, Mr **Neil Kinnock**, last night urged Tory MPs to stage a rebellion on Monday night when the Government will seek approval for the guillotine to cut short the committee stage of the Local Government Bill which abolishes the Greater London Council.

Mr Kinnock protested that the imposition of the guillotine was an outrage because the bill, abolishing the GLC and the six metropolitan county councils, would deprive 13 million electors of their democratic rights.

It is opposed by several Tory MPs, who want to see the GLC replaced with a city-wide authority for London. Mr Kinnock said: 'May I express the hope that all members opposed to this measure will join us in our efforts to prevent the guillotine falling on this bill'.

But the leader of the House, **Mr John Biffen**, who announced that there will be a three-hour debate on the guillotine motion in the Commons on Monday, denied that the Government was 'turning the Commons into a Reichstag'.

The committee on the bill still had 80 clauses to debate. After spending 110 hours it only reached Clause 16.

But the Government's real problems remain in the Lords, where it suffered a humiliating defeat on the paving legislation last year. There is no guillotine in the Lords and the Government is seeking as much time as possible to push it through the Upper House and to amend it, if necessary, in the Commons after any further government defeat to ensure that on April 1 1986 the GLC will cease to exist.

The GLC leader, Mr Ken Livingstone, visiting the Commons yesterday, said: 'The Government is gagging the Opposition with less than a quarter of the bill having been discussed'.

The Shadow Environment Secretary, **Dr John Cunningham**, denied that Labour had been wasting time and accused the Government of being scared about what will happen when the bill reaches the Lords.

The Guardian, 8 February 1985

- **Special standing committees** were introduced in 1980: these can investigate the issues behind a bill and may examine witnesses and experts. MPs are more informed as a result, but the process has only been used half-a-dozen times (e.g. for European legislation); more frequent use is often advocated.
- **Delegated legislation** is controversial (and could equally come under the heading of 'controlling the executive' below). It is also known as **indirect** or **secondary legislation**, because it allows ministers, local authorities and others to make detailed regulations, e.g. statutory instruments or by-laws, under powers delegated by Parliament in a parent Act. It thus turns ministers into law-makers, breaching the principle of 'separation of powers'. It has grown up because it allows more time, detail, expertise and flexibility in the law-making process. However, parliamentary scrutiny is inadequate. The Joint and Select Committees on Statutory Instruments have a heavy workload – around 2,000 items a year to examine, each ranging from a couple of paragraphs to a hundred pages or more. Delegated legislation passes through Parliament much more quickly than primary legislation; it can only be challenged it if is incomprehensible or seems illegal under the parent Act – its underlying principles cannot be questioned; and it can only be accepted or rejected as a whole, not amended. The restrictive regulations for board and lodging payments under the Social Security Act 1986, for example, were repeatedly rejected by both the Commons and the courts, but were simply rewritten and re-introduced by the government.

Controlling the executive

This is the most controversial issue of all. Some commentators, like former MP **Enoch Powell,** argue that the task of Parliament is simply to scrutinise and sustain government rather than 'control' it. Others, such as **Stuart Walkland**, say that Parliament should control government but cannot, for the following reasons:

(a)   Majority governments;
(b)   Party discipline;
(c)   Government control of parliamentary time;
(d)   Government secrecy and obfuscation, especially on finance;
(e)   Government control of civil service personnel and information;
(f)   The growth of delegated legislation;
(g)   The lack of power of committees and the Ombudsman;
(h)   Lack of resources and facilities for MPs;
(i)   The growing influence on government of extra-parliamentary bodies such as pressure groups and media.

- **The Opposition**, the second largest party in the Commons, is a formal part of the constitution: the leader, chief whip and two deputies of 'Her Majesty's Opposition' are paid a special salary; they have four civil servants to assist their parliamentary work, and are given special time and opportunities in Commons' procedures which are unavailable to other parties. The Leader of the Opposition is traditionally consulted on bi-partisan matters (e.g. the 1985 Anglo-Irish agreement), and is given a chauffeur-driven car. Since 1985, 20 Opposition Days are set aside in the Commons' yearly timetable for debate and criticism of government (replacing the old Supply Days); on 17 days, the topic is chosen by the leader of the Opposition, and the remaining three days are allocated to the leader of the second largest Opposition party.

   Nevertheless, the Opposition is clearly weak against a majority government. It cannot 'control' the executive; its main function now is to present itself to the electorate as the 'alternative government'. Frustration is demonstrated by low attendance of MPs (though committee work also takes its toll, with only about 70 MPs attending no committee meetings at all; and the mutual convenience of 'pairing' also allows MPs to absent themselves regularly from the Commons). Another outlet for MPs' frustration is rowdiness in the chamber; but this is not confined to the Opposition, and anyway is not nearly as bad as it was in the nineteenth century (today it is publicised and exaggerated by selective broadcasting). Lively debate may be seen as a legitimate tradition of the House. For some commentators, however, MPs' 'bad' behaviour is a symptom of the crisis of legitimacy developing in an unrepresentative, adversarial, executive-dominated House of Commons where the parliamentary process is slowly breaking down.

- **Question Time**, the noisiest and most publicised part of the Commons' day, epitomises government's accountability to Parliament. Around 50,000 questions are asked each year, and about 3,000 oral answers are given (the rest are written) at a cost of over £2 million; but many question the usefulness of the whole exercise, and it has been described as 'ritualised combat' and 'a Punch and Judy show'. The forty-eight hours' notice required for oral questions undermines their topicality; supplementary questions can be topical and also have the element of surprise, but they do not allow detailed discussion of an issue. Prime Minister's Question Time wastes precious minutes on formula questions and answers, about the PM's engagements that day, as a prelude to the supplementaries. Other ministers appear only about once a month under the rota system; and their chief skill often seems to

lie in evading the question, unless it is a 'plant' by the minister or by a supportive colleague to prompt an announcement or an opportunity for self-congratulation.

- **Select committees** (investigative committees) provide better opportunities for scrutiny, if not control, of government. Students of British government must be able to provide a topical assessment, especially of the fourteen departmental committees set up in 1979 by Norman St John Stevas. Their members are chosen by the House on the recommendation of the Commons Committee of Selection, though the whips do try to manipulate membership. Their expenditure is controlled by the Commons, not by the Treasury. They run for a whole Parliament, not just for a session. They attract growing media attention (e.g. the Trade and Industry committee's 1990 investigation of the sale of Rover to British Aerospace), absenteeism is low, and they have been able to extract more information from government: e.g. the Foreign Affairs Committee won access to the 'Crown Jewels' – classified documents on the sinking of the Belgrano during the Falklands conflict of 1982. Serving MPs have thus become better informed and more specialised. The government has sometimes acted on their recommendations: e.g. the Home Affairs Committee's reports on hard drugs and on the repeal of the 'sus' law (Vagrancy Act 1824). However, this last was promptly replaced by the stricter, but little known, Criminal Attempts Act 1981.

  The government often ignores the criticism and recommendations of the committees: e.g. the Employment Committee on the treatment of miners sacked during the 1984–5 strike; the Public Accounts and Defence Committees on the sale of the naval dockyards; the Environment Committee on building the Okehampton bypass through Dartmoor National Park; the Foreign Affairs Committee on leaving UNESCO etc. The committees lack adequate research and administrative resources, and, in practice, they lack the power to demand to see persons and papers. The Bank of England in 1986 refused to supply documents on the tin crisis to the Trade and Industry Committee, and Margaret Thatcher refused to allow William Whitelaw to give evidence to the Home Affairs Committee about a prison breakout. In the Westland affair, Trade and Industry Secretary, Leon Brittan, appeared before the Defence Committee but refused to answer eight questions; and Cabinet Secretary Sir Robert Armstrong appeared for all the civil servants involved, and simply stonewalled. Though the Defence Committee's report on the matter (1986) was highly critical, it was not debated in the Commons; and the government responded (through Armstrong) by imposing new restrictions on civil servants' evidence to the committees.

The government is particularly likely to ignore the committees when they divide on party lines (e.g. the Foreign Affairs Committee produced majority and minority reports on the Falklands); when they are united, they are criticised by radical MPs like Dennis Skinner for their 'sloppy consensus'. Michael Foot dislikes the whole structure of select committees, arguing that they detract energy and attention from the debating chamber as a whole. The Lord Chancellor's department is excluded from scrutiny.

In sum, most commentators agree that they have done little to shift the balance of power between executive and legislature, though they do provide more information, detailed scrutiny and public criticism of government.

> **The Departmental Committees**
>
> Agriculture
> Defence
> Education, Science and Arts
> Employment
> Energy
> Environment
> Foreign Affairs
> Home Affairs
> Scottish Affairs
> Social Services
> Trade and Industry
> Transport
> Treasury and Civil Service
> Welsh Affairs

- **Control of finance**: The House of Lords plays no part in this major aspect of executive accountability. The Commons has three days set aside in each session for discussion of government estimates of how much money is required by each department. The annual Budget and Finance Act provides the necessary government revenue through taxation and borrowing. The departmental committees examine the spending of each department (the old Expenditure committee was thus abolished in 1979). The Comptroller and Auditor General has, since the National Audit Act 1983, been independent of the Treasury; he audits government expenditure and reports to the Public Accounts Committee. This is a senior and influential backbench committee, traditionally chaired by an Opposition member. It can question civil servants and other witnesses, and is assisted by over 900 auditors and staff in the National Audit Office. It reports to the House, and its findings are publicised in the press.

  Nevertheless, the Public Accounts Committee said in 1987 that the Commons' control of government finance – 'Parliament's key constitutional function' – is 'largely a formality'. This is partly because a majority government can dominate the Commons, but also because the estimates and accounts provided by Whitehall are both too vague about key financial categories and objectives, and too complex on minor details. The budgets of the security and intelligence services (an estimated £1,000 million per year) are not subject to parliamentary scrutiny; nor are the nationalised industries. The Comptroller and Auditor General in 1987 also accused apathetic MPs of ignoring his many critical reports about government waste and mismanagement.

Representing the people

- The pros and cons of the electoral system (discussed in Chapter 3) are obviously central to this issue.
- A further point to consider is the issue of **devolution**: the delegating of some legislative or executive powers from central to regional bodies. Britain has a system of local government, but no local Parliaments. Despite the failure of the Scottish and Welsh referenda of 1979, the heat has not gone out of the devolution issue; an essay question such as '"Parliament is now failing the nation." Discuss.' (London, June 1983, P. 1.) could still prompt the response: which nation? In the 1987 election the Conservatives won only ten of Scotland's 72 seats, and some Scottish nationalists therefore argued that Westminster and Whitehall had no authority to control Scottish affairs. The setting up of the Commons departmental committees after the election was delayed because the opposition parties argued (unsuccessfully) against the government's right to keep its majority on the Scottish Affairs Committee despite its minority of Scottish seats. In January 1988 the Labour Party used one of its Opposition Days to promote its own devolution bill advocating tax-raising powers for a Scottish Parliament (which would also help to relieve the Commons' legislative workload).
- **Parliamentary privilege** is the exemption of MPs from some ordinary laws under the special laws and customs of Parliament. It is therefore a special category of constitutional law, which breaches 'the rule of law' and principle of legal equality. It was originally a defence against the power of the Crown, and is now justified on the grounds that MPs can better represent people if, for example, they have complete freedom of speech. Thus they are immune from slander or libel actions for words in spoken in Parliament. This may be used to expose wrongdoing, e.g. **Peter Wright's** allegations about MI5 in his banned book, *Spycatcher*, were repeated in the Commons in 1986 by Labour MP **Dale Campbell-Savours**, allowing the press to report them under the same cloak of privilege. However, this freedom may be abused by MPs; in 1980 **Geoffrey Rooker** MP accused a Rolls Royce executive of taking bribes, and later had to apologise; and in 1986 **Geoffrey Dickens** MP named two men suspected of child abuse, though neither was ultimately convicted.

    Other privileges, e.g. freedom from arrest, may now seem anachronistic or excessive. The right of Parliament to control its own proceedings is reasonable, but its right to try and to punish outsiders for 'contempt of Parliament' is controversial. This crime includes refusing to answer questions (e.g. Ian and Kevin Maxwell in 1991–2 before the Social Services Committee); pressurising MPs to vote in a certain way; publishing Commons' papers without permission; and speeches or articles which 'bring the House into odium, contempt or ridicule or lower its authority' ('Spitting Image', beware!). The 'trial', by the Committee of Privileges, is secret and invariably party political, with no procedural safeguards for the accused. The punishment is usually just a public rebuke in the House by the Speaker, but technically Parliament can fine or imprison offenders. Barrister **Geoffrey Robertson** is one critic of this aspect of Parliamentary privilege likening it to a 'kangaroo court'.

- **Televising** of the Commons (and its committees) was regularly debated in the House, and finally accepted in 1988. It enhances open government and freedom of the media; and many Labour MPs believe that TV, with its statutory duty of impartiality, will present a more balanced and fair view of party politics than does much of the British press. However, some MPs argued that it would encourage bad behaviour by MPs and public in the House, while others feared that selective broadcasting may trivialise, sensationalise or distort proceedings and undermine the authority of the Commons. Minority parties are under-represented in televised proceedings as they are in the Commons itself: thus the Liberal Democrats opposed the idea. However, the experiment of televising the Commons and its committees is clearly now here to stay.
- A related issue is the **lobby system**, which involves the briefing of specialist TV and press correspondents by MPs and ministers in Westminster and Whitehall on an unattributable basis, i.e. the media cannot name their sources. *The Independent*, *The Guardian* and *Scotsman* therefore did not use the system from 1986 until 1991 (post Thatcher). A survey of MPs in 1989 (by the Campaign for Freedom of Information) found that over 75% of the 200 who responded wished to see an end to the system of collective unattributable briefings. With the departure of Mrs Thatcher and her controversial press secretary **Bernard Ingham** in 1990, the lobby system has less often been perceived as a channel of media manipulation, misinformation and propaganda.

---

4.   Quick quiz. Briefly answer the following questions.

   1)   When did a monarch last refuse assent to a bill?
   2)   What is a White Paper?
   3)   Who is responsible for drafting government bills?

4) List the stages of legislation for public bills.
5) What is a joint committee?
6) What is *Hansard*?
7) Once elected, does the Speaker cease to be an MP?
8) List *three* functions of the Speaker.
9) Who is the present Speaker of the Commons?
10) What are Standing Orders?
11) What is a 'simple closure'?
12) What are 'the usual channels'?
13) List *three* functions of the whips.
14) What is 'pairing'?
15) What is meant by 'withdrawing the whip' from an MP?
16) Why might an MP seek a written rather than oral answer at Question Time?
17) What is the function of the Ombudsman?
18) What is the Consolidated Fund?
19) When was a government last defeated in the Commons on a vote of no confidence?
20) What is (a) the PLP and (b) the 1922 Committee?

---

5. Consider the possible reforms of the Commons listed (in no particular order) below.

(a) First, decide whether each is merely *procedural* or involves a *substantive* change in functions or powers. Now, decide which you would and would not advocate in an essay on the subject, and why.

(b) Consider whether one reform may require, generate or preclude another – i.e. ensure that your choices are consistent and compatible.

(c) Consider any possible problems arising from your chosen reforms; how would you counter or overcome them?

(d) Can you add any suggested reforms to this list?
  - Ombudsman: broader role (e.g. over police); more staff; more power over Whitehall; more publicity
  - Fixed-term elections
  - Full-time MPs
  - Compulsory registration/abolition of consultancy fees for MPs
  - Push-button or proxy voting for MPs in the House
  - Reform of electoral system (specify, and consider consequences)
  - Freedom of information for MPs and committees
  - More free votes in the House
  - Reform of parliamentary lobby system (abolition of secrecy)
  - Prohibition of retrospective law
  - More use of special standing committees
  - Devolution – Scotland/Wales/Ireland/English regions
  - Morning sittings
  - Fixed 10.00 p.m. adjournment
  - Better pay, research and office facilities for MPs

- More power (to scrutinise people and papers) and more publicity for select committees
- Abolition of all/obsolete parliamentary privileges
- Abolition of the guillotine
- Bills to be carried over from one session to the next
- Less control by whips of committee appointments
- Abolition of pairing
- More opportunities and (legal) assistance for private members' bills
- Reduction/abolition of notice for oral questions
- Better parliamentary scrutiny of delegated legislation
- An Opposition civil service

—— ESSAYS

1)   *Theme*   **House of Lords**

Q?   Should the House of Lords be abolished? Why have attempts at comprehensive reform of the House of Lords always failed?

(Simulated question.)

A✓   **Notes for guidance**

This is a two-part question; unless otherwise stated, assume half marks for each part.
Part 1 'Should the Lords be abolished?' – is evaluative; decide your conclusion at the planning stage and structure accordingly, putting your own case last.
Part 2 'Why …?' – is largely descriptive; your answer should centre on a list of reasons – 'Because …'
There is some scope for overlap between the two parts of the question; decide at the planning stage where best to put each point, and avoid repetition.

Essay plan

Part 1
1)   1983 Labour proposal: uni-cameral legislature.
2)   Crits. of Lords (case for abolition *or* mere reform):
      Non-elected, undemocratic, unaccountable, hereditary principle, Prime Ministerial patronage, unrepresentative, Conservative majority, low attendance, little power, poor check against elective dictatorship. Thus, if House lacks power, it is inadequate; if it has power, it is illegitimate. Opinion polls suggest majority support for reform, but not for abolition.
3)   Abolition

Case against	*Case for*
Would lose constitutional check: esp. veto over extending life of Parliament, and dismissal of judges. (Monarch's veto unsatisfactory.)	Check inadequate; majority government could change law to remove veto, or second chamber, first.

Delaying power valuable.	Rarely used since 1949; and not legitimate anyway.
Double scrutiny of bills is valuable safeguard; checks and balances in lib. dem., e.g. USA, France etc. bi-cameral.	Commons should do it properly. Should reform Commons. Denmark, Sweden, New Zealand and others uni-cameral.
Would require major reform of Commons for efficiency and constitutional checks.	Commons in need of major reform; abolition of Lords would provide impetus.
Would lose independent, leisurely and expert debate and scrutiny of Lords.	Should not be independent of voters. Again, Commons should have more time and expertise.
What about the judicial function of the Lords?	Should be separated out, as per liberal democratic theory.
Traditional authority of Lords.	No inherent virtue in the past.
'Representative' claims of Commons and government are also questionable.	True: should have PR, written and rigid constitution and Bill of Rights subject to referenda, instead of non-elected Lords.

Therefore, yes, Lords should be abolished.

Part 2

1) Attempts have not *always* failed: 1911 …
   Reforms since: 1949, 1958, 1963 … not 'comprehensive'.
   Failed attempt: Labour, 1969 …
   (Conservative proposal, 1978 – not attempted.)

2) Because
   (a) Arguments in favour of present chamber – case against abolition, above. Useful functions – veto, delay, amendment, debate, etc. Especially since Lords are now active against Conservative as well as Labour governments;
   (b) Lack of cross-party and intra-party consensus re. functions, powers and composition of a reformed chamber;
   (c) Democratised chamber could be rival to Commons, or obstructive;
   (d) All governments are reluctant to increase constraints against themselves;
   (e) Would be time-consuming and difficult, involving Commons, judiciary, Church and even monarchy. Governments have higher priorities, e.g. economic policy. Little public concern;
   (f) Prime Ministers of all parties find power of patronage useful;
   (g) Conservatives not enthusiastic about reform; minority parties (e.g. Liberal Democrats) have lacked opportunity;

3) **Conclusion:** Lack of political will for reform, though strong case for it; and abolition viable if alternative constitutional safeguards were introduced.

2) *Theme*   **Authority of Parliament**

Q?   Are there factors which are undermining the authority of Parliament in Britain?

(London, June 1980, P. 1.)

A✓   Plan

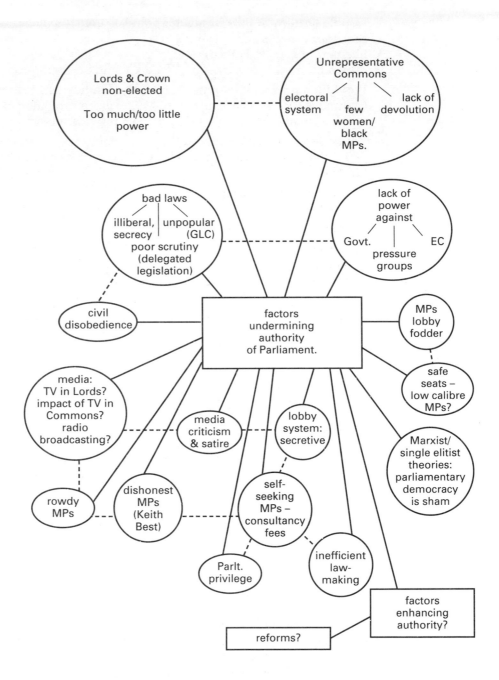

Additional essay tips

- The keyword in the above title is *authority*. If you write an answer about Parliament's lack of *power* – e.g. over the executive – it will often not be relevant. Instead, concentrate on factors which may be reducing the **legitimacy**, **reputation** and **status** of Parliament e.g. in the eyes of the electorate. Authority may shape power, or vice versa; be absolutely clear in defining and distinguishing the two concepts.

● **Note**   Crown, Lords and Commons are all relevant here.

---

6. Write a timed, structured essay using the diagrammatic plan on page 76.

---

7. Write at least one of the following essays.
Always write a brief plan first.

1) If you were asked to design a second chamber by some form of election, what would your response be?

(Oxford, June 1984, P. 1.)

2) Does the continued expansion of delegated legislation threaten the survival of the rule of law in Britain?

(Cambridge, June 1985, P. 1.)

3) Why was a new system of departmental select committees introduced in the House of Commons in 1979–80? How successful has this development been?

(JMB, June 1986, P. 1.)

4) In what ways and how successfully is Parliament able to control and hold accountable
   (a)   the civil service?   (10 marks)
   (b)   the government?   (15 marks)

(AEB, November 1989, P. 1.)

5) In what ways does the Commons seek to control finance? How effective are its procedures?

(Oxford and Cambridge, June 1990, P. 2.)

── GUIDE TO EXERCISES

Page 63

1.   Power; power; power; authority; power; authority.

Page 65

2.   1)   False.
     2)   False.
     3)   False – Lord Home was the first to renounce his peerage.
     4)   False.
     5)   False.

Page 72

4.   1)   1707 – Queen Anne, the Scotch Militia Bill.
     2)   An outline of proposed legislation, before publication of a bill.
     3)   The Parliamentary Counsel of 30 lawyers – part of government, not Parliament.

4) First reading, second reading, committee stage, report stage, third reading, amendments in the Upper House, royal assent.
5) A committee of MPs and peers combined.
6) The official record of proceedings in the Commons.
7) No.
8) (a) Decides allocation of time to parties and MPs.
   (b) Exercises casting vote on a bill where votes are tied; by convention, arranges for vote to be taken again.
   (c) Selects chairmen for, and allocates bills to, standing committees.
9) Currently Bernard Weatherill (1991).
10) Written rules on the conduct of Commons' business.
11) A time limit on debate in the Commons; the Speaker decides whether to allow a vote on it, and 100+ MPs must win a majority vote for motion to be carried.
12) The government and Opposition chief whips, who between them arrange special debates etc.
13) (a) Circulate weekly notice of Commons' business to MPs.
    (b) Arrange pairing, ensure that MPs vote as required, and count the votes.
    (c) Convey backbench opinion and recommendations for promotion to the party leadership.
14) Government and Opposition backbenchers arrange permanent 'pairs' at the beginning of each Parliament; they can then be mutually absent on important votes (with the permission of the whips).
15) Suspending or expelling the MP from the party.
16) More detailed information.
17) To investigate citizens' complaints of maladministration by government departments.
18) The government's account at the Bank of England.
19) 1979 – a minority Labour government.
20) (a) The Parliamentary Labour Party – all Labour front and backbenchers in the Commons.
    (b) All Conservative backbenchers; not frontbenchers.

—— REFERENCES

John Mackintosh, cited in W. B. Gwyn and R. Rose (eds), *Britain: Progress and Decline* (Macmillan, 1980).

Geoffrey Robertson, 'Out of Court' in *The Guardian* 24.1.83.

Stuart Walkland in S. A. Walkland and Michael Ryle, *The Commons in the Seventies* (Fontana, 1977).

Hugo Young, 'The Thud of Heads Against a Brick Wall' in *The Guardian* 17.11.87.

6 Executive: Monarchy, Prime Minister and Cabinet

> ## KEY ISSUES
>
> ▶ Parliamentary government: elective dictatorship?
>
> ▶ Monarchy: legal versus actual powers
> Arguments for and against the monarchy
> Uses/abuses of the royal prerogative
>
> ▶ Cabinet: Ministerial responsibility – to whom: the Crown,
> Prime Minister, Parliament or voters?
> Effectiveness of conventions of collective and individual
> responsibility
> Sources of Cabinet power: constraints and influences
>
> ▶ Prime Minister: powers and limitations
> Cabinet or Prime Ministerial government?
> Is British government becoming presidential?
> What was 'Thatcherism'?

── TOPIC NOTES

Key facts and concepts

The executive consists of: the **Crown**; the **political policy-makers** – Prime Minister, Cabinet and other ministers (around one hundred altogether); and the **administrators** – the civil servants, a hierarchy of non-elected, permanent, impartial and professional bureaucrats who administer the policies and machinery of government. The work of government is divided into around **50 government departments** – defence, employment, education etc. – and the ministerial heads of the 20 or so major departments are usually in the Cabinet.

In the British system of parliamentary government, the ministers are accountable to Parliament, and thus to the electorate, for the policies of government and the actions of government departments.

The monarchy

The **Crown** is the permanent, abstract institution which embodies the supreme power of the state. It is the formal head of all three branches of government (legislature, executive and judiciary) and all acts of state are done in the name of the Crown. The **monarchy** is the institution of hereditary, royal rule (as opposed to a **republic**, which is usually headed by an elected president). The **sovereign** or **monarch** is the person upon whom the Crown is conferred. In Britain, succession to the throne is determined by the Act of Settlement 1701; this states, for example, that male heirs take precedence over females, and that the monarch may not be, or marry, a Roman Catholic – outdated and offensive rules, according to some critics.

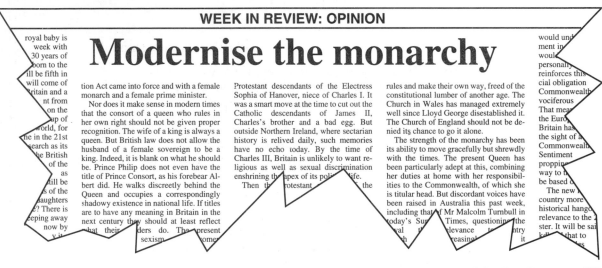

Sunday Times, 31 January 1988 © Times Newspapers 1988

The **royal prerogative** is the term given to the formal powers of the Crown. They are part of common law, and in theory are substantial (see list below). However, Britain no longer has an **absolute monarchy**, but a **constitutional monarchy**: an impartial (non-party political), largely symbolic head of state whose powers are exercised by, and on the advice of, ministers, in theory subordinate to the will of Parliament, the people and the rules of the constitution. This is meant to democratise the powers of the Crown and to keep the monarch out of political controversy. In the nineteenth century **Bagehot** classed the monarchy as a 'dignified' rather than 'efficient' part of the constitution, with much symbolical and ceremonial authority but little real power. Except in times of constitutional crisis, therefore, 'The Queen reigns, but does not rule'.

The royal prerogative

- Appointment and dismissal of the Prime Minister. In practice, usually governed by convention: the monarch chooses the leader of the majority party in the House of Commons, and the PM resigns if defeated in a general election or a vote of no confidence. However, if there is a hung Parliament or if the PM refuses to resign according to convention, the rules are unclear, and the monarch may exercise some real choice and power of appointment and dismissal.
- Other appointments and powers of patronage, e.g. ministers, peers, senior Church of England clergy, judges, civil servants, heads of the BBC and IBA, all honours and titles, etc. In practice, all are chosen or approved by the Prime Minister; only the Order of the Garter and Order of Merit are at the personal disposal of the monarch.

- Opening and dissolving of Parliament, and approval of statute law. In practice, the PM chooses the date of the election within the five-year term; the Queen simply participates in the ceremonies and reads the Queen's Speech – an outline of the government's legislative proposals written by the government. No monarch has refused royal assent for a bill since Queen Anne in 1707 (the Scotch Militia Bill).
- The granting of pardon: exercised by the Home Secretary.
- Declarations of war, treaties etc. may be made under the royal prerogative by proclamations or orders in council, without reference to Parliament. In practice exercised by the PM acting in the name of the Crown: e.g. Treaty of Accession 1972 making Britain a member of the EEC (Heath); the Falklands conflict 1982 (Thatcher); the banning of trade unions for civil servants at the government's intelligence gathering centre, Government Communications Headquarters (GCHQ) in 1984 (Thatcher); the Gulf War in 1991 (Major). Such actions do not require the approval of the monarch, and may also by-pass democratic accountability to Parliament.

The Royal Prerogative as a threat to the rule of law

Patrick McAuslan on a revived power that circumvents democracy

THE SUGGESTION, confirmed by the Prime Minister, that bugging and burgling by MI5 may be justifiable under the Royal Prerogative has clearly come as a surprise to many people, including Lord Denning and Merlyn Rees, both of whom vigorously repudiated such a notion in the letters column of this newspaper. It seems, however, that they are wrong.

The conventional view of the Royal Prerogative is that, following the Glorious Revolution of 1688, it was made subject to parliamentary control; and our constitution, based on parliamentary government under rule of law, dates from that time. How then can any actions which at first sight appear illegal, be justifiable, ie, legally supportable, by reference to this Royal Prerogative?

The fact is that the Royal Prerogative is alive and well and living for the most part in 10 Downing Street.

The authoritative jurist Albert Dicey defined the Royal Prerogative as "the residue of discretionary power left at any moment in the hands of the Crown, whether such power be in fact exercised by the Queen herself or by her ministers". It derives from the days before elected governments, when monarchs ruled the country and exercised powers over the citizenry. These powers, unique to the monarch, were his or her "prerogative" powers. Servants of the monarch, acting on his or her behalf, could also exercise the prerogative powers.

Modern elected governments govern in the Queen's name. Most of their powers are derived from the statute, and the constitutional struggles of the seventeenth century, confirmed by later judicial decisions, determined that prerogative powers could be displaced by Acts of Parliament and not vice versa, and that their use by elected governments was subject to parliamentary control and limited judicial supervision. But prerogative powers still exist and are still used by governments.

Much of the conduct of foreign affairs is carried on under the authority of the Royal Prerogative: for example, the declaration of war and the making of peace. Other examples of prerogative powers exercised by, or on the advice of, the government of the day are the granting of honours and the exercise of mercy. What currently gives cause for concern is that the Government appears willing to use such powers to circumvent actual or anticipated opposition to its policies; and the courts, though indicating a willingness in principle to control exercises of prerogative power, have in practice not done so.

The GCHQ case first alerted lawyers and others to the revived and aggressive use of prerogative powers by the Government. In January 1984, the Prime Minister unilaterally altered the terms of service of civil servants working in the GCHQ, forbidding them to be members of trade unions. In so acting, she exercised powers under the Royal Prerogative, for all civil servants are, *au fond*, servants of the Crown. She thus avoided the need for parliamentary approval.

The legality of her action was challenged in the courts, but the Lords, when the case eventually came before them, upheld her right to act, as she had done so on the grounds of national security. The decision provided powerful support for the use of the catch-all 'national security' argument as a justification for the use of prerogative powers.

Three years later, another unusual use of prerogative powers was sanctioned by the courts. In 1986, The Home Secretary issued a circular to chief constables inviting them to go behind the backs of their police authorities and obtain the support of HM Inspector of Constabulary, to try and bounce the authorities into agreeing to the chief constables' stocking supplies of plastic bullets and CS gas. In the event of any authority still being unwilling to allow such equipment to be stocked, the circular made it plain that the Home Office would nonetheless supply it.

The Northumbrian Police Authority challenged the lawfulness of this circular and the proposed action under it in the courts. The Divisional Court and the Court of Appeal found both to be lawful. The proposed action was justified as being an exercise of power under the Royal Prerogative: the prerogative of the maintenance of peace within the kingdom.

The judges gave the narrowest possible interpretation to the fundamental constitutional principle that where statute law and prerogative power cover the same subject matter, statute law always prevails. They said that since the 1964 Police Act did not specifically state that the Home Secretary could not supply police forces with equipment, it followed that the Act did not cover the whole subject, and prerogative powers were available to the Home Secretary to justify supply of equipment against the wishes of the police authority.

Legislation does not, and indeed cannot, cover absolutely all possible eventualities. The judgments in this case seem to be saying that if ministers find that they do not have power under a statute to take a certain action, they can nonetheless take action and justify it by reference to the Royal Prerogative. If they can in addition claim that the action taken is necessary in the national interest, then they will be free of any effective scrutiny.

Given these judicial decisions, it is easier to understand the claim that MI5 can justify its actions by reference to the Royal Prerogative. Officers of the security services could even be empowered to kill their fellow citizens, for one aspect of the Royal Prerogative is the defence of the realm. If there were any doubt, it should have been dispelled by the decision, announced yesterday, not to prosecute police officers who covered up unlawful killings in Northern Ireland. National security considerations were cited by the Attorney General as one reason for this.

Support may also be derived from the remarkable statement by Lord Donaldson, Master of the Rolls, in the Court of Appeal last Friday, that where members of the security services do commit illegal acts, there is always a prerogative power not to pursue criminal proceedings. This statement was confirmed by the Prime Minister herself in the House of Commons on Monday.

The present state of affairs is not consistent with any notion of constitutional democracy under the rule of law. The Government's willingness to use prerogative powers to get its way and national security to block scrutiny of what it is doing is as much a threat to parliamentary control of the executive as ever was James II's use of prerogative powers. It is, indeed, alarming that exactly 300 years after the Glorious Revolution, the executive is reviving the use of the prerogative to extend its powers over the citizenry.

The Independent, 27 January 1988

Crown immunity

The monarch, in her private capacity, is above the law. The legal immunity conferred by the royal prerogative may extend to institutions and servants of the Crown: e.g. in 1991 Home Secretary Kenneth Baker claimed Crown immunity when he was ruled to be in contempt of court for ignoring a court order against deportation of an asylum seeker. There is constitutional and legal debate among senior judges about whether Crown immunity extends to MI5 officers, allowing them to 'bug and burgle' without fear of prosecution; in 1988 Lord Donaldson (Master of the Rolls) seemed to suggest that they are in some ways above the law; Lord Hailsham (former Lord Chancellor) said that they are not.

Case for the monarchy

As the actual powers of the monarchy have declined, its symbolic and ceremonial functions have increased. The monarch is an impartial head of state, and thus a symbol of national unity, stability and continuity. As head of the Church of England [s]he promotes Christian morality and family life. The British monarch is also head of many Commonwealth countries; [s]he promotes good international relations and trade, while the pomp and ceremony of royal pageantry is good for tourism. The link with the Crown – royal assent, prerogative etc. – lends authority and legitimacy to Parliament and government. The Queen has long experience and exceptional knowledge of British and international politics which may be a valuable source of advice to governments and Prime Ministers. She does her job conscientiously and competently, and both monarch and monarchy are currently quite popular.

Case against the monarchy

Approval of the symbolic role of the monarchy is a conservative view which favours the status quo and fears progressive change. The monarchy has an ideological role in promoting class hierarchy, privilege, snobbery and deference, and its existence reduces British citizens to subjects. It is also anachronistic to have one established church in the modern, multi-cultural age. Heredity is no guarantee of merit, and the aristocracy and patronage perpetuated by the institution of monarchy are undemocratic. The popularity of the monarchy is said by critics to be largely a product of socialisation by the media, which trivialises the royal family while neglecting any pluralist debate about the political institution of the monarchy itself. The formal powers of the monarch, such as the royal assent, are redundant and should be abolished. The powers and immunities conferred on the Prime Minister and others by the royal prerogative are undemocratic, by-passing Parliament and breaching the 'rule of law'.

The **Civil List** – an annual grant from Parliament, by 1991 almost £8 million – pays for the personal income and households of leading members of the royal family, but not for the upkeep of the royal estates, yacht, train, plane, horses and carriages, travel etc. The monarch's exemption from taxation is also controversial, and was the target of an unsuccessful private member's bill introduced in 1991 by Liberal Democrat MP, **Simon Hughes**. The monarchy is therefore sometimes criticised on grounds of cost; but it also generates revenue (e.g. through tourism) and any alternative, such as an elected president, may have similar financial costs and benefits.

---

1. Briefly answer the following questions.

    1) Suggest why the powers of the Crown have not been formally transferred to the Prime Minister and other ministers.

    2) Suggest *three* exceptional circumstances in which the monarch may exercise real power.

3) Since the monarch usually has little real power, give reasons why the royal prerogative – the power of the Crown – is still controversial.

The Cabinet

The 20 or so most senior government ministers form the **Cabinet**, which grew out of the body of policy advisers to the monarch in the eighteenth century. According to current constitutional theory (since Bagehot), we have **Cabinet government**: collective policy-making by a united team of senior ministers with the Prime Minister *primus inter pares* (first among equals). All Cabinet ministers are MPs or peers, and most are heads of major government departments such as the Foreign Office and Treasury. The Prime Minister decides the size and composition of the Cabinet, and allocates portfolios, i.e. departmental responsibilities.

The Ministers of the Crown Act 1937 gives ministers (together with the Opposition Leader and Chief Whip) a special salary; but the Cabinet's composition, functions and powers are governed entirely by conventions. The two most important of these are the doctrines of **collective** and **individual ministerial responsibility**.

Collective responsibility

This doctrine rests on the assumption that Cabinet ministers make policy decisions collectively, and suggests that they should therefore publicly support and defend all government policy, and should be accountable for it to Parliament and thus to the electorate, e.g. through Question Time and votes of censure in the Commons. If ministers disagree so strongly with a policy that they cannot defend it in public, they should resign, as Sir Geoffrey Howe did in 1990 over Britain's approach to the EC. A united front, even it it is sometimes a façade, increases public confidence in the government and gives it strength and stability. More importantly, collective responsibility is central to the democratic accountability of government to Parliament and thus to the people.

Until 1990 this convention was said to be weakening; perhaps because of the rise of Prime Ministerial power, adversary politics and/or intra-party divisions, ministers since the 1970s have often disagreed publicly with government policy but have not resigned over it: e.g. Tony Benn (Labour radical) in the 1970s and Peter Walker (Conservative 'wet') in the 1980s. Michael Heseltine said that he resigned in 1986 because the Westland affair was not collectively discussed in Cabinet, and therefore he would not be bound by collective responsibility. Many dissident 'wets' were, however, sacked by Margaret Thatcher, including Ian Gilmour, Norman St John Stevas, James Prior and Francis Pym; and the resignations of Nigel Lawson and Geoffrey Howe in 1990 were clear examples of collective responsibility in operation.

Occasionally, the Prime Minister has been obliged to allow ministers to disagree publicly over an issue so controversial that the enforcement of collective responsibility would have risked mass resignations and the collapse of the government. Such **agreement to differ** occurred in 1975 over the EC referendum under Harold Wilson, and again in 1977 under James Callaghan over the European Assembly Elections Bill.

Individual responsibility

This doctrine rests on the assumption that ministerial heads of department are the chosen representatives of the people, while the non-elected civil servants who administer policy within each department are impartial, anonymous bureaucrats carrying out political orders. All ministers with portfolio should therefore be publicly accountable for all the actions of their department, and should resign in the event of serious error.

However, this convention is also weakening. The last minister to resign over a relatively minor error was Thomas Dugdale in 1954 over Crichel Down (farmland taken over by the Ministry of Agriculture during the war and not returned to the owner afterwards). In 1982 Foreign Secretary, Lord Carrington, resigned over the Falklands conflict, and Trade and Industry Secretary, Leon Brittan, took the blame for the leak of a confidential letter and resigned during the Westland affair; but in both of these cases, the very survival of the Prime Minister and government was at stake. In other cases, civil servants are becoming more accountable to Parliament (e.g. to the Ombudsman and select committees), while ministers have *not* resigned: e.g. Chancellor Nigel Lawson over the collapse of Johnson Matthey Bank in 1984, Northern Ireland Secretary James Prior over the mass escape of IRA prisoners in the same year and Home Secretary Kenneth Baker over the Brixton prison escapes in 1991. This may undermine the democratic accountability of government ministers, and openly embroil civil servants in controversial political matters. Individual responsibility may also cover personal impropriety: e.g. Cecil Parkinson who resigned over an affair with his secretary in 1983 (but was reappointed to Cabinet in 1987); Edwina Currie over her comments about salmonella in eggs (1988) and Nicholas Ridley over his anti-German remarks in a *Spectator* interview in 1990.

---

2.   Cabinet authority: sources and constraints.
     Which factors do you think are the most important?
     Can you add any others?

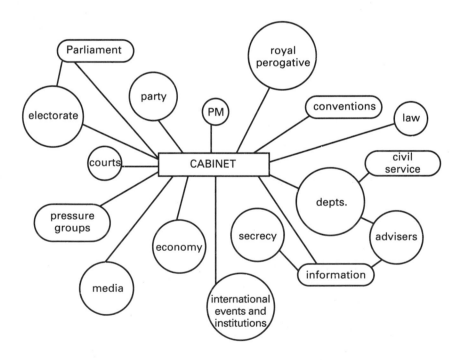

Prime Ministers 1900–92	
1900–2	Marquis of Salisbury (Cons.)
1902–5	Arthur Balfour (Cons.)
1905–8	Sir Henry Campbell-Bannerman (Lib.)
1908–16	Herbert Asquith (Lib.)
1916–22	David Lloyd George (Lib.)
	(War) coalition govt. with Cons.
1922–3	Andrew Bonar Law (Cons.)
1923–4	Stanley Baldwin (Cons.)
1924	James MacDonald (Lab.)
	Minority government.
1924–9	Stanley Baldwin (Cons.)
1929–35	James MacDonald (Lab.)
	Econ. crisis; coalition 'national government' 1931–5.
1935–7	Stanley Baldwin (Cons.)
1937–40	Neville Chamberlain (Cons.)
1940–5	Winston Churchill (Cons.)
	War coalition government.
1945–51	Clement Attlee (Lab.)
1951–5	Sir Winston Churchill (Cons.)
	Resigned 1955; PM Eden called and won election.
1955–7	Sir Anthony Eden (Cons.)
	Resigned over ill-health and Suez.
1957–63	Harold Macmillan (Cons.)
	Resigned 1963. No general election.
1963–4	Sir Alec Douglas-Home (Cons.)
1964–70	Harold Wilson (Lab.)
	Majority of four. Re-elected 1966.
1970–4	Edward Heath (Cons.)
1974–6	Harold Wilson (Lab.)
	Feb. 1974 minority government.
	Oct. 1974 election; majority of three.
	Resigned March 1976. No general election.
1976–9	James Callaghan (Lab.)
	1977–9 minority government. 'Lib-Lab Pact'.
	Defeated on vote of censure in Commons.
1979–90	Margaret Thatcher (Cons.)
	Resigned 1990. No general election.
1990–	John Major (Cons.)

The Prime Minister

By convention, the monarch chooses as Prime Minister the leader of the majority party in the Commons. The first Prime Minister in the modern sense is usually said to be Sir Robert Peel, who held office after the 1832 Reform Act which established the principle of executive accountability through Parliament to the electorate.

The **powers of the Prime Minister**, derived from the royal prerogative, rest entirely on convention:

1) Deciding the structure of government, e.g. creating, merging or splitting departments.

Sir Robert Peel (1788–1850).

2) Appointing and dismissing all ministers, selecting Cabinet ministers and allocating departmental responsibilities.
3) Deciding the agenda for Cabinet meetings, chairing Cabinet meetings, and summing up decisions reached in Cabinet.
4) Deciding the number, composition and terms of reference of Cabinet committees; and may chair important committees personally.
5) Co-ordinating government policy.
6) Political head of the civil service, ultimately responsible for numbers, duties and conditions of work.
7) Appointing top civil servants, judiciary, clergy, etc.; awarding peerages, honours and titles.
8) Representing the government and country at international summits etc.
9) Communicating government policy and advice to the monarch through weekly meetings.
10) Deciding the date of the general election within the five-year term.
11) Deciding the timetable of government legislation in the Commons; a function usually delegated to the Leader of the House, a senior Cabinet minister.
12) Leader of the party (this role differs somewhat within different parties).

According to the theory of Cabinet government the Prime Minister is simply first among equals, but a leader who can hire and fire all other ministers is clearly more than that. The conventional list of the PM's powers is extensive, and since the 1960s many commentators have perceived a trend towards Prime Ministerial rather than Cabinet government in Britain. However, the actual powers of a Prime Minister vary considerably according to circumstance; above all, they depend on **authority**.

Cabinet or Prime Ministerial government?

Former Labour minister **Richard Crossman**, in the 1960s, was among the first to assert that 'The post-war epoch has seen the final transformation of cabinet government into prime ministerial government'. He borrowed Bagehot's phraseology to argue that the Cabinet had joined the monarchy in 'dignified impotence', and cited three main reasons for the rise in the power of the PM:

1) The rise of disciplined parties.
2) The creation of the Cabinet Secretariat (1916) – the body of civil servants who administer the machinery of Cabinet, and who are largely under the control of the Prime Minister.
3) The unification of the civil service under the Prime Minister in 1919, which gave the PM effective control of the Whitehall bureaucracy.

Crossman later revised his thinking, but others have taken up the theme, including writers such as John Mackintosh and Hugo Young, and politicians such as Michael Heseltine (during the Westland affair) and Tony Benn. It is often difficult to assess the real balance of power within the executive because of the exceptional secrecy which shrouds the whole machinery of government and policy-making, but these commentators point to the following:

Factors enhancing Prime Ministerial power

- **Time:** The PM has no departmental responsibilities.
- **Control of Cabinet committees:** These, according to writer **Peter Hennessy**, are the real 'engine room' of British government. Their number, composition and terms of reference are secret, but there are believed to be about 135 committees now – fewer than under previous Prime Ministers such as Attlee. They may contain both ministers and/or civil servants; the PM decides whether they make recommendations to the full Cabinet or actually make policy decisions.

Some key Cabinet committees

EA	Economic affairs, energy policy, labour legislation. (Chaired by Prime Minister.)
OD	Overseas and defence policy, Northern Ireland. (Chaired by Prime Minister.)
H	Home affairs, social policy. (Chaired by Leader of the House.)
MISC 62	The 'Star Chamber' – decides departmental budgets.
PSIS	Permanent secretaries' steering committee on intelligence and security. (Chaired by Cabinet Secretary Sir Robin Butler.)

- **Political** and **administrative support** from political advisers and civil servants. The PM has effective control of the **Cabinet Office** – the group of civil servants within the Secretariat who organise Cabinet and committee meetings, draw up and circulate agendas, policy papers, reports and minutes, summon persons and liaise between departments. At its head is the Cabinet Secretary, who is also Head of the Civil Service and who works very closely with the PM. There is also the **Prime Minister's Office** at Number 10, with four sections made up of civil servants and political advisers: these are party political supporters brought in from industry, business, trade unions (with a Labour PM), journalism, etc. to give the PM partisan advice and support on policy options.

- Margaret Thatcher was also noted for her use of informal, *ad hoc* **groups** of policy advisers – ministers, civil servants, outside advisers and others combined – such as the Economic Seminar. These groups by-pass both Cabinet and the formal Cabinet committees, and are said to have made key decisions on, for instance, abolishing exchange controls (1979) and banning trade unions at GCHQ (1984).

- Prime Ministers have other informal sources of policy advice such as sympathetic **pressure groups** (e.g. for Thatcher, the Adam Smith Institute and, for Major, the Conservative Centre for Policy Studies).

The Prime Minister's Office at Number 10

Civil servants: official engagements, policy advice

PRIVATE OFFICE

POLITICAL OFFICE

MPs and political advisers: party links, policy advice

PRIME MINISTER

Civil servants: contact with media

PRESS OFFICE

POLICY UNIT

Political advisers: policy advice

Former minister **Francis Pym** has described this network of Prime Ministerial support groups as 'a government within a government'. Critics of Prime Ministerial power fear that these bodies do not simply advise on policy but help to make policy decisions; since they are non-elected, and by-pass Cabinet government, this may be seen as 'unconstitutional'.

In 1983 Margaret Thatcher abolished the 'Think Tank', the Central Policy Review Staff (CPRS), which had been set up within the Cabinet Office by Edward Heath in 1970 to advise Cabinet on long-term policy. It had been the source of some embarrassing leaks (e.g. a 1982 Think Tank report on welfare cuts) and perhaps it was deemed unnecessary. However, former Permanent Secretary Sir Douglas Wass (Reith Lectures, 1983) advocated a new Think Tank as an aid to Cabinet rather than Prime Ministerial government.

Many key policy decisions since the Second World War are said to have been made by the Prime Minister (usually with the advice and agreement of a few senior ministers, civil servants, policy advisers, etc.) rather than by the Cabinet as a whole.

Key examples of Prime Ministerial policies
The Budget, nuclear weapons, and intelligence and security, which have never been matters for Cabinet government.

Chamberlain: Appeasement (1938).
Eden: Suez (1956).
Wilson: Devaluation of the pound (1967).
Thatcher: The Falklands conflict (1982 – when Cabinet was suspended and replaced by a 'War Cabinet' – actually a Cabinet committee chaired by the PM), abolition of the Greater London and metropolitan councils (1985), the bombing of Libya by US planes from British bases (1986), the 'Spycatcher' affair (1986–8), the poll tax (1988), restructuring of the civil service (1988), inner cities policy (1988), etc.
Major: The Gulf 'War Cabinet' (1991).

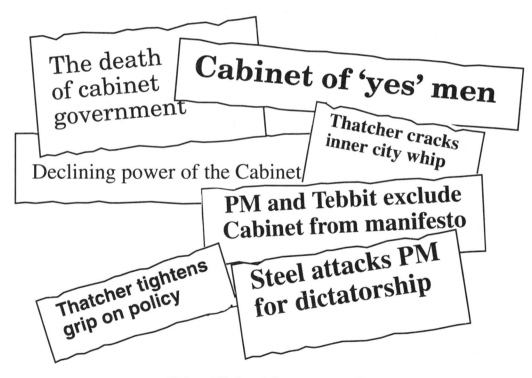

'Prime Ministerial government'?

The growing emphasis in British politics and the media on party leaders' individual personalities, styles and images has led some to suggest that British government is becoming '**presidential**'. However, a presidential system is based on separation of the executive and legislature; in the USA the President is separately elected by the people, and neither he nor his appointed executive team (also called Cabinet) are allowed to be members of Congress (the US equivalent of Parliament). The President may therefore lack a majority in Congress, and may thus be weaker than a British Prime Minister, e.g. George Bush's damaging clash with Congress over his budget in 1990. An outright presidential system therefore has additional checks and balances which are lacking in British parliamentary government.

Although arguments about Prime Ministerial government pre-date Thatcher, her style and image of leadership – variously described as 'strong' and 'authoritarian' – intensified the debate, especially since she was the first Prime Minister to have lent her name to an era. (See **Jones**.) However, Major's initial approach was clearly more Cabinet-oriented and consensual; and he obviously lacked her experience and assertiveness.

Suggested reforms to curb the powers of the Prime Minister include:

- A 'constitutional premiership' – outlining and limiting the powers of the PM (and perhaps also the Cabinet) in law;
- Election of the Cabinet by the parliamentary party;
- Transferring the PM's powers of patronage to the Commons;
- More political advisers for ministers;
- Ministers choosing their own senior departmental civil servants.

---

3. Read the outline of the Westland affair below, then write a list of the constitutional principles and problems of government which it seemed to raise – bearing in mind the conventions of ministerial responsibility, civil service neutrality and parliamentary government.

The Westland Affair: December 1985–January 1986

Westland Helicopter Company was in financial trouble, and was negotiating a merger with an American firm, Sikorsky; but **Defence Secretary, Michael Heseltine**, favoured a European bid for Westland. The Government had no official policy on the matter; it said it would leave Westland to decide. However, Heseltine suspected that **Prime Minister, Margaret Thatcher**, and **Leon Brittan, Secretary of the Department of Trade and Industry (DTI)**, favoured the American bid. He publicly accused the Prime Minister of suppressing Cabinet discussion of the issue, and of cancelling a Cabinet committee meeting on it; he also claimed that his protests in Cabinet about this had been omitted from the minutes by **Cabinet Secretary Sir Robert Armstrong** (12.12.85). The PM held a meeting of senior ministers and civil servants, including Armstrong and her **Press Secretary Bernard Ingham**, to discuss Heseltine's behaviour.

Heseltine wrote and published a letter warning against the American deal. The Prime Minister asked the **Solicitor General, Sir Patrick Mayhew** (a government law officer), to write a letter warning Heseltine that he might be overstating his case. The Prime Minister and Leon Brittan held separate meetings (5.1.86), and Westland were told by a DTI official that the Solicitor General's view would be made public. A decision was thus somehow made to leak the law officer's confidential letter (and so discredit Heseltine), against strong convention.

Two telephone conversations took place between DTI and No. 10 officials: **John Mogg, Brittan's Private Secretary to Charles Powell, Thatcher's PS; Colette Bowe, DTI Director of Information to Bernard Ingham**. In both cases, the DTI said that they were seeking authorisation to leak the Solicitor General's letter, while No. 10 said they were simply being informed of it – a coincidental misunderstanding. The PM was apparently not consulted throughout. Only the parts of the letter most damaging to Heseltine were leaked to the press by Bowe (6.1.86). DTI officials told Armstrong what had happened; again, apparently, Thatcher was not told. The **Attorney General, Sir Michael Havers**, threatened criminal proceedings against both the DTI and No. 10 over the leak of Mayhew's letter, and insisted on a formal inquiry. Armstrong set up a two-week inquiry, though he already knew what had happened. Thatcher said that she knew nothing of Brittan's role in the leak throughout, and denied any personal involvement in it.

In Cabinet (9.1.86), Thatcher said that any future statements by ministers about Westland must be cleared by the Cabinet Office, to maintain collective respons-ibility. Heseltine resigned, later saying 'Prime Ministerial will has replaced collective responsibility' and calling it 'unconstitutional'.

Under pressure from his own party, Leon Brittan resigned over the leak of the Solicitor General's letter. In two Commons' debates on the issue, the Opposition performed badly. It was reported that, before the second debate (27.1.86), the Prime Minister expressed fears that she might have to resign over the matter, but the government won decisively.

The Commons' Select Committee on Defence held an inquiry into the Westland affair. It failed to get evidence from the PM, or the Solicitor General – who said he was not accountable to Parliament – or from any civil servants involved except Armstrong, who was often evasive. Brittan refused to answer eight questions. The committee saw all non-classified papers, and some of its hearings were broadcast live on radio, but its critical report was issued just before the summer recess, and was not debated in Parliament. The government sought greater curbs on civil service evidence to parliamentary committees thereafter; and Armstrong issued a code of conduct for civil servants stressing their accountability solely to their ministers.

Westland was bought by the American firm Sikorsky.

Constraints on Prime Ministerial government

- **Authority** is the essential precondition of Prime Ministerial power. It derives from the electorate, the Commons, the Crown and, above all, the party. Unlike an American president, a British Prime Minister depends on party support and loyalty (e.g. Thatcher and the Commons' debate on Westland 27 January 1986, which amounted to a personal vote of confidence and conversely, of course, her resignation in 1990).

- Every Prime Ministerial power is also a **responsibility**; if it is misused, the PM may lose authority and even risk losing office: e.g. Eden over Suez, Macmillan's so-called 'night of the long knives' when he sacked seven Cabinet ministers at once (1962) at a time of economic problems and waning popularity, Heath over the miners' strike (1974) and Thatcher over Westland, the poll tax and the EC.

- There are constraints on the PM's **appointment** and **dismissal of ministers**: they must come from Parliament, should reflect the range of political feeling in the party, and they must also retain party support (Cecil Parkinson in 1983, Leon Brittan in 1986, and Ridley in 1990 did not). Too many re-shuffles suggest mis-judgement, disunity or incompetence.

- **Cabinet revolts** are rare, but significant: e.g. against Wilson's devaluation of the pound (1967) and Thatcher's proposed sale of British Leyland to US General Motors (1986).

- **Backbench revolts**: e.g. Wilson's Industrial Relations Bill 1969, and Thatcher's Shops Bill (Sunday trading) 1986.

- The **Lords**: e.g. the 'Paving Bill' 1984 (see Chapter 5).

- A Labour Prime Minister may be subject to additional party constraints, notably the National Executive Committee and annual conference. Also, Labour Shadow Cabinets are elected by fellow MPs, and will expect ministerial offices in a new government.

- **Pressure groups** may be a key constraint: e.g. the miners against Heath in 1974 and the public sector trade unions against Callaghan in the 'winter of discontent' 1978–9.

- The **media** and **civil service** may be a hindrance as well as a help, but a Prime Minister's effective power at any time depends on a variety of circumstances: personality and charisma, health and energy, size of majority, length of time in office and proximity of a general election, the state of the economy etc.

To quote former Prime Minister **Herbert Asquith**: 'The office of the Prime Minister is what its holder chooses and is able to make of it'. This stresses the flexibility of Prime Ministerial power, but also its limitations.

In sum, to expect or assume either Cabinet government or Prime Ministerial government, in any literal sense, may be too simplistic. The tasks of modern government are too many for a group of 20 or so busy (and more or less transient) ministers, never mind one person. Policy-making is a more or less pluralist process, dispersed throughout what **Madgwick** calls 'the central executive territory' – though the diverse groups of ministers, civil servants, advisers and experts involved may often be directed or even dominated by the Prime Minister. The key problems arising are:

(a)   The secrecy surrounding the policy-making process;

(b)   The fear that PM dominated policy-making may produce unbalanced or ill-judged policies, unchecked by Cabinet or Commons (given the strength of party discipline);

(c)   The fear that policy decisions are made by non-elected, unaccountable groups and individuals;

(d)   The perceived decline in ministerial accountability to Parliament and to the voters.

—— ESSAYS

1)   *Theme*   **Monarchy**

Q?   Are monarchy and democracy compatible?

(Cambridge, June 1986, P. 1.)

---

4.   Write a timed essay incorporating the points listed in the plan below (and adding your own arguments, names and examples).
Note that the title does not specify Britain; consider various types and styles of monarchy, e.g. Sweden, some African tribal societies, etc. Also bear in mind different interpretations of 'democracy' (see Chapter 2).

A✓   **Essay plan**

1)   Definitions … depends on type of monarchy (e.g. absolute or constitutional) and type of democracy (e.g. direct or indirect).

2)   Not compatible:
   (a)   If absolute monarchy – not 'people-power';
   (b)   Not elected;
   (c)   Aristocratic hierarchy against the interests of the majority;
   (d)   Promotes privilege and deference;
   (e)   Consent created by media and political socialisation;
   (f)   May mask significant conflicts of interest in society;
   (g)   Royal prerogative (whether used by monarch, PM and ministers or others) may by-pass Parliament and breach the 'rule of law';
   (h)   Promotes 'absolute premiership' – Prime Ministerial government.

3)   Compatible:
   (a)   Constitutional monarchy – subordinate to the ballot box;
   (b)   Need not preclude 'people-power';
   (c)   Sources of authority other than election: tradition, rules of the constitution, charisma, experience and expertise, *lack* of power;
   (d)   Consent;
   (e)   Promotes 'national interest' – unites country, enhances economy and tourism, etc.;
   (f)   Constitutional check against 'elective dictatorship';
   (g)   Alternatives? e.g. elected impartial president over PM and government (as in Eire), or fusion of 'efficient' and 'dignified' roles of executive in single premier (as in USA) – problems.

4)   **Conclusion:** Compatible, especially with indirect democracy; *but* British monarchy, and PM, royal prerogative etc., in need of reform: e.g. written constitution, 'constitutional premiership'.

●   **Note**   If you wish to conclude that they are *not* compatible, swop sections 2 and 3; always put your own case last.

2)   *Theme*   **Prime Minister**

Q?   'The powers of the Prime Minister do not explain his authority.' Discuss.

(London, February 1976, P. 1.)

A✓   **Examiners' comments**

'There are two conceptual points which need clarification for a good answer to this question: the difference between power and authority, and the idea that power is an ambiguous concept, i.e. that "the growing institutional power of the Prime Minister" as described by John Mackintosh does not in fact seem to guarantee effective power to influence events or opinion. Clarification of one of these concepts should earn an E or D grade; a C grade would require both. For an A or B grade to be awarded some thoughtful exemplification would be needed of the apparent paradox of politics that a man or government can have a lot of power without much authority, or a lot of authority without much formal power.'

Short plan

1)   Definitions: 'power' (P) versus 'authority' (A) …
     (Much P, little A: military junta.)
     (Much A, little P: British monarch.)
2)   Sources of PM's authority: electorate, party, Parliament, Crown, charisma? (Weber), state of economy, media …
3)   Therefore A → P rather than vice versa.
     (Briefly list conventional powers; e.g.s of practical limits.)
     Loss of A → loss of P: Eden, Heath, Thatcher … Revolts …
4)   *But* good use of P may increase A: Churchill?
     And misuse of P may decrease A: e.g. Macmillan 1962;
     Thatcher and GCHQ, Westland, Libyan bombing, EC etc.
5)   **Conclusion:** generally agree: A explains P, not vice versa.
     But use/misuse of P may then enhance or diminish A.

Note the *key difference* between the following two titles:

Q?   Explain the factors which a Prime Minister considers when selecting ministerial colleagues.

(AEB, November 1981, P. 1.)

Q?   What factors are likely to have most influence on a Prime Minister when deciding which ministerial offices to include in the Cabinet?

(JMB, June 1984, P. II.)

A✓   **Examiners' comments on second title**

'This was a very popular question, but many candidates either failed to read it properly, or chose to ignore the focus on "ministerial offices". Among those who did it correctly the better candidates did well. The question gave abundant scope for discussion of clientele departments vs. big spending departments; small vs. large cabinets; ministers without portfolio; super-departments etc. Most candidates attempted this question but many of them tried to adapt their "prepared" answer on the PM's choice of ministers. Others did not even attempt the adaptation.

3)   *Theme*   **Prime Ministerial government?**

Stimulus response questions

This type of exam question presents a prose passage, diagram or set of data (e.g.

electoral statistics), and asks students a number of questions *on and around* the issues raised in the passage. It is not simply 'data response', i.e. full information for all of the answers will not be found in the passage itself, students must know and show wider knowledge and evaluative skills in their answers. Sometimes marks allocated will be shown against each part-question, but if not students must judge how much time and attention to devote to each part of the whole question. You should therefore read it *all* through carefully first and consider how much and what information to put where; do not repeat yourself in different parts of the whole answer.

Q?   **Stimulus response question** (simulated example)

Read the passage below, then answer the questions which follow.

Those who argue that in Britain today we still have 'Cabinet government' point to the considerable practical constraints which operate on any Prime Minister's exercise of power; and also to the extra constraints which the party imposes on a Labour Prime Minister compared with a Conservative Prime Minister. Those who assert 'Prime Ministerial government', however, such as Tony Benn, argue that the powers of a modern Prime Minister are immense because they derive directly from the Crown and constitutionally do not require approval from Parliament. Such critics point to a PM's powers of patronage, powers to control the very structure and policies of government, the security services, the flow of information, international relations, war and peace, and even the precise date on which the people may be allowed to go to the ballot box. This, say the critics, is the real danger of the British Crown and monarchy today: not the flummery and family trivia which fills the pages of the tabloids, but the personal autocracy which it allows and empowers at the very heart of British democracy.

(a)   What constraints may, in practice, limit the powers of a Prime Minister?
(b)   Why and how might a Labour Prime Minister be more constrained by the party than a Conservative Prime Minister?
(c)   Comment on the view outlined at the end of the passage about the role of the British Crown and monarchy today.
(d)   Should Prime Ministerial power be lessened or not?
       If so, how?

A✓   **Suggested answer**

(a)   The many practical constraints on the powers of the PM centre on the need for authority from the people, Parliament, the party and the royal prerogative.
       The power of the PM to choose ministers is limited by the fact that they must come from Parliament (although a safe seat or a peerage may be given to a favoured individual, e.g. Lord Young 1984). Ministers should represent a balanced team in terms of age, experience and shades of thinking within the party if they are not to become alienated from the backbenchers.
       There are also clear constraints on the dismissal of ministers. Though a PM should 'be a good butcher', if [s]he sacks too many ministers too frequently it implies poor judgement in the first place, and the PM's authority will be undermined, as in Macmillan's 'night of the long knives' in 1962 when he sacked seven Cabinet ministers overnight.
       Cabinet revolts limit a PM's policy-making power. Consensus between PM and Cabinet is the norm; the outsider may wrongly perceive this as

Prime Ministerial domination, when, in fact, Cabinet is happy to accept PM leadership on most matters. When revolts do occur they may suggest misjudgement or mismanagement by a PM, e.g. in 1982 when the Cabinet refused to discuss a leaked Think Tank report advocating large NHS cuts before the 1983 election. However, although a Cabinet may be obstructive in the short term, a PM may win in the end, e.g. Thatcher and student loans.

The backbenchers may also be a constraint (e.g. Sunday trading 1986, and forcing the resignation of Leon Brittan), though they risk loss of promotion prospects. Parliament as a whole should be a key constraint; and the Lords have been more active in opposing government bills since the 1980s, but their power is limited.

Extra-parliamentary groups are also a constraint, though the power of the trade unions particularly has been curbed since the 1980s.

The real policy-making power of a PM depends on circumstances: the state of the economy, the size of the government's majority, the proximity of a general election; international events, the health, character and length of tenure of the PM him or herself etc.

(b) A Labour Shadow Cabinet is elected by Labour MPs, not chosen by the leader, and a Labour leader is obliged to take it with him/her into office; however, [s]he can re-shuffle after a year, and always has the freedom to allocate portfolios and to dismiss individual shadow/ministers. A Labour leader has to contend with the NEC and Conference which, according to party rules, have policy-making power. The NEC is the collective party head – writing the manifesto, appointing party officials, supervising party discipline etc. – and has no direct equivalent in the Conservative Party. Nor is the Conservative conference a policy-making body as such, but rather a sounding board for party opinion and a rally around the leader.

Moreover, the Conservative Party has a stronger philosophical tradition of loyalty to its leader, whereas the Labour Party lays greater stress on intra-party democracy (which can mean more visible disunity). However, that did not stop the Conservatives forcing Thatcher out of office. Also, the Conservatives are quicker to replace a leader out of office than are Labour. And finally, the institutional powers of a Prime Minister often, in practice, override theoretical party constraints, so the differences between a Labour and Conservative PM are not great in practice.

(c) The end of the passage suggests that (though the monarch as an individual may be beyond reproach) the conventional transfer of powers from the Crown to Prime Minister creates a Prime Ministerial autocracy, and that it is this constitutional arrangement which is the real 'danger' to British democracy.

On the one hand, the transfer of prerogative powers from monarch to ministers is intended to make the exercise of those powers democratic and accountable, because ministers are chosen from the majority party in the Commons and are collectively accountable to Parliament (e.g. through debates, votes, Question Time, committees, votes of censure etc.). This arrangement also lifts the monarch personally out of political controversy and party politics. He or she still has some limited power: e.g. choice of PM in a hung Parliament, dismissal of a PM (e.g. Gough Whitlam in Australia 1975), and granting of certain honours. For the most part, however, the role of the monarch today is largely symbolic and ceremonial – 'dignified' rather than 'efficient' as Bagehot put it. To that extent, the arrangement enhances 'representative and responsible government' and 'constitutional monarchy'.

On the other hand, the sweeping prerogative powers outlined in the passage are exercised, by ministers and especially Prime Minister, merely by convention. They therefore lack legal definition and limits, and may in practice be very flexible. A Prime Minister who can hire and fire all other ministers is clearly more than *primus inter pares*; the potential scope for corruption in the exercise of patronage is considerable (e.g. Lloyd George's sale of honours); and PMs can apparently break some conventional rules with impunity (e.g. the Westland affair).

(d)   I would conclude that the powers of a Prime Minister should be lessened, because Prime Ministerial autocracy is less democratically accountable to Parliament and the people than is collective Cabinet government; and because policies which are not debated and discussed by the whole Cabinet may prove to be 'banana skins' for the government – i.e. ill-judged, inept and unpopular or unworkable – e.g. GCHQ, the poll tax, student loans etc.

One solution would be a 'constitutional premiership' (Benn) where the powers of a Prime Minister are written and limited in law. Also, the MPs of the governing party could elect the Cabinet and approve portfolios. Cabinet ministers could choose their own top civil servants and have their own *cabinets* – bigger teams of advisers – as Kinnock has advocated. Freedom of information legislation would reduce the secrecy of the policy-making process and hence should enhance Cabinet government. Finally, a PM's powers of patronage should be transferred to the Commons (together with the replacement of the Lords by an elected second chamber), and new arrangements could be made for fixed-date general elections. These reforms combined would substantially remove the possibility of 'Prime Ministerial government' and enhance the democratic accountability of government as a whole.

---

6.   Write at least one of the following essays.
Always write a brief plan first.

1)   'In theory monarchy is indefensible in modern government; in practice no-one has invented a better system.' Discuss.

(Oxford, Summer 1986, P. 1.)

2)   To what extent does the British Cabinet system conform to the principle of 'collective responsibility'? Does this principle have any value?

(Oxford and Cambridge, June 1986, P. 2.)

3)   'A Prime Minister dominates British government only if the House of Commons and the Cabinet fail to assert themselves.' In what ways and with what success can the Cabinet or MPs of the government party resist the wishes of the Prime Minister?

(AEB, November 1989, P. 1.)

4)   What are the sources of a Prime Minister's powers? Evaluate the use Mrs Thatcher has made of these powers and compare it with that of any other British premier of recent years.

(Oxford and Cambridge, June 1989, P. 2.)

5) 'Full Cabinet meetings are becoming a mere rubber stamp for decisions made elsewhere.' How far is this true, and why?

(London, June 1989, P. 1.)

—— GUIDE TO EXERCISES

Page 82

1. 1) To legitimise the powers and actions of PM and ministers; to maintain flexibility; plus inertia.

   2) (a) 'Hung Parliament' – choice of PM.

   (b) If PM refuses to resign when government is defeated in the legislature on a vote of censure or major policy: e.g. Australia 1975 – Labour PM Gough Whitlam refused to resign when defeated on his Budget; the Governor General, acting for the Crown, dismissed him and replaced him with Opposition leader Malcolm Fraser, who immediately called a general election and won it, thus legitimising the Crown's action.

   (c) When to grant dissolution of Parliament: e.g. after defeat of a new minority government; in war, etc.

   3) Its use by ministers by-passes the elected Commons, and thus ministerial responsibility to Parliament is undermined; it breaches the central principle of the 'rule of law' that everyone is equal under the law; it may allow the security services to break the law with impunity.

Page 90

3. The Westland affair raised fears and allegations about the following issues:

   1) Prime Ministerial government versus Cabinet government and collective responsibility.
   2) PM's control of the Cabinet agenda.
   3) Manipulation of the Cabinet minutes by the Cabinet Secretary.
   4) Breach of collective responsibility and Cabinet secrecy by Heseltine.
   5) Disunity of government.
   6) Role of Cabinet committees in policy-making.
   7) Involvement of impartial civil servants in political matters by PM.
   8) Involvement of impartial law officer in political matters.
   9) Unconstitutional leak of law officer's confidential letter – breach of convention and possibly of law.
   10) Relationship, and friction, between No. 10 and departmental officials.
   11) Autonomy, power and political involvement of No. 10 officials.
   12) Lack of consultation/integrity of PM.
   13) Collective responsibility (Heseltine's resignation).
   14) Individual responsibility (Brittan's resignation).
   15) Influence of backbenchers on government.
   16) Lack of accountability of PM or officials for No. 10's involvement in leak.
   17) Parliamentary scrutiny and control of executive – role of Opposition.
   18) Powers and limitations of select committees.
   19) Government law officers' accountability to Parliament.
   20) The party system, discipline and loyalty in the Commons.

—— REFERENCES

Walter Bagehot, *The English Constitution* (Fontana, 1963).

Tony Benn, 'The Case for a Constitutional Premiership' in *Parliamentary Affairs* vol. xxxiii, no. 1, Winter 1980.

Richard Crossman, *Introduction to Bagehot's* The English Constitution (Fontana, 1963).

Peter Hennessy, *Whitehall* (Fontana, 1990).

Bill Jones (ed.), *Political issues in Britain Today* (Manchester University Press, 1987).

John Mackintosh (ed. P. G. Richards), *The Government and Politics of Britain* (Hutchinson, 1988).

Peter Madgwick, 'Prime Ministerial Power Revisited' in *Social Studies Review* May 1986.

Francis Pym, *The Politics of Consent* (Hamilton, 1984).

Hugo Young, *One of Us* (Macmillan, 1990).

7 The Civil Service

KEY ISSUES

▶ Theory and practice of 'bureaucracy'

▶ Civil service
  ● Constraints on personal and political freedoms; influence and power
  ● Neutrality; 'politicisation'
  ● Declining permanence and anonymity; declining ministerial responsibility
  ● The Rayner and Ibbs reforms; further reforms
  ● A political civil service?

▶ Secrecy and 'open government': arguments and reforms

—— TOPIC NOTES

Key facts and concepts

Civil servants are non-elected administrators and officials of the government. There are around 600,000 of them, and they form a hierarchy within each government department. At the top are the **higher civil service**: the Permanent Secretaries and other 'mandarins' (as they are often called, after the Chinese bureaucrats of old). Their functions include: giving information and policy advice to ministers, preparing policy papers and speeches, keeping the minister's official diaries and dealing with correspondence, organising and minuting meetings, anticipating parliamentary questions and preparing answers for ministers, consulting with outside interest groups, and running the departments. Further down the ladder are the administrative and clerical officials who administer the policies of government in Whitehall and around the country.

As **permanent**, non-elected, career officials who serve under successive governments of any party, civil servants are required to be **neutral**, i.e. they should not let political or personal bias influence their work. Non-elected civil servants are also not supposed to have policy-making power, though their advice – based on experience, and the possible costs, technical and administrative feasibility of different policy options etc. – may legitimately influence minister's decisions. Thus civil servants are meant to be **anonymous**, i.e. not publicly accountable for the work of the department; the minister in charge is answerable to Parliament and public for government policy and administration, according to the conventions of ministerial responsibility.

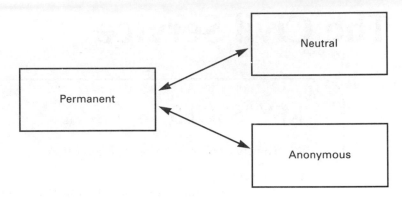

The British civil servant?

There are many restrictive rules designed to protect the neutrality, anonymity and integrity of civil servants; most were confirmed by the Masterman Committee on the Political Activities of Civil Servants 1949, and reviewed by the Armitage Committee 1978, and points (8) and (9) were introduced post-1979.

1) Though all civil servants may vote, none may stand for political office.
2) Though they may be members of the mainstream parties, none may be members or sympathisers of communist or fascist organisations, and the top 26% may not be politically active (e.g. campaigning for any party or pressure group).
3) Some may not travel 'behind the iron curtain' to socialist countries without permission (though this rule is changing as the 'iron curtain' comes down).
4) Some officials (e.g. in the Ministry of Defence and Foreign Office) may be subject to 'positive vetting', i.e. a secret investigation of their private lives and political sympathies.
5) They are all bound by the Official Secrets Act.
6) They may not speak to the media or write publicly about their work without permission.
7) For two years after leaving office, they should seek permission to work for private companies with which their department may have had dealings.
8) Officials in the Ministry of Defence were barred by the Thatcher administration from being members of the Campaign for Nuclear Disarmament.
9) Officials at Government Communications Headquarters (GCHQ) – the government's 'spy centre' – have been barred since 1984 from belonging to trade unions.

The **Fulton Report** (1968) on the structure and management of the civil service made a number of criticisms, prompting some reform.

1) The three tiers below the 'mandarins' were replaced in 1971 by a unified Administrative Group, to allow more flexible use of skills and easier promotion.
2) A Civil Service Department was created in 1968 to take over recruitment and management from the Treasury; but it was abolished in 1981 and control was centralised in the hands of the Treasury once again.
3) The Fulton Report advocated more specialisation of civil servants, based on professional qualifications and better management training. A Civil Service College was established to provide courses in management. However, higher civil servants still tend to be predominantly public school and Oxbridge educated arts graduates and generalists. Nevertheless, they develop specialist knowledge and

expertise in their work, and some critics say that they use their near-monopoly of official information to obstruct ministers and policies of which they disapprove.

4) Fulton recommended more personnel movement between the civil service and private industry and business. However, it is still hard to attract good people away from the private sector, where the pay and conditions of work may be better.

5) The whole machinery of government was said by Fulton (and others before and since) to be too secretive (see p. 107).

Critics such as **Crowther-Hunt** have suggested that the higher civil service succeeded in obstructing the proposals they disliked. This implies both power, and some common goal or bias; see below.

Criticisms and reforms

Bureaucracy and efficiency
Bureaucracy means the large-scale professional administration of any organisation, business or government. It is, in theory, characterised by appointment rather than election, permanence, hierarchy, consistent rules and procedures, impartial and impersonal methods, specialisation of functions, and division between the work and private lives of bureaucrats to prevent corruption or bias. The British civil service is sometimes said to be *too* bureaucratic, i.e. too inflexible, rule-bound, slow, costly, self-protective and obstructive – a negative image of 'faceless bureaucrats' and excessive 'red tape'. **Sir John Hoskyns**, a former policy adviser to Thatcher, has accused the Whitehall machine of lacking direction, drive and imagination: 'In organisational terms government is a creature without a brain' (Lecture to Institute of Directors, 28 September 1983).

The Conservative government under Thatcher sought to 'roll back the frontiers of state' and 'cut the bureaucracy' in accordance with its *laissez-faire* philosophy and its wish to cut public spending. Civil service numbers were reduced by over 100,000 to under 600,000, and politically sympathetic businessmen and industrialists were brought in to devise ways of making the civil service more efficient and management-minded. Sir (now Lord) Derek Rayner of Marks and Spencer set up an Efficiency Unit, a Management Information System for Ministers (MINIS) and a Financial Management Initiative. His successor as head of the Efficiency Unit, Sir Robin Ibbs of ICI, recommended the structural separation of the higher civil service, the policy advisers, from the administrators, who were to be devolved into semi-autonomous agencies headed by chief executives with considerable freedom and flexibility of management.

Criticisms of these proposals centred on fears of:

(a)   Loss of political (ministerial) accountability for policy administration;
(b)   Loss of co-ordination between policy advice and decision-making, and the administration of those policies;
(c)   Loss of incentive for administrative officials whose prospects of promotion to the top civil service may be reduced;
(d)   Loss of efficiency and morale in departments where staff cuts were high;
(e)   Loss of economies of scale, resulting in higher costs;
(f)   Loss of confidentiality within the administrative machine.

The actual changes (1988) were initially limited compared with the radical scope of Ibbs' proposals; they amounted to organisational and managerial reforms, rather than political or financial decentralisation. The 12 units (and 70,000 officials) first selected for hiving off, e.g. the Passport Office, the Meteorological Office, Her Majesty's Stationery Office, Jobcentres, royal parks and palaces, were either largely devolved already or were relatively insignificant sectors of Whitehall. Ibbs sought direct accountability of agency executives, but in fact the principle of individual ministerial responsibility was preserved, together with Treasury control of budgets. Nevertheless, by the end of 1990 over 30 executive agencies had been created, involving 80,000 civil servants, with around 30 more in the pipeline for 1991, and the Treasury and Civil Service Select Committee could describe Next Steps as 'the most radical reform of the public service this century'.

There does appear to be some blurring of the question of political responsibility, with Cabinet Secretary, Sir Robin Butler, saying in 1991 that ministers could not be expected to take responsibility for errors made by civil servants in executive agencies; and there is some dissatisfaction among officials at the centre who have lost day-to-day control.

Diversity of activities

SOME flavour of the diversity of government activities is conveyed by the list of agencies already created, and the current batch of candidates for agency status (with staff numbers alongside):

ALREADY HIVED OFF:
Building Research Establishment 680
Central Office of Information 740
Central Veterinary Laboratory 560
Civil Service College 200
Companies House 1,100
Registers of Scotland 1,000
Drivers and Vehicle Licensing Agency 5,300
Driving Standards Agency 2,100
Employment Service 33,800
Historic Royal Palaces................330
Her Majesty's Stationery Office 3,200
Hydrographic Office 890
Information Technology Services Agency 2,900
Insolvency Service 1,400
Intervention Board for Agricultural Produce 860
Laboratory of the Government Chemist 320
Land Registry......................10,800
Meteorological Office 2,250
National Engineering Laboratory 520
National Physical Laboratory......830
National Weights and Measures Laboratory 50
Natural Resources Institute.......330
Occupational Health Service.......100
Ordnance Survey....................2,550
Patent Office 1,150
QEII Conference Centre 60
Radiocommunications Centre ...460
Resettlement Agency 530
Royal Mint...............................970
Training and Employment Agency 1,700
Vehicle Certification Agency 70

Vehicle Inspectorate................1,600
Veterinary Medicines Directorate .70
Warren Spring Laboratory..........300
UNDER CONSIDERATION:
Cadw.......................................220
Central Science Laboratory 400
Central Statistical Office 1,000
Chessington Computer Centre ...430
Civil Service Commission...........340
Customs and Excise.............26,900
Defence Accounts Organisation...........................2,100
Defence Research Agency.....11,700
Farm and Countryside Services 2,550
Fisheries Enforcement Services 170
Forensic Science Service............580
Fuel Suppliers Branch 30
Historic Buildings and Monuments...............................570
Inland Revenue 60,400
Military Survey.........................850
NHS Estates 130
Passport Office 1,200
Planning Inspectorate 550
Pollution Inspectorate 210
Property Holdings 1,600
RAF Training 2,500
Royal Parks.............................570
Service Childrens Schools......1,000
Social Security Benefits.........68,200
Social Security Contributions 6,200
Social Security Operations (NICS)...................5,000
Valuation Office.....................5,700
Youth Treatment Service............220
Rating Division (NICS)..............270

Prisons, child support, and other parts of the Ministry of Defence are also under consideration.

The Independent, 31 October 1990

Power and influence

As non-elected officials, civil servants may influence ministers' policy decisions but they should not, in theory, have power themselves. However, critics such as **Kellner** and **Crowther-Hunt** argue that they derive power from many sources.

- Their large **numbers**, compared with ministers, who are busy with parliamentary and constituency as well as executive duties.
- Their **permanence**, compared with ministers who average two-and-a-half years in any one office.
- Their **experience** and **expertise**, deriving from permanence and also from access to **information** which even ministers may be denied because of the exceptional **secrecy** of the British system of government.
- Their departmental structure which, according to **Crossman** and others, may foster a common **departmental outlook** (e.g. pro-hanging in the Home Office) which ministers find hard to counter.
- Their network of **inter-departmental committees** which parallels the Cabinet committee network and which may enable officials effectively to pre-determine policy options before they reach ministers.
- Their effective **control of the administrative processes**, including the administration of any reforms to the machinery of Whitehall itself, such as the Fulton and Ibbs proposals.
- Their close involvement in **national security** and **intelligence matters**, e.g. in key Cabinet committees from which most ministers are entirely excluded.
- Their extensive powers of **patronage** over thousands of titles and appointments which are nominally the responsibility of the PM.
- British membership of the **EC**, which has increased the workload of ministers and has also necessitated much more preparation and co-ordination of policies by officials.

To quote former Cabinet Secretary **Lord William Armstrong**: 'The biggest and most pervasive influence is in setting the framework within which questions of policy are raised. It would have been enormously difficult for my minister to change the framework, and to that extent we had great power' (quoted in *The Times* 15 November 1976).

If civil servants have significant power to shape policy, it may not be realistic to expect individual ministers to take full responsibility for all policy decisions; and the apparent decline in ministerial resignations over policy and administrative errors (see Chapter 6) may reflect this.

A counter-argument is that complaints of excessive civil service power may simply suggest ministerial weakness or incompetence; many writers stress that officials like decisive and firm-minded ministers; and many former ministers such as Denis Healey and Peter Walker share this view.

Neutrality

Some critics argue that the civil service is *too* neutral: former Cabinet Secretary **Lord Bancroft** has argued that, far from being too powerful, civil servants are often too pliable and deferential to their ministers; **Lord Hailsham** has argued that official neutrality may mean excessive loyalty to the government of the day, promoting 'elective dictatorship'; and the constitutional writer **Nevil Johnson** believes that the mandarins' capacity to switch loyalties from one governing party and set of policies to another suggests a lack of integrity, and may not promote good government: 'Officials become so used to furthering any policy that they lose all faith and interest in the possibility of there being a good or a better policy' (pp. 99–100).

Others, however, allege that civil servants are both powerful and partisan; but the theme of these criticisms has changed over time.

1) From the first majority Labour government of 1945 through to the 1970s, Labour ministers tended to argue that senior officials were anti-Labour and pro-Conservative, because of their narrow class and educational background (70% public schools and Oxbridge). **Crossman** argued that civil servants were deliberately obstructive e.g. of Labour's nationalisation plans; and **Barbara Castle** has said that senior officials added clauses to the industrial relations White Paper 'In Place of Strife' (1969) trying to curb the trade unions, against the express wish of ministers. Hence the appointment by ministers since 1974 of party political advisers from academia, industry and trade unions, to counter or by-pass unsympathetic civil servants. It has been suggested, however (e.g. by former Conservative minister **Michael Heseltine** in **Young and Sloman**), that the real obstruction to radical Labour policies came from right-wing Labour Prime Ministers such as Wilson and Callaghan.

2) In the 1970s and '80s ministers of both main parties often argued that their officials were not party political as such, but were centrist and hostile to radicalism, whether of the left or the right. **Benn** wrote of 'established Whitehall policy' promoting consensus politics, and **Nicholas Ridley** said that his Conservative government's privatisation plans were met with official 'procrastination, inactivity and sabotage'. Even former Permanent Secretary, **Sir Anthony Part**, has said that the civil service 'always hopes that it's influencing ministers to the common ground' (quoted in *The Times* 5 December 1980).

Civil service centrism, if it exists, may derive from a particular official perception of the national interest, or simply from a desire for continuity of policy for long-term stability, administrative convenience, bureaucratic self-interest or political safety.

3) Writers such as **Simpson** (and many Opposition politicians) have argued that senior officials were 'politicised' under Thatcher to act – against their constitutional neutrality – in support of the Conservative government. Critics point to:

(a) The premature dismissal of former Cabinet Secretary Sir Ian Bancroft – a rare event in the top ranks of the civil service.

(b) The close involvement of Bancroft's successor, Sir Robert Armstrong, in the Westland affair, and in the 'Spycatcher' case where he spoke for the government in the Australian courts and admitted to being 'economical with the truth'.

(c) The alleged involvement of other top officials in party political matters: e.g. The PM's Press Secretary Bernard Ingham and Private Secretary Charles Powell in Westland, and Ingham in party meetings about the Government's defence policies. Critics also cite the publication by officials of material 'promoting' (rather than simply explaining) controversial policies such as the poll tax and NHS reforms; and the improper use of MI5 staff and information in a party political campaign to discredit CND, according to former MI5 official Cathy Massiter.

(d) The unusual degree of personal interest which Mrs Thatcher took in senior official appointments, and her well-known tendency to ask 'Is he one of us?'. Critics cite Treasury Permanent Secretary Peter Middleton and Defence Permanent Secretary Clive Whitmore as 'political appointments'. (They also stress that, simply because of her long premiership, by 1990 Thatcher had overseen the appointment of 24 out of the 27 top Permanent Secretaries.) Even the professional body of top civil servants, the First Division Association, said, 'There is evidence that the traditional even-handedness of very senior officials is being undermined' (quoted in *The Financial Times* 27 February 1985).

(e) Some political opponents (e.g. **Roy Jenkins** in a speech in the Lords in 1988) link the alleged 'politicisation' of the civil service to a perceived 'Thatcherite' onslaught on other Establishment institutions such as the Church of England, the BBC, the universities and the judiciary.

The Westland affair, especially, demonstrated that the line between 'political' ministers and 'neutral' civil servants is a very fine one indeed. However, the specific allegation of political motivation in appointments is hard to prove or disprove. Mrs Thatcher and others said that she simply sought people with drive and energy, and disliked the tradition of Buggins' Turn, i.e. promotion by seniority; this might have fuelled some resentment among senior officials. Moreover, people like Armstrong and Ingham all worked with Labour governments for many years; and the present Cabinet Secretary,

Sir Robin Butler has a demanding and multi-faceted role as Cabinet Secretary.

Sir Robin Butler, is not known as a Thatcherite. The 'politicisation' argument is therefore not clear-cut; but note that it stresses PM more than civil service power.

---

1. Some commentators perceive or predict a loss of civil service anonymity and/or permanence, arising either from 'politicisation' or from other constitutional and political developments.

   1) Suggest possible reasons and evidence for loss of (a) anonymity and (b) permanence, now or in the future.

   2) What might be the implications of any such trends for ministerial responsibility?

Some of those who believe that the senior civil service is or was being covertly politicised (e.g. Tony Benn) advocate reform of the executive to enhance traditional civil service neutrality, anonymity and ministerial responsibility (both collective and individual). Others (e.g. the First Division Association, John Hoskyns and Dr William Plowden, a former senior civil servant and now Director General of the Royal Institute of Public Administration) have instead suggested introducing an overtly political higher civil service (perhaps the top three ranks only), along the lines of the US system where officials are party political appointees who come and go with the government of the day.

---

2. 1) Write a list of possible reforms which might enhance the traditional roles and relationships of civil servants and ministers.

   2) Write a case for, and a case against, appointing top civil servants on an overtly party political basis.

Secrecy

The criticism of excessive secrecy is levelled not just against the civil service, but against the whole machinery of British government. **Crossman** called it 'the British disease'; examples include:

- The **Official Secrets Act 1911**, intended originally to be temporary, was passed by Parliament in a single day at the height of a German spy scare, and its most contentious clause was Section 2, which made secret all official information, however harmless. The Franks Committee 1972 recommended repeal of Section 2, but as late as 1984 it was used to prosecute and imprison a junior civil servant, Sarah Tisdall, for passing to *The Guardian* the date of arrival of Cruise missiles in Britain. However, when senior civil servant Clive Ponting was prosecuted in 1985 for passing to Tam Dalyell MP details of the sinking of the Belgrano during the Falklands conflict, he was acquitted; and Section 2 seemed so discredited as to be almost unenforceable. Instead, the government then tried to use the civil law of confidentiality to suppress embarrassing information, such as the book *Spycatcher* by former MI5 official Peter Wright.

  A Conservative backbencher, Richard Shepherd, introduced a private member's bill in 1988 to reform the secrecy laws, not in any radical way, but the government imposed an unprecedented three-line whip against it, and it was defeated. The government then produced its own **Official Secrets Act 1989**; it replaces the blanket 1911 Section 2 with six broad categories of information where unauthorised disclosure may be prosecuted; but it does not permit a public interest defence for exposing wrong-doing (Ponting's defence) nor a defence of prior publication (*Spycatcher*).

- The **Public Records Act 1958** forbids the publication of any government papers for a minimum of 30 years (the so-called '30-year rule').

- The **secrecy of the policy-making processes**, Cabinet committee system and Cabinet meetings themselves, as well as the restrictions surrounding official information given to Parliament, and the publication of former ministers' memoirs (since the Crossman Diaries 1975) etc.

- The **secrecy of the lobby system**, where ministers and civil servants give political correspondents daily briefings whose sources cannot be named (hence the use of phrases like 'sources close to Downing Street', which usually means the Prime Minister's Press Secretary). *The Guardian* and *The Independent* refused from 1986 until 1991 to abide by these rules of secrecy, and therefore did not participate in the lobby system. The British executive and media together also operate a system of voluntary self-censorship based on non-legal guidelines known as the '**D-Notice system**' (D for defence), which is unique in peacetime for a 'liberal democracy'.

- There have also been frequent allegations of the **improper withholding of information by government from Parliament**: e.g. the sinking of the Belgrano during the Falklands conflict, the Zircon spy satellite project (1987), the Westland affair (1986), the payment of 'sweeteners' to British Aerospace to buy Rover (1990) and the development of new nuclear weapons such as Chevaline and Trident.

More **open government** is therefore advocated e.g. by the Labour Party and Liberal Democrats, Clive Ponting, and the Campaign for Freedom of Information which was established in 1984 and whose members include former top civil servants such as Sir Douglas Wass and Sir Patrick Nairne. They seek not only reform of the secrecy laws, but also a fully-fledged Freedom of Information Act which would make public any official information that was not specifically classified – the opposite of the present system. They point to the operation of such open government in the USA, Sweden, Australia and many other Western countries.

---

3.   Suggest a case for, and a case against, more open government in Britain.

—— ESSAYS

1)   *Theme*   **Civil service power**

Consider the two titles below.

Q?   Is the civil service really 'secret government' as some assert?

(London, June 1982, P. 1.)

Q?   Does the power of the modern Civil Service mean that the concept of ministerial responsibility is a sham?

(Oxford and Cambridge, 1983, P. O.)

A✓   **Notes for guidance**

The theme of these two titles is very similar: that the civil service has policy-making power, contrary to theory and to appearances.

The first title suggests that this power is 'secret', i.e. hidden behind the cloak of ministerial responsibility. The general secrecy of the system is relevant in so far as it may bolster civil service power; but 'secrecy' *as such* is not the core issue here.

The second title goes further to suggest that ministerial responsibility is a 'sham', implying a deliberate pretence. Consider whether the accusation may be levelled against civil servants and/or ministers. It also refers to the 'modern' civil service, perhaps implying some change (increase) over time in the role and power of officials – discuss possible reasons and evidence for any such change.

For both titles, bear in mind the need to discuss the following points:

- The theory of civil service influence and ministerial power;
- Names and arguments of those who defend the civil service and deny civil service 'power'. If you disagree with the titles, this section should go at the *end* of the essay;
- Names of critics who allege civil service power;
- Perceived sources of civil service power;
- Different types of power, e.g. through policy advice or administration;
- Suggested examples of 'civil service policy-making';
- Allegations of civil service bias, and their changing nature;
- The apparent decline in ministerial resignations over policy and administrative errors, with examples; does this imply that civil service 'power' is not 'secret' but is formally recognised, i.e. no 'sham'? Consider also examples where ministerial responsibility has been upheld;
- The perceived decline in civil service anonymity, with examples; does this also imply no 'secret government' or 'sham'?;
- The alleged 'politicisation' of the civil service by Thatcher; does this imply civil service pliability and/or power? e.g. Consider and discuss the role of civil servants/ministers/PM in the Westland affair;
- The implications of Whitehall reforms (e.g. Ibbs) for civil service/ministerial power and accountability;

- If critical of the status quo, suggest reform(s): either to enhance the 'traditional' role of the civil service, or to make them overtly accountable for their 'power'.

2)   *Theme*   **Civil Service reform**

Q?   'Given the dominance of civil servants in policy implementation one might question whether radical reform of the civil service could ever be achieved.' Evaluate recent attempts to reform the civil service in the light of this statement.

(JMB, June 1986, P. II.)

A✓   **Examiners' comments**

'This popular question was found by candidates to be difficult. There were two reasons for this: (a) linking together the two parts of what was not an easy question; (b) lack of understanding on the part of many candidates of the term "implementation". Consequently many candidates really produced two answers within one: one discussing minister/civil service relationships without any real focus on implementation; the second discussing civil service reform, without any real focus on civil service power (never mind implementation). In consequence a measure of latitude was exercised in marking this question, particularly to reward candidates who were well-prepared but yet still found difficulty in focusing on the specific question.'

Additional essay tips

- The title quote states that civil servants effectively control the execution of policy, including reform of Whitehall; and that they might use their administrative power to obstruct reform of the civil service itself.
- The focus on reform also implies defects, past or present; briefly outline the main criticisms which reformers have sought to address.
- 'Recent reforms' to be evaluated should include: the Fulton report, and, since the 1980s, cuts in civil service numbers, abolition of the Civil Service Department, banning of trade unions at GCHQ, the Rayner reforms, the restructuring which followed Ibbs' proposals, and alleged 'politicisation' of senior civil servants.
- Stress role of PM; and consider possible reasons for resistance to reform.

3)   *Theme*   **A political civil service?**

Q?   State a case for and a case against having a more political, that is a less politically neutral, civil service.

(London, February 1976, P. 1.)

A✓   **Examiners' comments**

'A bare pass would be achieved by a simple and lop-sided advocacy of either "the Civil Service frustrates the intentions of the party manifesto" or "politics must at all costs be kept out of administration or we will have no objectivity and a spoils system". A candidate will fail if he is not even lop-sided but tries to fly on one wing alone. These "for and against" questions are designed to test empathy and the ability to present reasons and justifications on both sides. The average candidate will see the difficulties on both sides: lack of drive and thrust, but the danger of a political bureaucracy leading to a one-party state. The candidate who gains either grade A or B will know something of political advisers and will see that the distinction between "involvement" and "neutrality" is not obvious; like lawyers, civil servants support their clients in a most partisan way. The good candidate will also distinguish between civil servants supporting or criticising a Minister privately and having a public voice.'

---

4. In the light of the examiners' comments above, and your own knowledge of the subject, try to assess, mark and grade the student's essay below as if you were the examiner. The essay is reprinted as the student wrote it, under timed conditions.

State a case for and a case against having a more political, that is a less politically neutral, civil service.

In theory the British civil service, specifically the most senior officials, the mandarins (who make up around 600 of the civil service) should be permanent, anonymous and neutral. The permanence means that it is a career job and that the mandarins serve under successive governments. The anonymity of the civil service means that they are not publicly accountable and accountable only privately to their ministers, the PM, the Ombudsman or the departmental committees, they are not permitted to talk to the media about their work or personal views. The bulk of this question, however, is concerned with their neutrality. This means that they should be impartial, non-party political and, as Sir Douglas Wass puts it, they should be loyal, but not enthusiastic to the minister or policy of the day.

The argument in favour of a political civil service centres around the criticism that the civil service has been 'politicised'. It is argued that this occurred in Mrs Thatcher's term of office, specific examples being former Cabinet Secretary Sir Robert Armstrong, who acted on behalf of the government in the 'Spycatcher' court hearings and admitted to being 'economical with the truth'; and press secretary Bernard Ingham. The likes of Plowden and Ponting, as well as the First Division Association (the civil service union), have argued that in Britain we already have a political civil service and that it should be made open, rather than continue with an arguable 'myth' of civil service neutrality.

In addition to the arguments that the civil service is already political are the actual arguments in favour of a political system of civil service. It has been argued by critics of the present system that the 'neutral' officials are too pliable and indifferent in their government administration (Bancroft). They have been seen to be equally supportive of the policies of one government and then another government that may propose opposing ideas. Whilst this may be seen as a fulfilment of the neutral and permanent theories of the civil service, it may mean that little attention is placed upon the immediate concerns of the day. It is also argued by Nevil Johnson that this apparent indifference shows a lack of integrity on the part of the civil service; and if they were overtly politicised they would have greater motivation.

Those in favour of politicising the civil service look to the USA and France. It is arguable that such systems allow for greater commitment on the part of the bureaucrats and that they enhance the strength and efficiency of the government of the day. In such a system the bureaucrats come and go with the government of the day so that their loyalties are not divided.

The arguments against politicising concentrate on the lack of continuity and the dangers of a 'one-party state'. Whilst, for example, Tony Benn may criticise the present system in Britain, he regards the American political bureaucracy as a 'spoils system'. Critics of politicising the civil service argue that a political civil service entails lack of job security, since once the government of the day is defeated in an election, the officials would lose their jobs. This might entail a reduction in the quality of officials since the job prospects are not good. Therefore it might be difficult to attract qualified individuals. Critics of politicisation also concentrate on the fact that a lack of permanence and continuity means that the officials cannot gain any expertise and are as ill-equipped as their ministers. The critics of a political civil service (e.g. Wass) also state that it may prevent long-term planning that the present system may enjoy.

I conclude that the drawbacks of politicising the civil service are too dangerous, and take Wass's arguments that there should be an Opposition civil service (on temporary secondment) to prevent a possible one-party system due to too much bias in government. I also propose a constitutional premiership so that the officials are more accountable to their own ministers and less dependent upon the will of the particular PM involved.

4) *Theme* **Open government**

Q? Discuss the arguments for and against the introduction of a Freedom of Information Act in Britain.

(JMB, June 1986, P. 1.)

A✓ **Short plan for guidance**

Range of current secrecy provisions; e.g.s ...
Critics of present degree of secrecy ...

Case against

1) All governments are reluctant to increase checks against themselves.
2) Freedom of Information Act would increase powers of non-elected, and some say 'unrepresentative', judges in deciding extent of open government.
3) Could inhibit honest advice from officials to ministers.
4) Could lead to political appointment of officials to avoid public knowledge of internal friction or unsympathetic advice.
5) Open government may undermine ministerial responsibility to Parliament if actions of civil servants become more public.
6) Could make government less efficient. **Lord Bancroft**: 'Government is difficult enough without having to halt continually while people peer up the governmental kilts'.
7) Could be costly to administer.
8) Existing provisions – e.g. data protection laws, Green Papers, new departmental committees etc. – are adequate.

Case for

1) Present secrecy laws run counter to principle of open government and informed choice in liberal democracy.
2) Public 'right to know' stressed by judges in 'Spycatcher' case.
3) Range of existing secrecy provisions may discredit law and make it hard to protect genuine secrets.
4) Secrecy may undermine ministerial responsibility to Parliament if MPs lack information about government policies.
5) Flexibility of present law allows government to define limits of national

security; but a government concerned with protecting itself may not be best placed to decide what should properly be kept secret. **Lord Donaldson**: '... very easy for the Government to confuse the national interest with the Government interest'.

6) Double standards of present system – where ministers may leak on an unattributable basis, but civil servants may be prosecuted – fuels resentment in civil service and may encourage leaks by officials.

7) Civil servants who suspect government malpractice (e.g. Ponting) have no recourse but to leak and/or to resign.

8) Excessive secrecy may undermine the authority of government in the eyes of the public.

9) Excessive secrecy may hide waste, inefficiency or corruption – e.g. loss of £212 million through mismanagement in Crown Agents Affair (Fay Report 1977); loss of £3.5 billion each year through long-term mismanagement and fraud in the Ministry of Defence (Public Accounts Committee Report 1988).

10) Pursuit of excessive secrecy (e.g. through the courts) may waste taxpayers' money in legal costs.

11) Pressure groups need more official information to represent their members/causes adequately; and media need information to inform the public and scrutinise government.

12) Academic research about British government and politics hampered by undue secrecy.

13) Opinion polls indicate majority support for freedom of information.

14) More informed debate about policies may produce better policies, and/or more consensus politics.

15) Freedom of information legislation appears to work well in USA etc.

Conclusion: Arguments for Freedom of Information Act outweigh those against.

● **Note**   If you wish to conclude against a Freedom of Information Act, put the 'case against' last.

---

5. Write at least one of the following essays.
   Always write a brief plan first.

   1) How and by whom are new policies initiated in Britain?
                                                    (AEB, June 1990, P. 1.)

   2) 'The problem of devising a new "official secrets" Act is that the public interest requires that national security be protected, but the democratic interest requires that ministers and civil servants should not be able to cover up their mistakes.' Discuss.
                                          (Oxford and Cambridge, June 1989, P. 2.)

   3) Discuss the main ways in which senior civil servants contribute to the political process in Britain.
                                                (Cambridge, June 1989, P. 1.)

   4) Has the Civil Service been politicised?
                                             (London, January 1991, P. 1.)

   5) Is government secrecy compatible with democracy?
                                               (Oxford, Summer 1980, P. II.)

—— GUIDE TO EXERCISES

Page 106

1. 1) (a) Decline in civil service anonymity:
    (i)   More accountable to Parliament since creation of Ombudsman (1967) and departmental select committees (1979).
    (ii) Senior officials are increasingly public spokesmen for the government in the media and the courts, e.g. Armstrong in the 'Spycatcher' case.
    (iii) Officials are more often publicly named and sometimes blamed for policy errors: e.g. by administrative tribunal over collapse of Vehicle and General Insurance Co. (1971); Westland (1986).
    (iv) More media coverage and communication: e.g. Peter Hennessy's *Whitehall*, ministerial and official memoirs.
    (v)   Financial Management Initiative (1982), and creation of executive agencies (1988), were both designed to give senior officials more autonomy over budgets and management, which may suggest more direct accountability of officials e.g. to Parliament.
    (vi) Leaks by officials publicly prosecuted, e.g. Tisdall and Ponting.
    (a) Decline in civil service permanence:
    (i)   Cuts in numbers – loss of job security.
    (ii) Sacking of Bancroft.
    (iii) Perception of 'political' appointments may prompt replacement of key senior officials by a new government or PM (as Major replaced Press Secretary Bernard Ingham), producing a political civil service *de facto*.
    (iv) Restructuring might ultimately lead to privatisation of some administrative units, and loss of civil service status and permanence for those staff.
    2) May reduce ministerial accountability to Parliament.

Page 106

2. 1) Possible reforms:
    (a) Ministers (rather than PM and civil servants themselves) appointing and dismissing their own officials.
    (b) More political advisers for ministers (perhaps in advisory bodies like the French *cabinets*).
    (c) Access by ministers and advisers to official committees and files.
    (d) More open government.
    (e) Control of Cabinet Office by Cabinet (rather than by PM).
    (f) Greater adherence to convention of individual ministerial responsibility.
    (g) Stronger parliamentary control of executive – e.g. more power and publicity for Ombudsman and select committees.
    (h) Withdrawal from EC (Benn).
    2) Case for and against a political civil service: see essay 3) on page 109.

Page 108

3. Case for and against open government: see primarily essay 4) on page 111; but remember that open government is a broad concept. As well as freedom of

information legislation, it may refer to the openness of parliamentary, policy-making and judicial processes, meetings and committees, the lobby system, police and security services, public appointments, etc.

Page 110

4. The student's essay was a little short; it should have said more on reasons for the principle of civil service neutrality (deriving from permanence), and on allegations of civil service bias before Thatcher's premiership (e.g. in the 1960s). Conclusion could also have been more fully explained. However, the essay was well-structured, relevant throughout and made good use of prominent names and arguments. It was graded B- in a class exercise.

—— REFERENCES

Lord Bancroft, *In Defence of the Mandarins* in *The Guardian* 2.10.83.

Barbara Castle, *The Castle Diaries, 1974–76* (1984).

R. H. S. Crossman (ed. A. Howard), *The Crossman Diaries* (Condensed Version) (Magnum Books, 1979).

Lord Hailsham, *The Dilemma of Democracy* (Collins, 1978).

Peter Hennessy, *Whitehall* (Fontana, 1990).

Nevil Johnson, *In Search of the Constitution* (Methuen, 1977).

P. Kellner and N. Crowther-Hunt, *The Civil Servants* (MacDonald and Jane's, 1980).

David Simpson, *Politicisation of the Civil Service* (Longman, 1989).

H. Young and A. Sloman, *No, Minister: An Inquiry into the Civil Service* (BBC, 1982).

8 Local Government

> ## KEY ISSUES
>
> ► Functions of local government and councillors
>   Accountability of local government
>   Pros and cons of local government
>   Central-local government relations
>   Local government versus parliamentary democracy
>   Local government finance
>   Controls on local government
>
> ► Devolution

—— TOPIC NOTES

Key facts and concepts

Local government entails the election of local people to run local services such as education, housing, refuse collection etc. The structure of local government in the United Kingdom is a mixture of single-tier and two-tier local authorities.

The **Local Government Act 1985**, enacted on 1 April 1986, abolished the Greater London Council and the six Metropolitan county councils (Greater Manchester, South and West Yorkshire, West Midlands, Merseyside, Tyne and Wear). Central government argued that they were too costly and remote from the local communities. Their functions passed either to the 32 London borough councils, or to district councils in the Metropolitan areas, or to joint boards of district and borough councillors, or to quangos (e.g. London Regional Transport Board), or to central government. London is therefore now the only European capital without a city-wide elected executive. The GLC and Metropolitan councils fought strongly against abolition, arguing that they were more democratic, efficient and co-ordinated than the new arrangements which, they said, would actually be more costly. All of the abolished councils were Labour led, and the issue was very much party political.

Since abolition was a Conservative manifesto proposal in the 1983 election, the government argued that it had a mandate to carry out the policy, although public opinion polls indicated around 70% opposition to it. The May 1985 local elections were thus a possible obstacle to abolition, since they were bound to be treated as a referendum on abolition, and the Conservatives were likely to fare badly; the government therefore proposed to bring forward abolition and to give powers to

The Structure and Major Functions of Local Government

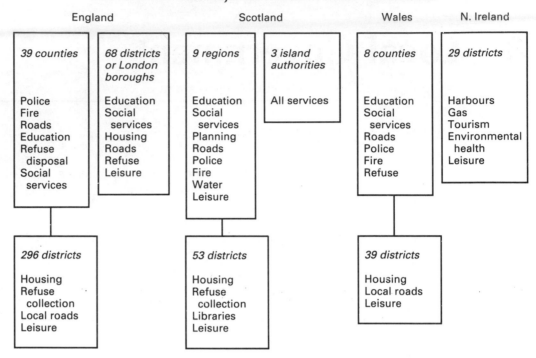

| England | | Scotland | | Wales | N. Ireland |

39 counties

Police
Fire
Roads
Education
Refuse
 disposal
Social
 services

*68 districts
or London
boroughs*

Education
Social
 services
Housing
Roads
Refuse
Leisure

9 regions

Education
Social
 services
Planning
Roads
Police
Fire
Water
Leisure

*3 island
authorities*

All services

8 counties

Education
Social
 services
Roads
Police
Fire
Refuse

29 districts

Harbours
Gas
Tourism
Environmental
 health
Leisure

296 districts

Housing
Refuse
 collection
Local roads
Leisure

53 districts

Housing
Refuse
 collection
Libraries
Leisure

39 districts

Housing
Local roads
Leisure

nominated district and borough councillors until the new arrangements were established. This proposal – enshrined in the Local Government (Interim Provisions) Bill 1984, known as the 'Paving Bill' – was defeated by the Lords on the grounds that it had no mandate (unlike abolition itself). The government therefore simply deferred the elections.

There are around 25,000 county, district and borough councillors. They are elected for fixed four-year terms to local areas known as **wards** (rather than **constituencies**). In London, all seats are contested together every four years. In the Metropolitan districts one-third of the seats are contested each year, with county council elections in the fourth year. The non-Metropolitan districts choose either method. Councillors are part-time and are paid expenses and attendance allowances only; they therefore tend to be atypical of the electorate, many of whom lack the time or money for local political involvement. Around 17% of councillors are women. Councillors are usually party political like MPs, but there are many more independents (around 15%), and there are many hung councils where no one party has an absolute majority.

What are the functions and powers of a local councillor? How do they differ from those of an MP?

A councillor is a member of a local executive body, whereas an MP is a member of the national legislature. Both are elected to represent a local area; but a ward is smaller than a constituency, and whereas a councillor is purely local, an MP is expected to represent both constituency and national interests (according to the Burkean view). An MP is a legislator, and local councils, like everyone else, should work within the law of the land ('rule of law'). MPs may pass laws – such as the Local Government Act 1985 – which alter the powers of local councils or even abolish them completely. MPs are also meant to scrutinise and control the executive, both central and local; councillors are therefore subordinate to MPs. The only kind of law which councillors may make is delegated legislation, e.g. local government by-laws. Their functions are **executive** rather than **legislative**: providing local services such as education, housing, refuse collection, fire and police, roads and harbours, leisure and social services. Some of these are 'mandatory', i.e. local government is obliged by law to carry out certain functions, such as housing the homeless; others are 'permissive', i.e. optional, such as providing local libraries and nurseries.

Local government is advised and administered by appointed officials who are full-time, paid and permanent. As with the central civil service, the distinction between advice, administration and policy-making may be blurred, and the officials are sometimes accused of having power without public accountability.

---

1.   List *five* advantages, and *five* disadvantages, of local government.

Local government finance

Local government spending (e.g. on building and running schools, council housing, roads, and providing services like homes for the elderly, parks and gardens, plus the administrative costs of local government itself) totals around £30 billion, nearly one quarter of all public expenditure.

Capital spending (e.g. on new roads) is financed by borrowing from central government and banks etc., and by selling assets such as land.

Revenue (day-to-day running costs, wages etc.) is financed by a number of sources.

● **Grants** from central government. These have increased from about 50% to over 75% of revenue, with increasing central control under the community charge system (see next page).

- **Payments for services**, e.g. council house rents.
- Until 1989/90, local rates levied on business and domestic properties. These were replaced (1989 in Scotland, 1990 in England and Wales) by the **community charge** or **poll tax** – a flat-rate charge paid by every adult, unconnected with property.

This measure, the **Local Government Finance Act 1988**, was highly controversial; 38 government backbenchers rebelled in favour of Conservative MP Michael Mates' amendment proposing an income-related charge, but it failed. Ministers sought unsuccessfully to have the bill categorised as a 'money bill' to prevent intervention by the Lords; they then pulled out the 'backwoodsmen' (at a cost to taxpayers of over £40,000 in peers' attendance allowances) to produce a vote in the Lords of 317 to 183 against an income-related scheme. A clause in the bill prohibiting judicial review of ministerial power was condemned by Lord Denning as 'unconstitutional'. Rates on business properties were replaced by the **uniform business rate**, centrally fixed and collected, then redistributed to councils in the form of grants.

Case for the community charge

The old rating system was iniquitous – a family of four adults could be paying the same as the lone pensioner next door. Out of an electorate of 35 million only 18 million paid rates at all, and only 12 million paid the full contribution. A rating revaluation in Scotland in 1985 produced large increases (many over 50%) and a political outcry; revaluation in England and Wales, delayed since 1973, did not happen. The community charge is equitable in the sense that, in principle, everyone pays the same. Students and those on income support etc. may claim rebates of up to 80%. Some are wholly exempt: people in hostels, nursing homes, residential care homes, severely mentally ill, people sleeping rough, most monks and nuns, 18-year-olds still at school, and prisoners except those imprisoned for non-payment of the community charge itself.

Case against the community charge

The community charge is inequitable in that it is a regressive tax, flat-rate regardless of income. The last attempt in Britain to levy a poll tax, in the fourteenth century, was followed by a census which found that the population had mysteriously shrunk by a quarter, and it generated the 1381 Peasants' Revolt and the beating to death of two ministers responsible. The only known equivalent now is said to be the Nyasaland hut tax. A 'Committee of a hundred', including several MPs, was formed in Scotland pledged to civil disobedience and non-payment of the charge.

The recent protests against the community charge are not without precedent. Here Richard III is seen meeting rebels at Greenwich during the Peasants' Revolt generated by the imposition of the poll tax in 1381.

It is costly to collect – around twice as much as rates. It is easier to evade than a tax on property. The principle of flat-rate equity is undermined by rebates and concessions; while the principle of taxing the person rather than property is undermined by double poll tax demands on people with second homes. The community charge register is compiled from various sources, including the electoral register, and some people have therefore not registered to vote in the hope of evading the poll tax. Critics such as the pressure group Liberty also feared the need for 'Big Brother' surveillance tactics and an 'army of snoopers' to keep the register accurate and up-to-date, culminating in compulsory national identity cards. (This last has not happened.)

Like the rates, the poll tax may be 'capped', i.e. central government can impose a limit on the maximum levied, which contradicts the principle of local responsibility and accountability for spending levels. This also undermines the mandate of local authorities, and some councillors have said that they could not then afford to provide mandatory services. Lambeth local council was one of the twenty-one authorities – none of them Conservative controlled – capped in 1990; it took the government to court to question the legality of the capping procedures, and won. Parliament therefore had to amend the law in 1991 to require government to clarify the capping regulations so that local councils could know how to avoid being capped. Nevertheless, the regulations themselves were not deemed illegal, though they were perceived by critics as being motivated by party politics (like the abolition of the Labour-led GLC and Metropolitan councils): for example, in 1990 they enabled Conservative-controlled Berkshire to escape capping despite a 20.6% spending increase, while Labour-controlled Brent with a 1.4% rise in spending was capped. When John Major became Prime Minister he appointed as Environment Secretary Michael Heseltine, a long-standing opponent of the poll tax, who pledged a fundamental review of the system. In

1991 the government announced that the poll tax would be abolished in 1993 and replaced by a banded property tax – in effect, a return to something similar to the old rating system.

Controls on local government

Parliament. Local authorities are created by statute, and all powers must be granted by law. There were 58 items of local government legislation in the ten years after 1979.

Courts may rule local authorities *ultra vires*, i.e. acting beyond their legal powers. For example, in the 1981 GLC 'Fares Fair' case, the courts ruled public transport fare cuts illegal under the Transport (London) Act 1969 which required economical services (interpreted by the courts to mean non-subsidised). There was more controversy in the mid-1980s when Liverpool and Lambeth councillors over-stepped the rate-capping limits, were surcharged for illegal expenditure, bankrupted and hence barred from office for five years. (However, the courts can also, of course, rule against central government's actions and in favour of local government: e.g. in 1985 when the Environment Department took money away from the GLC prior to abolition to set up London Regional Transport, the High Court ruled that £50 million too much had been taken, which the judge described as 'unlawful, irrational and procedurally improper'. The difference here was that central government used its majority in Parliament to rewrite and backdate the law to legalise its own illegality.)

Central government intervenes to control overall public spending – hence e.g. compulsory competitive tendering of some local services such as refuse collection; to ensure consistency of standards across the country, e.g. in education; and to co-ordinate local functions, e.g. planning. Methods include:

(a)   Financial control: grants, audits (via the Audit Commission for Local Authorities in England and Wales, established in 1983 and appointed by the Environment Secretary), capping, power of veto over capital spending projects etc.;

(b)   Ministerial approval required in many areas, e.g. education (the Education Reform Act 1988 granted the Secretary of State 366 new powers);

(c)   Inspection by relevant department, e.g. police, fire, education;

(d)   Appeals against local authority action, e.g. to the Environment Secretary against planning decisions;

(e)   Inquiries, e.g. the Widdicombe Inquiry into the Conduct of Local Authority Business, whose 1985 report resulted in legislation curbing 'twin-tracking' where an officer of one authority is an elected member of another; barring around 70,000 local government officers from public political activity; the prohibition of 'political' advertising by local authorities (such as the GLC's campaign against abolition, which cost £10 million); a ban on the appointment of all party political advisers by local authorities; and a compulsory register of councillors' financial interests;

(f)   The Commissioners for Local Administration – three local ombudsmen established in 1972 – who investigate public complaints of maladministration against local authorities;

(g)   Central government can remove local authorities' power ('default') as in 1972 when Labour-controlled Clay Cross council refused to increase council house rents as required by the Housing Finance Act of that year, the Conservative Government sent in a Housing Commissioner. Or, through Parliamentary legislation, whole local authorities can themselves be abolished.

It may be argued that this undermines local democracy and the mandate of local authorities; but local elections are often about national parties, policies and issues; and the turnout is usually low – around 40% – perhaps, of course, precisely because local councils are seen as weak and insignificant.

The consequences of growing central control of local government since 1979 have been growing legal and financial constraints, loss of local power and increasing centralisation. For example, the Local Government Act 1988 extended compulsory competitive tendering of some services, e.g. refuse collection, street cleaning and catering; it also included the controversial Clause 28 (a backbench amendment) forbidding local authorities from promoting homosexuality. The forced sale of council houses has been operative since 1980, but local authorities are not allowed to spend most of the resulting revenue. There has been legislation allowing council tenants and schools to opt out of local government control, the imposition of non-elected Housing Action Trusts (HATs) to run some urban council estates (Housing Act 1988), the establishment of city technology colleges outside of local authority control, and the abolition of the Inner London Education Authority (ILEA) in 1990. Many of the changes were imposed rather than being the product of local or political consensus. They were made easier by a long-running Conservative party and press campaign against the so-called 'loony left' in local Labour councils.

GOLDSMITHS' MEDIA RESEARCH GROUP
The Press and the Loony Left

A NEW STYLE of investigative journalism has developed which itself needs investigating. A small number of partisan newspapers have produced a series of bizarre reports – about left-wing councils in London – which have either been conjured out of thin air or have contained more artificial additives than true ingredients.

One recurrent theme of these reports is that 'loony left' councils are hypersensitive to imagined racial and sexist slurs to a point bordering on paranoia. For example, the London Standard (February 27, 1986) published a startling report that Hackney council had officially renamed manholes as 'access chambers'. The report featured an irate engineer, Tom Jordan, who allegedly had received a memorandum from the council containing the new decree.

The report was pure fiction. The council had not authorised the renaming of manholes, nor sent out a memorandum to that effect. It did not even employ an engineer called Tom Jordan. But this did not prevent the story from being recycled in nine other newspapers, including the pro-Labour Daily Mirror, where Keith Waterhouse denounced Hackney councillors as 'barking mad'.

The source of the story was the Fleet Street News Agency. The editor at the time was Leif Kalfayan (now at the Daily Mail) who claims that 'Tom Jordan' was tracked down 'at some engineering depot that we got out of the directory enquiries or the telephone book'. The story, he insists, originated from the Hackney Gazette, which Tim Cooper, the newspaper's local government correspondent, strongly denies. The Hackney Gazette has never carried the story.

In a similar vein, the Sun (November 22, 1986) disclosed that Camden council had ordered its employees not to call each other 'sunshine' because the council supposed it to be racist. The article alleged that council chiefs had sent a memorandum to 'key members of the social services department' banning the word, and that a white worker who had called a black colleague 'sunshine' faced dismissal.

Again this report (which was recycled by the Daily Mail) was a fiction; no memorandum on this subject had been issued by the council and no white worker faced the sack for calling a black colleague 'sunshine'. The author of the Sun article, Dina Malik, refused our invitation to justify what she wrote. But her report would appear to be a garbled version of an incident that occurred more than a year before in which a black worker had been called to a disciplinary hearing for a number of reasons, including calling his white manager 'sunshine' in a derogatory manner.

Another recurring tabloid theme is that left-wing councils are obsessively preoccupied with minority interests at the expense of those of the white, heterosexual majority. Working to this prepared story line, the Sun (February 20, 1987) ran a major investigative report headlined 'Freebie trip for blacks but white kids must pay. Barmy Brent does it again' (which was again recycled in the Daily Mail). The Sun article alleged that 'a loony left council is splashing out at least £9,000 to send a group of black teenagers on an expenses-paid jaunt to Communist Cuba.' The report was seemingly corroborated by 'youth worker Shirley Williams' who said 'blacks are getting the subsidised places because we really only want to take them'.

The report is untrue. A voluntary organisation, Caribbean Exchange, has been trying to raise funds for the trip. But Brent council has not offered to subsidise the trip, and the Caribbean Exchange is no more part of the council than the local boy scouts and girl guides, which are also affiliated to its Youth and Communities Service.

The story which got the widest publicity and which has come to encapsulate the tabloid image of the 'loony left' was the alleged banning of the nursery rhyme Baa Baa Black Sheep. The story appears to have surfaced originally in the Daily Star (February 15, 1986), which claimed that Beavers Play Group in Hackney had suppressed the rhyme. This was reworked by the Sun (February 20, 1986) into 'loony left-wing councillors have banned children from reciting the nursery rhyme'.

In fact, the council had not banned the rhyme. All that happened is that the parent-run Beavers Play Group had sometimes sung a humorous alternative version of the rhyme, beginning 'Baa Baa White Sheep ...' and ending 'and one for the little boy (or girl) with holes in his (or her) socks', as well as singing the conventional version of the rhyme.

The story was given a new twist by Anthony Doran in the Daily Mail (October 9, 1986), who reported that Haringey council had banned the rhyme at a racism awareness course which play leaders in the borough had been instructed to attend. This report was repeated in a large number of other papers. In fact, the council issued no such ban. It is not even clear that the rhyme was even discussed at the racism course, where attendance was voluntary.

Out of all the papers which repeated the story, only the Yorkshire Evening Press had the grace to print a retraction, acknowledging that it had relied on 'an inaccurate report'.

Perhaps the final irony is that the story eventually became almost true, although in another borough. Nursery teachers did effectively ban the rhyme at one Islington school, perhaps believing, due to press publicity, that it was the policy of left-wing councils to forbid it. But on this occasion, Islington council's denial that it had banned the rhyme or promoted its ban was widely reported.

Coverage of London councils has been particularly inaccurate and distorted in four papers – the Sun, Daily Mail, Mail on Sunday and the London Evening Standard. Their more lurid and misleading reports on 'loony left' authorities have been regularly repeated in local newspapers up and down the country. They have also been incorporated into briefings issued by the Conservative Party Central Office. These four papers have thus played a key role in mass-producing the 'London effect'. The local elections on Thursday may show whether this effect extends beyond London.

The Guardian, 4 May 1987

Devolution

Devolution means the delegation or passing down of some legislative and/or executive functions of central government to local bodies, while the national government remains responsible for major national issues such as defence. The local bodies are subordinate to the central legislature or executive, which can readily retrieve their powers. **Federalism**, on the other hand, entails greater local autonomy. Here the regions allocate certain national powers to a central body, and they are in theory equal to it. Thus central government cannot readily increase its powers at the expense of the regions or federal states. The USA and Australia are examples of federal systems. **Separatism** means complete political independence.

The United Kingdom has elements of executive devolution in local government, and Scotland and Wales have their own Secretaries of State with Cabinet status. Scotland's legal and educational systems are also quite distinct. There is, however, no legislative devolution; Westminster has been the sole UK legislature since the suspension in 1972 of the Northern Irish Parliament, Stormont, and the introduction of 'direct rule' because of the growing political conflict in Northern Ireland at that time.

Encouraged by the rise of nationalist feeling in Scotland and Wales since the late 1960s, all of the major parties except the Conservatives advocate devolution for Scotland and Wales, and the Liberal Democrats also propose elected local legislatures for the regions of England. A Labour Government in 1977 introduced a Devolution Bill, and held referenda on the issue in Scotland and Wales in 1979. Wales voted against; Scotland voted in favour, but the 'yes' vote amounted to only 32.5% of the total electorate, and the bill required approval by at least 40% of the electorate (a backbench amendment). The proposals were withdrawn, but devolution is still an important issue in UK politics. In Scotland especially, where the Conservative Party won only ten of the 72 seats in the 1987 election, many voters question or deny the authority of Westminster and Whitehall.

1987 manifesto policies on local government and devolution

Conservative ▶

LOCAL GOVERNMENT AND INNER CITIES

The Conservative view of local government is that local people should look after the interests of the local community which they were elected to serve, maintaining and improving essential services at a price people can afford. That is an honourable tradition of public service, still upheld by councillors in most local authorities.

But the abuses of left-wing Labour councils have shocked the nation. The Labour Party leadership pretends that this is a problem in only a few London boroughs. The truth is that the far Left control town halls in many of our cities.

The extremists have gained power in these areas partly because too few ratepayers have an interest in voting for responsible councillors pursuing sensible policies. Many people benefit from local services yet make little or no contribution towards them: this throws too heavy a burden on too few shoulders.

There is much else wrong with the present system of domestic rates. They seem unfair and arbitrary. And companies are left with little protection against huge rate rises levied by councils controlled by Labour, Liberals and Social Democrats, which drive them out of business and destroy jobs.

We have acted to protect ratepayers' interests in a number of ways. The wasteful and unnecessary tier of the GLC and metropolitan counties has been eliminated – to the substantial benefit of ratepayers. Our rate-capping legislation – so bitterly opposed by the Labour, SDP and Liberal parties in Parliament – has protected ratepayers from huge rate increases. This year alone, twenty councils will be rate-capped – nineteen of them Labour and one controlled by the Liberals and the SDP – saving ratepayers several hundred million pounds.

We will now tackle the roots of the problem. We will reform local government finance to strengthen local democracy and accountability.

Local electors must be able to decide the level of service they want and how much they are prepared to pay for it.

We will legislate in the first Session of the new Parliament to abolish the unfair domestic rating system and replace rates with a fairer Community Charge.

This will be a fixed rate charge for local services paid by those over the age of 18, except the mentally ill and elderly people living in homes and hospitals. The less-well-off and students will not have to pay the full charge – but everyone will be aware of the costs as well as the benefits of local services. This should encourage people to take a greater interest in the policies of their local council and in getting value for money. Business ratepayers will pay a Unified Business Rate at a standard rate pegged to inflation.

We will require local authorities to put out to tender a range of services, including refuse collection, the cleaning of streets and buildings, vehicle maintenance, catering and ground maintenance.

Ratepayers expect councils to provide their services as efficiently as possible. Yet some local authorities steadfastly oppose private sector companies tendering for services even though they could provide them more cheaply and more effectively. The independent Audit Commission has estimated that some £500 million a year could be saved if all councils followed the practices of the best – sums which could be used to lower rates or improve services.

The Widdicombe Report into the conduct of local authority business painted a disturbing picture of the breakdown of democratic processes in a number of councils. We will take action to strengthen democratic processes in local authorities.

Labour
▼

We will:

- Set up an Environmental Protection Service and a Wildlife and Countryside Service.
- Extend the planning system to cover agricultural forestry and water developments requiring them, and industry, to take account of environmental considerations.
- Invest more in land reclamation and cleaning up, in recycling and conservation, in development of new products, processes and pollution control equipment. This will not only make the country cleaner but will create jobs as well.
- Take action to deal with acid rain.
- Stop radio-active discharges into our seas and oppose the dumping of nuclear waste at sea.
- Provide for better monitoring, inspection and enforcement of pollution control, to cover areas ranging from air pollution to beaches, from hazardous chemicals to food additives, and from water quality to vehicle emissions.
- Protect green belts and other specially designated areas.
- Bring in a new Wildlife and Countryside Act and provide for public access to all common land, mountain, moor and heath.
- End all forms of organised hunting with hounds. Special account will be tak... of the conditions applying in N... Parks. These changes will ... shooting and fishing.
- Update animal pr... for example, ... experime...

Protect green belts

STR...

Strategic authority for London

We will halt the cuts in rate support grant and end financial penalties. We will make the legal liabilities of councillors similar to those of Ministers and Company Directors by ending surcharge and disqualification except for criminal offences.

We will abolish the Rates Act and repeal the legislation which established the poll tax in Scotland.

Repeal the poll tax in Scotland

We will give local authorities the necessary powers to enable them to build on existing successful initiatives for enterprise and employment, to develop new technologies and to train young people.

Labour will examine the structure of local government to ensure that it is democratic and effective. We will establish a new Quality Commission to ensure the spread of 'best practice', efficiency and high standards of local authority provision and response to the public.

Establish a new Quality Commission

NEW LIFE FOR INNER CITIES

Except where it has turned areas over to speculators so that they can create luxury accommodation at astronomical prices, this government has left inner-city areas to rot.

Experience has shown that the Conservatives' City Action Teams have never had the means or the purpose of making any real impact on inner city problems.

Tory cuts in funding and in housing, together with mass unemployment, have turned too many of our urban areas into dingy, hopeless places.

Yet the people who live there, given the chance, have the zest and initiative to make these areas thrive socially and economically.

Labour will launch a drive against inner-

for changes in the structure of Scottish local government.

WALES

Wales and Welsh economy will clearly benefit from Labour's programme for investment in jobs and vital services. In addition, the Welsh Development Agency will be given greater powers and funds – and there will be a new Wales Economic Planning Council. Welsh agriculture will benefit from our measures to help the livestock farmers – especially the marginal and hill farmers.

A separate Arts Council for Wales will be established and the development of the use and choice of the Welsh language will be encouraged.

Welsh Development Agency

NORTHERN IRELAND

Labour's policies for economic renewal are essential to combat the record unemployment and social deprivation in Northern Ireland and to encourage the economic development which is fundamental to the security community.

We believe in a united Ireland: to be achieved peacefully, democratically, and by consent. We consequently sup... the Anglo-Irish Agreement and its... there should be ... ent that constitutional ... n the without the ... land people ... the wit... ty

Support the Anglo-Irish Agreement

city deprivation both as a way of generating employment and as a means of making such areas safer and better places to live.

Labour's approach will be to develop the partnership between central and local government, with the direct participation of the voluntary and private sectors.

We will:

- Give local authorities in key areas the power to declare Public Action Zones. In these areas, local councils will have additional resources and powers to undertake programmes of investment. Land will be identified for housing, jobs and amenities and extra government resources allocated to help with comprehensive regeneration. Local people will be fully consulted about their needs and ideas.

Declare Public Action Zones

- Strengthen the Urban Programme and Partnership Schemes.
- Make Urban Development Grants available for local needs.
- Increase resources for reclaiming derelict land.

RURAL AREAS

Under the Tories, the problems of the rural areas have become steadily more serious – the lack of jobs, the poor housing, and the loss of buses, post offices, shops and schools.

Labour will give our rural communities the chance to thrive again. Our policies include better public transport, new mobile facilities for health care and social services – and extra help to keep open local schools and post offices.

New mobile facilities for health care and social services

—— ESSAYS

1)   *Theme*   **Local government**

1)   **Q?**   Account for recent attempts by central government to assert greater control over local government.

(London, June 1986, P. 1.)

2)   **Q?**   Discuss the arguments for and against recent extensions of central control over local government.

(London, June 1987, P. 1.)

A✓   **Notes for guidance**

Whereas the first title above requires a list of reasons for growing central government control over local government, the second title requires an evaluation of the arguments for and against such growing control, and is therefore more difficult.

---

2.   Consider the list of points below, all of which could form an answer to the second title. Which would *not* be necessary for the first title?

Methods and examples of growing central control over local government: rate-capping, community charge-capping, uniform business rate, surcharging of councillors through the courts, abolition of GLC and metropolitan counties, compulsory tendering of some services, removal and restraint of powers in education and housing, city technology colleges, Housing Action Trusts (HATs) etc.

- The UK is a unitary state – central power may always give or take power to and from the regions.
- Central government intervenes at local level to ensure:
  control of overall public spending;
  consistency of provision of services across country;
  co-ordination of local functions and services.
- Local government may thwart mandate of central government – and the latter is stronger because turnout at local elections is low.
- Prior to rates reform, only a minority of voters paid rates and local government was insufficiently accountable for its spending. Local businesses also paid disproportionate costs.
- Local authorities have sometimes gone beyond their local mandate to involve themselves in national issues such as defence.
- Two or more tiers of local government may be excessively costly, bureaucratic and remote from local communities.
- Local government may avoid necessary but painful financial measures in pursuit of political popularity; it may therefore be very costly and inefficient.
- Local government has a mandate from local electors.
- Local government provides checks and balances against 'elective dictatorship' of majority central government in a sovereign, unitary Parliament.
- Local government elections provide a test of public opinion between general elections.
- Local government allows democratic participation at local level.
- Local government provides a training and recruitment ground for central government and Parliament.

- Local government knows local needs.
- Local government provides services relatively cost-effectively; transfer of powers to the centre or to quangos etc. may increase costs, reduce democratic accountability and ignore local needs.
- Central government intervention may simply be party political.

Q? 'The strongest justification for elected local government is its claim to be an effective provider of services.' Evaluate this claim in the light of recent central government policies towards local government.

(JMB, June 1986, P. II.)

A✓ **Examiners' comments**

'This popular question created all sorts of difficulties. Many candidates interpreted this as "the question" on abolition of Metros and failed to relate it to any other recent central government policies. Significantly many candidates from the Metropolitan areas showed a somewhat blinkered approach. There was often a total lack of recognition that different circumstances pertained outside the Metropolitan areas, i.e. that districts in non-metropolitan areas had different functions, that non-metropolitan county councils had not been abolished, etc. There were also many confused accounts of financial controls and rate-capping. This is admittedly, not an easy subject, but sadly there seemed to have been less searching out of relevant materials on this subject than, by contrast, there seemingly had been for privatisation.'

Q? How and why is local democracy limited in the UK?

(London, June 1988, P. 1.)

A✓ **Examiners' comments**

'Most candidates demonstrated a reasonable knowledge of how local democracy is limited in the United Kingdom, with the better answers pointing to recent examples such as rate-capping and the abolition of the metropolitan counties. The "why" part of the question produced some good answers couched in terms of the unitary nature of the UK constitution. High marks were available for those who understood the conflict between local and national democracy. A good example of how the second part should have been tackled was given by one candidate who began as follows:

"Local democracy in the UK is limited primarily because the UK is a unitary state. That is to say, all power is derived from the centre and may be taken back if the government so decides. This century local government has been given the responsibility for education and housing by central government, but the central government has also taken back from local government responsibility for running local hospitals".

The candidate then went on to discuss the problem of conflicting mandates and the need for central government to ensure uniformity of provision and to control public expenditure.'

Q? Why not abolish local government altogether?

(Cambridge, June 1985, P. 1.)

A✓ **Notes for guidance**

Like many other titles, this one centres largely on the broad arguments for and against local government, outlined above. The introduction should point out, with examples, that local government in the UK is increasingly limited in function and weak in its powers, and that there is a case for carrying this shift of power through to its logical conclusion. However, this may be effectively to say that central government has curtailed local government so much that it is virtually impotent, and may as well be abolished altogether – a self-fulfilling prophecy which may be logical, but may not be 'democratic'.

Q? How great could the powers of regional parliaments become without there ceasing to be a British state?

(London, February 1976, P. 1.)

A✓ **Examiners' comments**

The answer should turn on some clear understanding of "state". The weakest possible definition would not be compatible with Scotland described as "simply a member of the Commonwealth"; legal separation followed by practical integration could still retain a weak sense of the state. In a strong sense, it implies the continuing power to act decisively in defence, foreign relations and in response to internal crises; this could well be threatened by various levels of "home rule". Some of these notions must be specified, even hypothetically, for the award of a grade B or an A.

Skeletal essay plan

1) History of calls for legislative devolution – to regions of England as well as to Scotland, Wales and Northern Ireland …
2) The concept of 'state': definitions and problems …
3) Degrees of devolved power: local law; local spending; local revenue-raising; lack of 'override' by Westminster; capacity to legislate for administrative/ legal/political/financial autonomy.
4) Possibility that limited devolution, and resulting local dissatisfaction, could generate calls for greater autonomy and hence ultimate break-up of UK – 'thin end of the wedge' argument.
5) **Conclusion:** Essence of 'state' is political sovereignty, i.e. control of defence, national security, international relations and military matters. In practical terms, ultimate control of purse-strings is key to political control by centre. (It is, of course, debatable whether there *should* continue to be a British state; there is a case for complete separatism, at least of the four countries of the UK, if not the regions of England.)

---

3. Write at least one of the following essays.
    Always write a brief plan first.

    1) 'The main trouble with local government is that it is neither democratic nor properly accountable.' Discuss in the light of recent problems.

    (London, June 1985, P. 1.)

    2) It has been argued that the rating system was an inefficient, unfair and increasingly unworkable method of raising local revenue. Is the Community Charge or 'poll tax' an improvement?

    (Oxford and Cambridge, June 1990, P. 2.)

3) 'Local government is no longer local.' Is this true?

(Cambridge, June 1986, P. 1.)

4) Should local government be given greater independence from central government control?

(Oxford, Summer 1986, P. 1.)

5) 'The rise of nationalist sentiment in Scotland and Wales is in reality no more than a protest against economic decline and the remoteness of central government.'
(a) How accurately does the statement explain the support for Scottish and Welsh nationalist parties since 1970?   (12 marks)
(b) How great a challenge has nationalism presented to the political homogeneity of Britain since 1970?   (13 marks)

(AEB, June 1987, P. 1.)

—— GUIDE TO EXERCISES

Page 117

1. Five advantages of local government:
    1) Know local needs;
    2) Allow element of local democracy, accountability and political participation;
    3) Impose checks and balances on centre;
    4) Provide training and recruitment ground for centre;
    5) May be more cost-effective than central bureaucracy.

    Five disadvantages of local government:
    1) May thwart [stronger?] mandate of central government;
    2) May mean inconsistent and uncoordinated provision of services across country;
    3) May be unduly costly;
    4) May mean local 'elective dictatorship' of one strong and/or radical party on a minority vote;
    5) Strong local government is contrary to the constitutional principles of a unitary state.

Page 124

2. There are 15 points listed altogether; the last eight would not be necessary in answer to the first title.

—— REFERENCES

Alan Alexander, 'The decline of local government' in *Contemporary Record* vol. 2, no. 6, Summer 1989.

Barrie Houlihan, *The Politics of Local Government* (Longman, 1986).

David J. Wilson, 'More Power to the Centre? The Changing Nature of Central Government/Local Authority Relationships' in *Talking Politics*, vol. 3, no. 1, Autumn 1990.

9 The Legal System and Civil Rights

KEY ISSUES

▶ The 'rule of law': theory and practice
Civil disobedience: arguments for and against

▶ Judicial independence and impartiality
The courts and Parliament
The courts and the executive

▶ The police
  ● Powers, impartiality and accountability
  ● Public order and politics

▶ Civil rights and freedoms
Degrees, limits and trends
Relationships between freedom and equality
A Bill of Rights: arguments for and against

—— TOPIC NOTES

Key facts and concepts

The law

Laws are the rules of state which, unlike conventions, are enforceable in the courts. There are many different **types of law** (see Chapter 2), including statute law, common law, case law, EC law and delegated legislation.

---

1. Give a precise definition and topical example of each of the *five* types of law mentioned above.

Civil law concerns disputes between individuals or groups in society. The aggrieved individual (or company etc.) decides whether to take proceedings, and the aim is compensation.

Criminal law concerns offences against society or state, and the aim of proceedings is punishment. The offence may be the same (e.g. assault) but under criminal law the Director of Public Prosecutions may take action even if the victim does not desire it. The legal processes are different and are often in different types of courts, e.g. county courts and the High Court for civil cases, and magistrates' courts and Crown courts for criminal cases. Civil cases (e.g. divorce, bankruptcy) are rarely heard before a jury. Jury trial is a feature of criminal cases in the Crown courts; but 98% of all criminal cases begin and end in a magistrate's court, with no jury. Moreover, under successive statutes such as the Criminal Justice Acts of 1988 and 1991, a growing number of criminal charges (e.g. obstruction, breach of the peace and common assault) have lost the right to jury trial in the Crown courts, despite the widely-held principle that 'trial by one's peers' is 'the lamp that shows that freedom lives' (to quote former judge **Lord Devlin**).

The '**rule of law**' (see Chapter 2): The phrase was coined by **A. V. Dicey** (1885), and the concept, which seeks to equate law and justice, is said to be central to any constitutional democracy. However, it is best seen as a statement of an ideal (or as a list of ideal principles), to which many legal systems may aspire; but, in Britain and other countries, all of its key principles are consistently breached in practice.

---

2. a) List *six* basic principles of the 'rule of law'.
    b) Give at least *two* examples of breaches of each principle in the English legal system.

Law, justice and morality

Something is 'legal' if it is in accordance with the law of the land; whereas something is 'just' if it is deemed fair and equitable. The idea of the 'rule of law' seeks to equate law and justice, but sometimes the law may be regarded as unjust: e.g. the legal immunities of diplomats, legal tax avoidance, imprisonment before trial (remand), the high costs of litigation, etc. Conversely, an action may be seen as just, though illegal: e.g. personal retribution – 'an eye for an eye'; breaking the law to prevent a greater crime; the Robin

Hood principle (stealing from the rich to give to the poor); just violence against an unjust state (one man's 'terrorist' is another man's 'freedom fighter'), etc.

Similarly, an action that is deemed 'moral' – ethically right and proper – may be illegal: e.g. 'draft-dodging' (refusing conscription into the army, e.g. on religious grounds); anti-nuclear protests such as trespassing in nuclear bases; euthanasia ('mercy-killing'); Sikhs refusing to wear motor-cycle helmets in place of their turbans, etc. Or what is considered an 'immoral' action may be legal: e.g. suicide, adultery, divorce or abortion.

All three concepts are subjective; even whether an action is legal or illegal is often a matter of debate between senior judges. However, perceived conflicts between law, justice and morality are sometimes used to justify **civil disobedience**: deliberate, peaceful law-breaking as an act of public, political protest. Some examples are: cannabis 'smoke-ins' in Hyde Park; the obstruction by the pressure group Greenpeace of nuclear waste discharges into the North Sea; the refusal of some local councils (e.g. Liverpool and Lambeth) to obey central government's rate-capping laws; public refusals to pay the poll tax; secondary picketing by trade unions such as the National Union of Seamen; and the freeing of animals from research laboratories by the Animal Liberation Front.

---

3. 1) Find *five* further examples of civil disobedience by pressure groups or individuals.

2) What arguments were used to justify the action in each case?

3) List *three* key arguments for, and *three* arguments against, civil disobedience.

The courts

The **European Court of Justice at Luxembourg** enforces European Community law, e.g. against Britain's discriminatory retirement ages for men and women, pollution of British beaches etc.

The **European Court of Human Rights at Strasbourg**: This is nothing to do with the EC. It enforces the 1950 European Convention for the Protection of Human Rights, ratified by 21 countries including the UK. It has ruled against British Governments on phone tapping by government agencies, corporal punishment in state schools, torture of prisoners in Northern Ireland, press censorship, discrimination against women and ethnic minorities, and many other matters. The British government has lost more cases at Strasbourg than any other, largely because Britain has no Bill of Rights, does not enforce the European Convention in its own courts, and because much government action is based simply on convention rather than on law.

The courts and Parliament

Parliament is sovereign: the British courts therefore cannot challenge the law of Parliament; they can only interpret and enforce statute law as it is written. However, Parliament's law may be unclear or ambiguous; in a test case, the judges must interpret the law precisely, which can allow a very creative judicial role amounting effectively to law-making. The courts and Parliament may clash when the courts interpret a statute in a way which Parliament did not intend. Parliament may then rewrite the law; it can thus 'legalise illegality' or set aside court decisions.

Lord Denning, formerly a very senior (and controversial) judge, has argued that judges should be able to veto parliamentary statutes:

'Every judge on his appointment discards all politics and all prejudices. You need have no fear. The judges of England have always in the past – and I hope always will – be vigilant in guarding our freedoms. Someone must be trusted. Let it be the judges' (Dimbleby Lecture, 'Misuse of Power', 1980).

He gave the hypothetical example of any attempt by the Commons to abolish the House of Lords, which seemed, to some critics, to demonstrate the very 'politics and prejudices' he sought to deny. Also, without a written constitution or Bill of Rights, there are no clear, consistent and overriding constitutional principles against which judges could challenge parliamentary statutes.

Civil and Criminal Courts in England and Wales

House of Lords

Lord Chancellor and Law Lords
No jury

*Appeal
Permission needed*

Court of Appeal

Civil Division
Master of the rolls and
Lords Justices of Appeal
No jury

Criminal Division
Lord Chief Justice and
Lords Justices of Appeal
No jury

Appeal

Appeal

High Court

Family
Division

Chancery
Division

Queen's Bench
Division

Occasional jury

Crown courts

Single recorder or judge
Jury trial

Appeal

*Appeal on points of law
in minor cases*

*Commit for trial
or appeal*

County courts

Circuit judge
No jury

Magistrates' courts

JPs; stipendiary magistrates
in some cities
No jury

The courts and the executive

Administrative law: This is the whole package of laws which apply to executive and other public bodies. There is no distinct body of administrative law or courts in Britain (unlike e.g. France). However, the ordinary courts may hear civil or criminal actions against central or local government members or departments. They may declare the orders or actions of a minister or department to be *ultra vires*, i.e. beyond their legal powers, either because of what was done or because of the way in which it was done.

Such **judicial review** of executive action has increased since three significant rulings against the government in 1976, concerning attempts to ban Laker Skytrain, to stop people buying TV licences early to avoid a price increase, and to hasten the introduction of comprehensive schools in Tameside. Those were all rulings against a Labour government, but the 1980s' Conservative government was overruled by the British courts more often than any other. However, any central government usually has a majority in a sovereign Parliament, and therefore if it is ruled illegal by the courts it may use Parliament to rewrite the law and so legalise itself. It may even backdate the rewritten law so that the government was never technically illegal – so-called 'retrospective law'. Some examples are: Environment Secretary Nicholas Ridley taking £50 million too much from the GLC to finance the new London Regional Transport body (1985), increasing toll charges for the Severn Bridge (1986), and authorising the building of the Okehampton by-pass through Dartmoor National Park (1986); DHSS Secretary Norman Fowler imposing cuts in board and lodging allowances, and cuts in opticians' fees (1986), etc.

The Local Government Act 1987 retrospectively legalised central government's grant allocations to local authorities, which, it was discovered, had been technically illegal since 1981. The Act also contains a so-called 'ouster clause' barring judicial review of the new regulations; this was said by Lord Denning to be an 'unconstitutional' attempt to place government above the rule of law, and he led an unsuccessful revolt against the clause in the Lords. In 1990 the European Court of Human Rights ruled illegal the detention without charge of three men for over four days under the Prevention of Terrorism Act, but the British government said that it would ignore the ruling (**derogation**).

The courts' control of central government is therefore limited, and is bound up with the issue of **parliamentary sovereignty**. It is also debatable how far non-elected and arguably unrepresentative judges *should* control 'democratic' public bodies. This issue has also been central to judicial rulings against local councils: e.g. GLC's 'Fares Fair' policy (1982), and the surcharging of Liverpool and Lambeth councillors who breached the rate-capping laws (1985).

The judges

There is a hierarchy of judges in the British courts, from magistrates (JPs) who are lay people rather than trained lawyers, through recorders (part-time judges), and judges in the Crown courts up to the most senior judges in the House of Lords.

The independence of the judiciary

According to the 'rule of law', justice should be an end in itself, and judges should not be subject to political pressure from the legislature or executive, nor should they be partial or prejudiced in their interpretation or enforcement of the law. To this end:

1) The judiciary should be separate from the other branches of government, in accordance with **Montesquieu**'s principle of the 'separation of powers'.

2) Judicial appointments should be based on merit, not on political patronage.
3) Senior judges have security of tenure: under the Act of Settlement 1701, they can only be removed by a resolution in both Houses of Parliament (which has never yet happened).
4) Judges receive fixed salaries paid from the Consolidated Fund and not subject to political debate in Parliament.
5) Judges' decisions should not be questioned in Parliament.
6) Judges' remarks in court (like those of lawyers, witnesses and jury members) are not liable to legal actions for damages.

---

4. How far are these principles of judicial independence upheld? Can you give specific instances where any principles are, or have been, breached?

Many commentators, such as **J. A. G. Griffith**, question how far judges are, or can be, 'non-political'. This concept has at least four dimensions: separation of powers; freedom from external political pressure; lack of personal or political prejudice; and lack of involvement in any political role. Judges are often said to be unavoidably political, in one sense or another, for the following reasons.

- Judges' social background – 97% male, 80% public school and Oxbridge – their above-average age, and the nature of their legal training (still steeped in nineteenth-century Victorian values), all of which may foster a conservative, if not Conservative (i.e. party political), outlook. Judges' comments especially on class, race and gender have often caused controversy.
- Overlaps between judiciary, legislature and executive: e.g. the Lord Chancellor, Law Lords, Prime Ministerial appointment of senior judges, commissions of inquiry headed by judges (e.g. the Scarman Inquiry into the 1981 Brixton riots) etc.
- 'Judges are part of the machinery of authority within the State and as such cannot avoid the making of political decisions' (Griffith, 1985, p. 195). Also as part of the

Judging the judges

state, judges may have a particular view of the national interest; in cases of dispute between state and citizen, they may 'show themselves more executive-minded than the executive' (Lord Atkin) – especially on issues of national security and official secrecy such as the banning of trade unions at GCHQ, and the Tisdall and Ponting cases; and also in key industrial disputes such as the 1984–5 miners' strike.

- Judges must review executive actions under administrative law – an unavoidably 'political' role.
- Judges must enforce statutes which sometimes seem overtly party-political: e.g. the employment and Trade Union Acts of the 1980s, the rate- and charge-capping legislation etc.
- Marxists such as **Miliband** argue that the whole legal system in a capitalist country like Britain is necessarily class-based, and that judges are, unavoidably, part of the political superstructure which protects private property and profit for a minority ruling class.

The political nature of the judiciary is both enhanced and highlighted by 'judicial creativity'. Either judges must interpret statute law or, where none exists, they must make and enforce common law. For example, in 1961 a man called Shaw published a directory of prostitutes, and the Law Lords invented an interesting new common law of 'conspiracy to corrupt public morals' under which to prosecute him.

The other side of the coin of judicial independence is judicial unaccountability. Election of judges, either by the general public or by an electoral college of lawyers, is therefore sometimes suggested. Note that this could make judges more, rather than less, political.

The police

There are around 200,000 police in Britain (of whom around 10% are women and 1% are black). Their job is to enforce the criminal law 'on the ground': to prevent crime, apprehend criminals and maintain public order. Their numbers, pay and powers increased substantially in the 1980s. Essay questions on this topic focus on the following issues.

Public order

This concept implies legal, peaceful, controllable behaviour especially of crowds in public places, e.g. pickets, marches and demonstrations. The maintenance of public order is therefore the most overtly political role of the police. The Public Order Act 1936 outlawed quasi-military organisations and unofficial political uniforms (e.g. fascist blackshirts); it bans offensive weapons (which the police have taken to include nail files, combs and keys); and it covers threatening, abusive or insulting language, breach of the peace, public nuisance and obstruction of the highway or of the police. The Public Order Act 1986 provides new definitions and sentences for disorderly behaviour, unlawful assembly, affray and rioting; it requires organisers of marches to give the police seven days' notice; and it allows senior police officers to stipulate the time, place and numbers involved in meetings and marches, and to ban demonstrations if they threaten public disorder or 'serious disruption to the local community'. The danger of such discretionary policing powers, according to some observers such as the pressure group Liberty, is that they may be exercised in an inconsistent, arbitrary or excessive way, e.g. against young and black people, peace protestors and 'hippy' travellers.

Controversy has surrounded policing tactics in many public order incidents: e.g. during an anti-National Front demonstration in 1979, teacher Blair Peach was killed by

Yard pays £376,000 to wronged citizens

Police pay £350 damages for woman's 'terror' ride

Met faces riot charges

Police guilty of hippy attack

INJURED, FINED

Police 'at fault' in student clash

Discretionary policing – use or abuse of power?

a Special Patrol Group officer, but no one was disciplined or prosecuted. After riots in Brixton and Toxteth (1981) and in Handsworth and Tottenham (1985), the police allegedly broke into people's homes, unlawfully assaulted people and detained children for days without informing their families. During the miners' strike (1984–5) there were over 500 official complaints against the police of illegal detention, assault, criminal damage to homes, strip-searching of miners' wives and tapping of union members' phones – but no prosecutions or disciplinary charges resulted. In blocking the Peace Convoy at Stonehenge in 1985, the police attacked women and children and wantonly destroyed their property according to the owner of the land, Lord Cardigan. Twenty-four of the travellers finally won over £25,000 damages against Wiltshire police in 1991. Following a peaceful demonstration at Manchester University (1985), police allegedly assaulted student Stephen Shaw, burnt him with cigarettes and repeatedly threatened him until he fled the country. In 1986 officers from a police patrol van assaulted five innocent schoolboys in Holloway Road; and violent policing of the Wapping picket lines in the same year was described by critics as a 'police riot'.

There is also concern about assaults and deaths in police custody: e.g. Liddle Towers, Jimmy Kelly, John Mikkleson and James Davey (no prosecutions or disciplinary charges resulted in any case). The misuse of firearms and shooting of innocent people by the police is also criticised: e.g. Steven Waldorf (mistaken for a robber) was shot at 14 times whilst sitting in his car (1983); six-year-old John Shorthouse was killed in his bed while police were searching for his father; Cherry Groce was shot and paralysed in her home while police were looking for her son; and four others died in separate incidents in the last three months of 1991. Better police training is often recommended by critics.

Impartiality

Like judges, the police are supposed to enforce the law impartially. However, the Scarman Report found police racialism to be one factor underlying the 1981 Brixton riots, and a study of the London Metropolitan Police by the Policy Studies Institute in 1983 found routine racialism, sexism, a 'cult of violence', a disregard for the law and the rules of police procedure, and a readiness to cover up for colleagues' wrong-doing.

Home Office statistics also suggest the possibility of police bias: for example, blacks are ten times more likely than whites to be stopped and searched on suspicion (though they constitute only 4% of the population).

Police Constable Blakelock was killed during a riot on the Broadwater Farm estate in Tottenham in 1985. In the ensuing trial of Winston Silcott and two others, the judge criticised the 'oppressive behaviour' of the police handling the interrogations, and many since campaigned for the freeing of the three men, believing them to be innocent. The 1991 appeal resulted in the acquittal of Silcott within two hours and the release of the other two shortly afterwards.

There has been persistent evidence of police corruption since the 1970s, when over 450 officers were removed from the Met., but Operation Countryman, the inquiry set up by the Home Secretary to investigate corruption in the London force, was eventually abandoned because of alleged obstruction and concealment of evidence by senior officers.

The Guildford Four – Gerard Conlon and others – were released in 1989 after wrongly serving 14 years for IRA pub bombings. The similar case of the Birmingham Six caused equal disquiet. Some officers involved in that case were in the West Midlands Serious Crime Squad, which was disbanded by its Chief Constable in 1989 after repeated evidence of fabrication of evidence, false confessions, assault and intimidation resulting in dubious convictions. The West Midlands inquiry almost doubled the workload of the Police Complaints Authority; the Appeal Court has since quashed the sentences of some of those interrogated by the Squad, and others in 1991 still awaited appeal. Major inquiries into at least 40 other local forces were also underway in 1990.

The Birmingham Six, with hands raised in victory, on the day of their release, 15 March 1991.

Writer **Stuart Hall** has noted the growth of a powerful 'bobby lobby' since the 1970s, with the Police Federation issuing press adverts advocating capital punishment, and the Association of Chief Police Officers campaigning actively for tougher public order laws, stiffer sentencing and more police weaponry – all politically sensitive proposals. MPs such as Eldon Griffiths are also employed as spokesmen for the Police Federation. Despite this, opinion polls consistently indicate falling public confidence in the police, especially in the late 1980s and early 1990s at a time of record rising crime rates.

There have been increasingly frequent references since the 1980s to the growth of a **police state** in Britain, from commentators as diverse as Arthur Scargill, Lord Scarman, Lord Gifford QC and the Bishop of Durham. This concept implies a state where the law is arbitrarily enforced by the police who are themselves largely above the law, authoritarian and militaristic, with extensive powers of stop, search, detention, interrogation, use of force and secret surveillance, operating in support of government and state and with the tacit or open support of government and judiciary (see also **Roger Scruton**'s definition below).

Writers such as **Robert Reiner** have noted some disturbing trends in British policing: increasing numbers and powers, use of force, militarisation, politicisation, centralisation, arbitrary and discriminatory law enforcement, lack of accountability, and secret surveillance of legal groups such as trade unions, CND and Liberty. However, the degree of police power and accountability is perceptibly different in Britain from e.g. South Africa or Chile.

> **police state.** A state in which political stability has come to be, or to seem to be, dependent upon police supervision of the ordinary citizen, and in which the police are given powers suitable to that. The police force is extended, and operates secretly, with powers to detain for interrogation without charge, to search, to interrupt correspondence and to tap telephone calls, and in general to keep detailed records on citizens accused of no crime, in order to enforce measures designed to extinguish all opposition to the government and its institutions. The powers here may not be legally granted, but that is not normally an obstacle, since there is a presumption that there is no rule of law in these circumstances, and the acquisition of large *de facto* powers by the police will simply be one aspect of a widespread defiance of natural justice.
>
> R. Scruton, *Dictionary of Political Thought*

Accountability

The 43 regional police forces in England and Wales are controlled by:

1) The **Home Secretary**, at the national level.
2) At local level, each regional force except London is linked to a **local council police committee** comprising two-thirds elected councillors and one-third non-elected magistrates, who are partially responsible – together with central government and the local Chief Constables – for police pay, equipment, overall structure and strategy. However, some committees (such as Manchester and Merseyside) have objected to their lack of control e.g. over police acquisition of plastic bullets and CS gas. The Labour Party advocates more local, democratic control of the police, especially in London; but, again, this could also mean more 'political' control of the police.
3) **Civil and criminal law**: The Met. police alone pay out over £500,000 per year in civil cases of wrongful arrest, assault and malicious prosecution; and two officers, Hamish Montgomery and Patrick Shevlin, were given life sentences in 1988 for the killing of Owen Roberts in police custody. The **Police and Criminal Evidence Act 1984** extended police powers of stop and search, seizure of evidence, detention without charge (for up to 96 hours) and interrogation; but it also codified and set limits on those powers in statute law for the first time.

4)   The **Police Complaints Authority** (PCA), established under the 1984 Act, is chaired (1991) by former Ombudsman Sir Cecil Clothier and none of its members are police officers; but all of its investigations are still carried out by the police themselves, an arrangement which even the Police Federation has come to oppose because of public mistrust of the system. Around 16,000 complaints are made to the PCA each year of police assault, illegal detention etc., but under 10% result in any further legal or disciplinary proceedings.

Civil rights and freedoms

Rights are entitlements, e.g. to some kind of freedom or equality. **Natural rights** are those to which, according to some philosophers, everyone is entitled; **civil rights** are those granted to citizens by a particular state or government, and they may differ widely from one society to another.

Different political ideologies adopt different views on rights and freedoms: liberals tend to stress individual rights and positive freedoms which should be enhanced by state action if necessary – e.g. the right to own private property, and the freedom from sexual or racial discrimination, protected by law. Socialists tend to stress collective rights (e.g. freedom of assembly or industrial action for trade unions), and economic, political or social equalities; and socialists are often (more or less) opposed to private property.

Freedom and equality may conflict; for example, the freedom to choose between private or public health or education (a liberal tenet) may conflict with the goal of equal access to health care or equal educational opportunities (a socialist tenet). Similarly, progressive taxation in pursuit of greater economic equality or welfare (a socialist principle) may conflict with the freedom of individuals to spend their own money as they wish (a conservative principle).

Conflict may also arise between individual and collective freedoms: for example, the collective right to strike against the individual's right to strike-break was a source of acute conflict within mining families and communities during the 1984–5 dispute.

Law, by its nature, may both enhance and constrain freedom: for example, it may protect the individual against violence, theft or discrimination, but it also limits individual freedom of action in those spheres. Is discrimination – sexual, religious or racial – an individual right or a social wrong?

Some laws in Britain are often seen as excessive constraints on individual or collective freedoms, and this view is sometimes used to justify civil disobedience. For example, civil servants Sarah Tisdall and Clive Ponting in 1984 both deliberately breached Section 2 of the 1911 Official Secrets Act; and trade unions such as the miners, seamen and print-workers have been taken to court over 'secondary picketing', illegal since 1980.

---

5.   Consider the following list of rights and freedoms. For each, can you say what limits currently exist in British law and practice? What limits, if any, do you think there *should* be on each, and why? Do some rights conflict with others? Can you add to the list?

- The right to life
- The right to death
- Freedom of assembly
- Freedom of movement
- The right to strike
- Freedom of speech
- Freedom of information
- Freedom of the media
- The right to privacy
- Freedom of religious conscience
- Freedom from arbitrary arrest or imprisonment
- Freedom from discrimination
- Legal equality
- Political equality
- Equal educational opportunities
- The right to work
- The right to housing

A Bill of Rights for Britain?

In Britain, few rights are guaranteed in law; such rights as citizens have tend to be negative, i.e. they are allowed to do something if there is no law against it. Unlike most Western democracies, Britain has no Bill of Rights – a legal document outlining and guaranteeing in law a list of citizens' basic entitlements, freedoms and equalities.

Case for a Bill of Rights

- According to some observers (e.g. Liberty and Charter 88), basic civil liberties in Britain are always under threat with a majority government in a sovereign Parliament in effective control of a flexible, unwritten constitution. They say that the growing political emphasis on law and order in the 1980s and 1990s, together with growing police powers, bureaucracy and a conservative judiciary, have all added to the threat.

- The situation in Northern Ireland – where rights of political activity and legal equality, residence, movement, privacy, jury trial, freedom from arbitrary detention and from 'cruel and inhuman punishment' etc. have all been abridged – demonstrates the fragility of basic liberties in the UK.

- The 'rule of law' demands a clear statement of citizens' rights and duties, which is lacking in Britain.

- A Bill of Rights would impose legal limits on governments' actions, which are currently often guided only by convention and are therefore effectively above or beyond the law.

- With no domestic Bill of Rights, recourse to the European Court is often necessary, but is very time-consuming and costly.

- Since Britain is already a signatory of the European Convention, it would be simple and logical to incorporate it into domestic law.

Case against a Bill of Rights

- Which rights should be entrenched? How general or specific should they be? Political consensus would be hard to achieve.

- How entrenched should a Bill of Rights be? Should it have the status of an ordinary statute? Critics fear excessive rigidity.

- Many existing laws would conflict with it, e.g. the Police Act, Prevention of Terrorism Act, Clause 28 of the Local Government Act 1988, Clause 25 of the Criminal Justice Act 1991 etc. (although this is precisely why defenders of civil rights want to see them entrenched).

- All governments are reluctant to increase constraints against themselves and against the state.

- It could be hard to reconcile majority and minority rights, or collective versus individual rights, or freedom and equality.

- Left-wingers are suspicious of a Bill of Rights which would probably entrench 'liberal' principles such as property rights and undermine 'socialist' principles such as trade union rights.

- Many do not, in Lord Denning's words, 'trust the judges' to interpret and enforce a Bill of Rights in a liberal and progressive way, because they see judges as unrepresentative, conservative and 'executive-minded'. A rigid Bill of Rights would transfer sovereignty from elected MPs to non-elected judges, and it could also make judges more overtly political.

- Every Bill of Rights has some qualifying clause allowing for the restriction of rights, e.g. 'in the national interest', and some are scarcely worth the paper on which they are written.

- Rights in Britain are often said to be adequately protected already through Parliament and the Ombudsman, the 'rule of law'; the courts (including the European Courts), administrative tribunals, pressure groups and the media, etc.

—— ESSAYS

1) *Theme* **Law-breaking**

Note the different scope of the five titles below (all taken from the London Board): from those which cover law-breaking in all its forms, through those which focus more narrowly on civil disobedience, i.e. peaceful, political law-breaking, to those which concern only violent law-breaking.

(a) **Q?** Are there circumstances in which we should break the law?

(London, February 1976, P. 1.)

A✓ Examiners' comments

'This question must not be turned into a "good old Rule of Law" or a "Conscience is King" rhapsody. "Circumstances" is the key word. Some general rules must be advanced (minimal), plausible examples given (average), and some attempt at defining criteria to judge between *law* and *justice* would carry more marks. The better candidate will attempt to define what is meant by 'law' and will see that both the example of breaking a general rule and of enduring needlessly a lawful injustice are to be considered.'

(b) **Q?** What forms of protest against government do you consider legitimate, and what forms illegitimate?

(London, June 1984, P. 1.)

A✓ **Examiners' comments**

'Many candidates attempted this question and were able to offer an account of different forms of dissent. Difficulties arose over distinguishing the basis of legitimacy and most candidates concentrated their answers on legality. The better candidates were able to raise problems concerning the issues that Greenpeace posed at Sellafield – about protest that breaks the law but that raises the question that, while such protest may be unlawful, is it necessarily illegitimate?'

(c) **Q?** Is there ever a case for civil disobedience?

(London, June 1979, P. 1.)

(d) **Q?** Can any recent instance of direct action by a pressure group in defiance of the law be justified?

(London, June 1985, P. 1.)

(e) **Q?** How tolerant should we be towards threats to overthrow the state by violence?

(London, June 1978, P. 1.)

Additional essay tips on each title (a) to (e)

(a) 'Should' is a strong word, implying not simply a right but a duty to break the law.

(b) This title seeks a personal evaluation of various methods of political protest, with some explicit and reasoned line-drawing: e.g 'I would condone illegal "leaking" of official secrets to expose wrong-doing, but I would not condone unprovoked violence against the police because …' etc.

(c) This title requires a balanced assessment of both the 'case for' and the 'case against' civil disobedience; but the word 'ever' would make it hard to conclude with a blanket 'no'.

(d) This title specifies law-breaking by *pressure groups*; examples of law-breaking by other individuals and organisations would not be relevant, however accurate or topical they may be. Several examples of illegal action by different pressure groups may be discussed here; not just one.

(e) 'We' may mean the state, society or both; and a distinction could be made between real and uttered 'threats'. Where more than one interpretation of a title seems possible, always point this out explicitly in the introduction; and always cover *every* possible interpretation in your answer, to gain most marks.

2) *Theme* **The judges**

Q? Evaluate the allegation that in recent years the implementation of government policies has been assisted by 'Tory judges'.

(AEB, June 1986, P. 1.)

---

6. Use the examiners' comments and the plan below to write a full answer to this question.

A✓   **Examiners' comments**

'Weak answers simply stated the constitutional position of the judiciary in Britain, but the majority covered one or more of the recent cases such as Greenham Common, Ponting, Fares Fair, Tisdall, Liverpool, Lambeth, GCHQ and the NUM. However, very few were able to indicate the substance of the alleged bias in the judiciary or the ways in which any such bias may have affected the outcome of these cases specifically. Surprisingly few candidates covered the interpretation of industrial relations law even though several made reference to the NUM and SOGAT 82. The very few good answers discussed these cases in the context of the laws under which prosecutions had been brought, and also noted the importance of the judiciary's ability to "create" law by developing common law. They also linked the Lord Chancellor's patronage to the question as well as the common socio-economic background of the legal profession.'

Essay plan

1) Theory of judicial independence and impartiality …
    List of ways in which it is protected … e.g.s of each …
2) Case against title: rulings against Cons. governments
    (including explanation of 'judicial review' and *ultra vires*). e.g.s: First GCHQ hearing; 'Spycatcher'; Ridley v. GLC etc.
3) Case for title: rulings in favour of Cons. government.
    e.g.s: Tisdall, Ponting, GCHQ.
    Rulings against Labour executives: three key 1976 cases; Fares Fair, Liverpool, Lambeth etc.
    Other 'anti-left' rulings: NUM, Wapping, CND, Greenham Common, anti-apartheid and racial cases …
4) Possible reasons for right-wing bias in judges:
    (a) Socio-economic background …
    (b) Legal training …
    (c) Political patronage …
    (d) Party political laws …
5) Are judges 'executive-minded', i.e. pro-state, regardless of party, rather than pro-Conservative? Possible reasons:
    (a) 'Part of machinery of state' (Griffith);
    (b) Overlaps between judiciary, executive and legislature …
    (c) Dual role of law;
    (d) Marxist argument (Miliband) …
6) Judges are in a position of political power because of:
    (a) Law enforcement role …
    (b) Relative unaccountability …
    (c) 'Judicial creativity' …
7) **Suggested conclusion:** 'In conclusion I would argue that judges exercise an unavoidably "political" role in interpreting and enforcing the law, especially in cases involving central or local government, and in sensitive "political trials" (**Hain**) such as those involving key pressure groups. I would also agree with Lord Atkin that judges tend to be "executive-minded", given their position as part of the machinery of the state. It is a bit too simplistic to call them "tame Tory judges" as Labour MP Martin Flannery did over the 1984–5 miners' strike; after all, the last Conservative government has been ruled against more often than any other. However, British judges do seem to be predominantly Conservative; Lord Templeman estimated (on Radio 4 in

April 1988) that only 10–15% of them – "a diminishing number" – were Labour supporters.

'On balance I would therefore agree with the title, and I would support calls from Griffith and others for lawyers and judges to be recruited from a wider social background, with more extensive and progressive legal training. Also, the appointment of senior judges should be done by an all-party committee of lawyer-MPs in the Commons rather than by the Lord Chancellor and PM.'

3)   *Theme*   **The police**

Q?   'If the public are to be protected by the police, they must also be protected from the police.' Discuss.

(Oxford, Summer 1981, P. 1.)

---

7.   On questions like this, to quote the examiners, 'emotional reaction too often replaces hard analysis'. Use your textbooks and local library to research the incidents, issues and sources listed below; then consider carefully how you would use them in an answer to the above essay title.

- Public Order Acts 1936 and 1986
- Brixton and Toxteth riots 1981
- Report of an Inquiry by Lord Scarman: 'The Brixton Disorders', Cmnd. 8427 (HMSO Nov. 1981)
- The shooting of Steven Waldorf, 1983
- Policy Studies Institute Report on the Met., 1983
- Police 'racialism': e.g. the enforcement of the 'sus' laws
- Miners' strike 1984/5
- Police and Criminal Evidence Act 1984
- Robert Reiner: 'Is Britain Turning Into a Police State?' in *New Society* 2 August 1984
- Roger Scruton: *A Dictionary of Political Thought* (Pan, 1983), p. 358 on the concept of 'police state'
- Report by Labour Party Working Group; 'Protecting the Citizen', 1985
- The Metropolitan Police: *The Principles of Policing and Guidance for Professional Behaviour*, 1985
- Association of Chief Police Officers: *Public Order Tactical Options*, 1985
- Stonehenge 'hippy convoy' incident 1985
- Broadwater Farm disturbances 1985
- Holloway Road incident 1986
- Wapping disturbances 1986
- Guildford Four, Birmingham Six, West Midlands cases ...

---

4)   *Theme*   **Civil rights**

Q?   Besides Parliament, what bodies best preserve and enhance civil liberties?

(London, June 1978, P. 1.)

A ✓   Essay plan

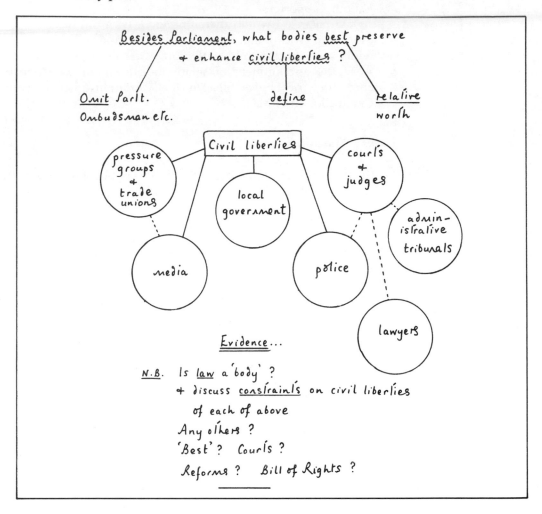

Besides <u>Parliament</u>, what bodies <u>best</u> preserve
+ enhance <u>civil liberties</u>?

<u>Omit</u> Parlt.   <u>define</u>   <u>relative</u>
Ombudsman etc.   worth

Civil liberties

pressure groups + trade unions

local government

courts + judges

media

police

admin-istrative tribunals

lawyers

<u>Evidence</u>...

<u>N.B.</u>   Is <u>law</u> a 'body'?
+ discuss <u>constraints</u> on civil liberties
of each of above
Any others?
'Best'? Courts?
Reforms? Bill of Rights?

---

8.   Write at least one of the following essays.
Always write a brief plan first.

1)   What are the main threats to the rule of law in contemporary Britain?
(Cambridge, June 1986, P. 1.)

2)   'The obligation to obey the law is always conditional – even in a democracy.' Discuss.
(Oxford and Cambridge, June 1990, P. 1.)

3)   Should the courts have more power over Parliament?
(London, June 1985, P. 1.)

4)   Should the police be more subject to democratic control?
(Oxford, Summer 1986, P. 1.)

5)   Consider the extent to which British judges undertake a political role and assess their suitability to do so.
(AEB, June 1989, P. 1.)

—— GUIDE TO EXERCISES

Page 128

1. 1) Statute law: Acts of Parliament, e.g. Criminal Justice Act 1991.
   2) Common law: 'common custom of the realm', established and enforced by the judges since the twelfth century, e.g. public rights to common land and footpaths.
   3) Case law: 'Judge-made law' – judicial interpretations of statute, common and other forms of law which set a precedent for future cases, e.g. the GCHQ case 1984.
   4) EC law: European Community legislation, which takes precedence over all domestic law, e.g. on some tariffs and taxes (such as VAT).
   5) Delegated legislation: law made by bodies other than Parliament under authority passed down (delegated) by Parliament, e.g. local authority by-laws.

Page 129

2. Principles and breaches of the 'rule of law':

   1) Everyone, including government, should be equally subject to the same law. Exceptions: GCHQ (1984); Local Government Act 1987 (see p. 132); legal immunities of diplomats, MPs etc.; cost of litigation – 'The law, like the Ritz Hotel, is open to all' (Lord Justice Darling).
   2) There should be a clear statement of people's rights and duties under the law. Exceptions: no Bill of Rights; quantity and complexity of law; retrospective law; plethora of conventions.
   3) There should be fair, consistent and open court procedures. Exceptions: inconsistent sentencing; secret trials e.g. Bettany spy trial (1984); different rules for different courts e.g. administrative and deportation tribunals and coroners' courts.
   4) Justice should be an end in itself, with no arbitrary law or government. Exceptions: alleged police bias e.g. in enforcing public order laws; retrospective law; delegated legislation e.g. Social Security Act 1986.
   5) No one should be subject to legal penalty unless [s]he has broken the law – innocent till proven guilty. Exceptions: remand before trial, the 'sus' laws; 'trial by media' (e.g. 'Yorkshire Ripper' Peter Sutcliffe).
   6) There should be an independent and impartial judiciary. Exceptions: lack of separation of powers; political patronage; alleged judicial bias.

Page 130

3. 3) Arguments for/against civil disobedience:
   - (a) The law is/not democratic.
   - (b) There are/not legal and effective methods of protest.
   - (c) The law does/not protect our rights and freedoms.

Page 133

4. Independence of judiciary; breaches of principles:
   1) Lord Chancellor, Law Lords, judges heading executive inquiries e.g. Lord Justice Woolf on prison riots.

2) Allegations of political patronage, e.g. Lord John Donaldson's promotion since 1979 by Conservative PM.
3) No breach of principle.
4) Rowdy debates in Parliament over large pay increases for judges e.g. in 1985.
5) Labour MP Martin Flannery referred to 'tame Tory judges' in 1984–5 miners' strike; Mrs Thatcher criticised low sentence imposed on child rapist by Judge Stanley Price in 1982.
6) No breach of principle.

Page 138

5. For example, the law or practice on: murder; capital punishment; abortion; euthanasia; treason and sedition; libel and slander; official secrets; obscenity and pornography; race relations and sexual discrimination; immigration; political and religious extremism; personal privacy; personal morality; homosexuality; the electoral deposit; picketing; remand; the 'sus' laws (suspicion); the costs of litigation; state and public schooling; unemployment; homelessness; poverty and welfare.

—— REFERENCES

Lord Denning, Dimbleby Lecture: 'Misuse of Power', 1980.
J. A. G. Griffith, *The Politics of the Judiciary* (Fontana, 1985).
Peter Hain, *Political Trials in Britain* (Penguin, 1984).
Stuart Hall et al., *Policing the Crisis* (Macmillan, 1979).
Ralph Miliband, *The State in Capitalist Society* (Quartet, 1969).
Robert Reiner, 'Is Britain Turning Into a Police State'? in *New Society*, 2.8.84.
Robert Scruton, *A Dictionary of Political Thought* (Pan, 1983).

10 Public Opinion, Pressure Groups and Media

KEY ISSUES

► Definition and measurement of 'public opinion'.
How far should governments heed public opinion?

► Pressure groups: power and influence; reasons for success
or failure; help or hindrance to democracy.

► Trade unions: power; links with the Labour Party; changing
role since 1960s and 1970s.

► Mass media: ownership, control and bias; influence on the
political agenda and public opinion.

— TOPIC NOTES

Key facts and concepts

Public opinion

In a democracy it is usually assumed that government should be responsive to **public opinion**, but this is a very difficult concept to define or measure. It is best defined as the majority view on a given issue at a given time; but if opinion is divided several ways there may be no majority view; or the view of a vocal or powerful minority may dominate.

Public opinion may be expressed or assessed through elections, referenda (e.g. in 1975 on remaining in the EC; and in 1979 in Scotland and Wales on devolution), through letters to the press or to MPs, pressure group activity or opinion polls. However, a distorted impression of public opinion may be conveyed, for example, by tactical voting, abstention, unequal degrees of political activism by different sections of the public (e.g. the middle classes tend to be more politically active than the working class). Public opinion polls may question an unrepresentative sample of people; they may offer limited options as answers; or they may shape the very thing they are trying to measure, simply by posing questions about an issue which some people may never have considered before. Political parties often carry out their own polls; and they may publish misleading results in an effort to boost their own vote. It is sometimes suggested that even professional opinion polls should be banned in the days before an election, because they may influence the result of the election itself: for example, if one party seems very strong – or very weak – its supporters may not bother to vote at all.

Though public opinion is difficult to define or measure, it may influence Parliament or government: e.g. the so-called 'greening' of the Conservative government from the late 1980s, when they paid increasing attention to environmental issues, reflecting growing public concern and pressure group activity. However, it may be argued that politicians should not follow every whim of public opinion, because it may be ill-informed, selfish, fickle, emotional or irrational. Parliament's consistent rejection of capital punishment since the 1960s may be one example of this.

Distinguish between political influence and political power.

'Influence' is persuasive effect on others' ideas or actions; it may or may not be intended, organised or perceived, but it is based on reasoned agreement, respect etc., and is therefore closer to authority than to power. 'Power' is the ability to make decisions, to act, or to get others to do something through threat or use of sanctions – rewards or punishments, even force or violence. It implies coercion rather than consent. If farmers or water workers can cut off food or water supplies, that is power; whereas a persuasive publicity campaign by Comic Relief or CND is simply influence.

Pressure groups

Pressure groups are organisations which seek to promote a cause or to protect a section of society, often by influencing government, Parliament or the public. Unlike parties, they do not stand candidates for election, and their aims and membership are often narrower; but they do often have close links with political parties.

Two main types of pressure group are:

(a) **Promotional** or **cause groups**, which seek to promote a specific cause, e.g. CND (Campaign for Nuclear Disarmament), Shelter (housing), Friends of the Earth (environment);

(b) **Protective** or **sectional** or **interest groups**, which seek to protect the interests of their own members as a particular section of society, e.g. trade unions and professional associations such as the NUM (National Union of Mineworkers), the Law Society (solicitors), the CBI (Confederation of British Industry) etc.

Some groups are hybrid, i.e. a mixture of both types: e.g. the Automobile Association and Royal Automobile Club seek to protect their own members and to promote the cause of motoring and the wider interests of all motorists. Some pressure groups may be temporary, and will disband if they achieve their aims – e.g. preventing nuclear waste-dumping in a local area.

There has been a huge growth in the number and influence of pressure groups in the twentieth century for a number of reasons:

● The principle of public participation and influence in political decision-making, established with universal suffrage;

- The weakness of individual as opposed to collective influence and organisation;
- The expanding role of government and state in public affairs, and rising public expectations of government intervention and activity;
- New pressure groups being formed to oppose existing ones, e.g. FOREST (The Freedom Organisation for the Enjoyment of Smoking Tobacco) to counter the anti-smoking group ASH (Action on Smoking and Health); pro- and anti-abortion groups, etc.

Pressure groups vary enormously in power and influence, depending on their type, size, membership, financial resources, links with parties, methods, media coverage and current trends in government policy (e.g. CND became the fastest growing pressure group in the country in the early 1980s as US and British governments pursued a strongly pro-nuclear line and built up stocks of Cruise and other nuclear weapons). Large groups are not necessarily the most powerful. Protective groups tend to have more sanctions available to them than promotional groups, and hence more power – e.g. the members of a key economic interest group may withdraw their labour or capital. Promotional groups may have considerable *influence* on public opinion, but even the largest, such as CND, lack *power* to change government policy.

Methods

The most powerful groups, such as the National Farmers' Union, often have **direct links** with government and civil service, in a relationship of mutual need – i.e. for information, expertise and influence. Such groups rarely need to resort to public lobbying, street demonstrations etc.; the most powerful and influential groups are therefore often, paradoxically, the least visible. A few groups, such as the farmers, have the statutory right to be consulted on relevant legislation and policy initiatives. (An example of the farming lobby's influence was the resignation of Junior Health Minister Edwina Currie, followed by new government subsidies to egg producers, after her remark in 1988 that 'most egg production' in this country was contaminated by salmonella.)

Many groups work **through Parliament and MPs** by:

- **Financing political parties**: The Labour Party is funded largely by trade unions such as the TGWU; the Conservative government introduced legislation in 1984 to give trade union members a say on political donations. The Conservative Party has been accused of using covert channels such as British United Industrialists to channel corporate cash donations to the party. A Labour amendment to the Companies Bill, giving company shareholders a say on political donations to the Conservative Party, was accepted by the Lords in 1989 but defeated in the Commons.
- **Lobbying MPs** in Parliament, through letters, leaflets, petitions, free gifts, dinners, trips and parties, and personal consultancy fees to MPs (e.g. Conservative MP Vivian Bendall receives £3,000 per year from the London Taxi Drivers' Association).
- **Sponsoring MPs**: Many trade unions pay some part of a local Labour party's election campaign costs in return for support by a Labour MP – e.g. Neil Kinnock is sponsored by the Transport and General Workers' Union (which sponsors a total of 32 Labour MPs).
- **Drafting** and **promoting private members' bills**: e.g. David Steel's 1967 Abortion Act was largely drafted by the Abortion Law Reform Association, and successive amendment bills (e.g. by John Corrie, David Alton and Anne Widdicombe) were backed by anti-abortion groups such as the Society for the Protection of the Unborn Child (SPUC).

- **Seeking to influence government legislation**: e.g. the Lords' Day Observance Society mobilised MPs into opposing Sunday trading in 1986.
- **Hiring professional lobbyists**, to promote a cause among MPs. Full details and figures are unclear, because the Register of Members' Interests often lacks detail; but there are now over 50 PR firms involved in political lobbying for fees in the region of £10 million a year, and some MPs (e.g. Bob Cryer) fear potential conflict of interests and an appearance of 'bribery'.

Often a last resort for the least powerful but most visible cause groups is to seek to influence government indirectly through the **mobilisation of public opinion**: e.g. Child Poverty Action Group, Shelter and Greenpeace. Methods used include conducting or publicising opinion polls, petitions, pickets, leaflets and letters, media adverts, demonstrations and staged public events, such as Friends of the Earth dumping thousands of 'non-returnable' bottles on the doorstep of Schweppes to protest against waste. Concern is sometimes expressed where such tactics are emotive, obstructive, illegal or violent.

> THE LAW STILL ALLOWS PEOPLE TO SQUIRT WEEDKILLER IN A BABY'S EYES, INJECT IT WITH POISON, GROW CANCERS ON ITS BACK, BURN ITS SKIN OFF, EXPOSE IT TO RADIATION AND EVENTUALLY KILL IT, IN UNRELIABLE EXPERIMENTS.
>
> SO LONG AS IT'S ONLY AN ANIMAL.
>
> BUT YOU CAN HELP STOP IT.
>
> YOU DON'T HAVE TO BUY PRODUCTS TESTED ON ANIMALS.
>
> **National Anti-Vivisection Society**

Pressure groups may use **civil disobedience** (see Chapter 9) to gain publicity for their cause: e.g. CND members trespassing and cutting the perimeter wire at nuclear bases, refusing to pay taxes towards nuclear weapons and staging mass street 'die-ins' (obstruction). Sometimes groups resort to the threat or use of **violence**: e.g. the Animal Liberation Front planting bombs at animal experimentation centres and at shops which sell fur products. They would argue that it is fair to counter violence with violence; and such methods may also win more publicity and response than legal, peaceful methods, which raises questions about the role and responsibility of the media in their coverage of public participation and protest.

---

1. Select any *four* pressure groups – two protective and two promotional. Write brief notes on each, under the following headings:

   (a) Aims.
   (b) Characteristics: size, type of membership, sources of finance, links with political parties.

(c)   Methods.
(d)   'Successful' or 'unsuccessful'? By what criteria?
(e)   Reasons for success or failure.

Trade Unions

A **trade union** is a protective organisation of workers which aims to protect its members' pay and working conditions. There are several types:

(a)   Craft unions, e.g. the National Graphical Association.
(b)   Industrial unions, e.g. the National Union of Mineworkers.
(c)   General unions, e.g. the Transport and General Workers' Union.
(d)   White-collar unions, e.g. the National Association of Local Government Officers.

Generally, the more skilled and specialised are its members, the more 'powerful' is the union.

Arthur Scargill, NUM President, facing the challenges of the 1990s.

In the 1960s and 1970s, during the period of 'consensus politics', trade unions were closely involved with governments, both Labour and Conservative, in shaping economic and industrial policy. Examples of trade union influence or power during this period were:

●   The Labour government's abandonment of the 1969 White Paper 'In Place of Strife' in the face of trade union opposition.
●   The 1974 miners' strike which is often credited with bringing down the Heath government.
●   The Labour Party's repeal in 1974 of the Industrial Relations Act 1971, and abolition of the Industrial Relations Court, in response to strong trade union opposition.

- The 1978–9 'winter of discontent' – public sector strikes over pay restraint – which contributed to Callaghan's defeat in the 1979 election.
- The involvement of the trade unions in bodies such as the Advisory, Conciliation and Arbitration Service (ACAS) and the National Economic Development Council ('Neddy').

This **'corporatist'** approach was rejected by the Thatcher governments of the 1980s.

The theme of exam essay questions on this topic has therefore changed over the last ten years from the 'excessive power' of trade unions to their 'loss of power'. This is because economic recession and high unemployment in the late 1970s and 1980s, together with a series of legislative changes, have combined to weaken most trade unions.

Legislation in the 1980s

Employment Act 1980
Limited sympathy and secondary action, i.e. action other than that between workers and their own employers, at their own place of work in a dispute only about pay or conditions of work.

Employment Act 1982
Prohibited sympathy and secondary action, secondary and mass picketing. Required secret ballots for maintaining a closed shop (where 80% must be in favour). Rendered trade unions liable for damages for breach of contract arising from industrial action.

Trade Union Act 1984
Required secret ballots before industrial action, and for maintaining a political fund (i.e. contributions to the Labour Party). Allowed fines and 'sequestration', i.e. freezing and seizure of union funds by courts for illegal action or contempt of court.

Employment Act 1988
Required unions balloting on industrial action in separate workplaces to win a majority vote in every workplace. Prohibited unions from disciplining strike-breakers even if a clear majority have voted for strike action. Employers still allowed to sack strikers even after a ballot in favour of action. Established a trade union Commissioner to fund cases against unions in courts. Required periodic re-election by secret ballot of all union officers.

Employment Act 1989
Prohibited the pre-entry closed shop.

The defeat of the miners in 1985, after a year-long strike over pit closures, was seen by the government and trade unions alike as a watershed in the decline of trade unions' power and rights. (In the four years from the end of the strike to March 1989, for example, the South Wales mining industry was reduced from 28 pits and 24,000 men to nine pits and 6,000 men.)

The most powerful trade unions now are the professional associations such as the Bar (barristers), Law Society (solicitors) and British Medical Association (doctors), which have a legal monopoly on their own professional services, regulate entry to their own professions, and often have the dual function of protecting and disciplining their own members. Concern about the latter aspect of their role, and the possible conflicts of interest which may arise from it, prompted the setting up in 1991 of an ombudsman for the legal services.

2. What is meant by the following terms (all of which are related to the issue of trade unions)?

   1) Block vote.

   2) Closed shop.

   3) Corporatism.

   4) Functional representation.

   5) Sequestration.

Media

The main theme of essays on the media is how far they shape public opinion or the political agenda (see Essays section, p. 163). Questions are also asked on the related themes of ownership, control and possible bias of the media. The main viewpoints on the topic are the liberal or pluralist views on the one hand, and the radical-critical, socialist or Marxist views on the other.

A distinction must be made between the press and broadcasting media; TV and radio are obliged by law to be non-party political, whereas the press are not. However, some radical left-wing critics (e.g. **Miliband** and **Tunstall**) perceive a broader, and consistent, conservative bias in all mainstream media, including TV and radio. They attribute this largely to the concentrated and 'Establishment' nature of media ownership and control. Given the high cost of launching a new mass medium (e.g. it cost £20 million to launch *The Independent* in 1986), the owners tend to come from a narrow economic and social background which is not inclined to radicalism. Media ownership is also becoming more, rather than less, concentrated, with growing overlaps between different forms of media (see table on page 154). This should be curbed by anti-monopoly regulation but, for example, when Rupert Murdoch took over Times Newspapers from Thomson in 1981, and *Today* in 1987, the government refused reference to the Monopoly and Mergers Commission, and approved the mergers. The high costs of the 'new technology revolution' in the media (i.e. direct printing by computer, satellite and cable broadcasting) may raise costs and narrow ownership still further.

". . . and now Murdoch's put in a bid for the Monopolies Commission . . ."

The Guardian, 7 July 1987

It is therefore unsurprising, according to socialist critics such as Tunstall, that the British press is largely and overtly Conservative; only the Mirror Group is explicitly pro-Labour, and only *The Independent* did not back any political party during the 1987 election. Marxist critics such as Miliband argue, however, that the party political balance of the media is irrelevant, since all are broadly supportive of the status quo.

Pluralist views, conversely, stress the diversity of the media, from *Living Marxism* (Revolutionary Communist Party) to *Bulldog* (National Front).

Top ten groups of weekly newspapers by circulation
(The top ten controllers of groups publishing weekly and bi-weekly newspapers at 31 December 1989 by aggregate circulation.)

| Controller | Number of titles | | Circulation | | TOTALS | |
	PAID	FREE	PAID	FREE	Number	Circulation
Reed International plc	40	111	413	5,434	151	5,847
International Thomson Organisation Ltd (Toronto)	39	105	229	3,758	144	3,987
United Newspapers plc	47	55	362	2,348	102	2,710
EMAP plc	62	52	863	1,724	114	2,587
Yellow Advertiser Newspaper Group Ltd	11	38	76	2,288	49	2,364
Pearson plc	32	49	310	1,921	81	2,231
Daily Mail & General Trust plc	22	38	322	1,736	60	2,058
Argus Press Group	34	30	317	1,274	64	1,591
The Guardian & Manchester Evening News plc	33	26	238	1,274	59	1,512
Southern Newspapers plc	8	24	101	1,328	32	1,429

Source: The Press Council of Great Britain 1990.

Several A level essay topics, including the previous one – trade unions and their 'declining power' – were illustrated by Murdoch's 1986 'Wapping revolution', when he moved the *Sunday Times* and *News of the World* from Fleet Street to Wapping to be printed by new computer technology, eliminating the old crafts of the printers and excluding the unions. Some 5,500 workers were dismissed; there were mass secondary pickets and demonstrations at Wapping; these were illegal under the 1980 and 1982 Employment Acts, therefore the Sogat union had all of its funds sequestrated. Nineteen-year-old picket Michael Delaney was hit and killed by one of TNT's 32-tonne lorries; although the jury returned a verdict of unlawful killing, the DPP said that there was no case to answer. Eighteen police officers were prosecuted for excessive violence on the picket lines, but most of the charges were dropped after long delays in bringing the cases to court.

Political controls on the media

Note (and point out explicitly in essays) that political controls may include *economic* sanctions which are used for *political* ends, e.g. to influence or dictate the political or social content of the media.

Ownership
Lord Beaverbrook to the Royal Commission on the Press 1949: 'I run the *Daily Express* purely for the purpose of making propaganda, and for no other motive'. Also Stanley Baldwin's criticism of Lords Beaverbrook and Rothermere in 1931, that they sought 'power without responsibility, the prerogative of the harlot throughout the ages'.

Advertising
Over £70 million per year worth of advertising sold in the two-minute break of 'News at Ten'. May prompt direct pressure on media content, e.g. in 1980 WD & HO Wills withdrew £500,000 of advertising from the *Sunday Times* because of an anti-smoking

article by their health correspondent. Or it may prompt indirect pressure through the ratings battle, e.g. when *The Star* plummeted downmarket in 1987, Tesco withdrew its advertising, circulation fell, and the Express group changed its policy.

Censorship by distributors
WH Smith long refused to stock *Private Eye* and *Gay News* on the grounds that they were 'abhorrent, though lawful'.

Direct censorship by government
For example: Falklands, Gulf War: curbs on news reports, pictures, MoD disinformation etc.

Government pressure
For example, through the penalty imposed on the BBC licence fee in 1979 after BBC interviews with the IRA and INLA; through threat of grant cuts, e.g. by Eden over BBC coverage of Suez. Also the postponing of 'Real Lives' by the BBC in 1985 after a letter from Home Secretary Leon Brittan; criticism of the BBC by Norman Tebbit over coverage of Libya in 1986; strong government pressure and alleged manipulation of information over Thames TV's 'Death on the Rock' (about shooting of unarmed IRA activists in Gibralter). Such pressure is not new, nor confined to one party: e.g. Harold Wilson persuaded the BBC not to show 'Steptoe and Son' on the night of the 1964 election in case it kept Labour voters at home.

Allegedly political appointments
BBC chairman Marmaduke Hussey and director general Michael Checkland; Lord Chalfont, deputy chairman of IBA ('The most flagrant example yet of the politicisation of Government appointments' – Lord Bonham Carter, formerly on the BBC board of governors); Lord Rees-Mogg, chairman of Broadcasting Standards Council set up in 1990.

Legal constraints
(a) Broadcasting laws allow the Home Secretary complete control over all broadcasting content; thus e.g. Home Office curbs in 1988 on direct reporting of Irish activists; criticised particularly because the ban covered legal political parties such as Sinn Fein who, as well as the National Union of Journalists, later challenged it in the courts on the grounds that it prevented the broadcasting media from upholding their legal obligation of balance and impartiality.
(b) Official Secrets Act (under which police raided BBC Scotland in 1987 to seize tapes on the 'Secret Society' programme about Zircon project; MI5 vet some broadcasting staff and have agents permanently employed within the national broadcasting companies).
(c) Prevention of Terrorism Act (renewed annually).
(d) Police and Criminal Evidence Act 1984 (under which journalists have been obliged to hand over unpublished photographs, e.g. of the Wapping disturbances and riots).
(e) Libel laws.
(f) Contempt of Court Act 1981.
(g) Obscenity laws.
(h) Race Relations Acts.
(i) Laws of sedition, incitement to disaffection and treason etc.
(j) Two relevant private members' bills were introduced in the 1989 session: John Browne's Privacy Bill and Tony Worthington's Right of Reply Bill. Both failed.

A combination of all of the above factors has generated much **'self-censorship'** especially by broadcasters: e.g. 1926 General Strike (when **Lord Reith** said, 'Since the BBC is a national institution and since the Government in this crisis is acting for the people ... the BBC is for the Government in the crisis too'); 1936 abdication crisis; 1956 Suez affair, 1982 Falklands conflict and 1991 Gulf War; 1963 Profumo affair, cancellation of E.P. Thompson's 1981 anti-nuclear Dimbleby lecture; the BBC banning for 20 years the anti-nuclear film 'The War Game' as 'too horrific, especially for viewers of limited intelligence'; over 30 programmes on Northern Ireland dropped since 1969; 'The Untouchables', about links between senior police and a notorious gangster, banned by the BBC and eventually shown by Granada; BBC postponing and vetting of 'Secret Society' series in 1987; former minister John Biffen's description, in a BBC interview February 1989, of No. 10 press secretary Bernard Ingham as 'merely the sewer, not the sewerage' – cut out of broadcast by senior editor; many plays about sensitive topics postponed, cut or banned, e.g. 'Tumbledown' (Falklands), 'Mates' (teenage homosexuality), 'Leftover People' (unemployment); and an Omnibus programme (BBC February 1981) on media censorship, censored to exclude references to previous censorship.

Radical critics therefore cite Ernest Bevin's comment in a Cabinet debate about media censorship: 'Why bother to muzzle sheep?'

The **lobby system**, whereby political journalists meet politicians and civil servants at Westminster for daily 'unattributable briefings', has been criticised e.g. by **Hennessy** for its secretiveness, mutual dependency and scope for news manipulation and misinformation (e.g. budget leaks). *The Independent*, *The Guardian* and *The Scotsman* did not participate from 1986 until 1991.

The **Press Complaints Commission** which replaced the Press Council in 1990 as a voluntary self-regulating body investigates complaints of bias, cheque-book journalism, invasion of privacy etc., and may censure newspapers, e.g. criticism of *The Sun* in 1986 for attempting 'seriously and improperly' to influence the outcome of the 1984 Chesterfield by-election, won by Tony Benn. Critics fear that it may prove to be a watchdog without teeth, and that statutory control of the press may be necessary.

Sun soars away to top complaints league

RICHARD BROOKS

THE *SUN* has soared to the top of the Press Council's daily paper complaints league for 1987.

Another News International title, the *News of the World*, had most complaints among the Sundays.

The figures for last year, due to be published soon, will show a 50 per cent increase in the number of adjudicated complaints. Forty-one were upheld against national dailies (26 in 1986), and 18 (nine in 1986) against Sunday nationals.

The Press Council's general secretary, Mr Kenneth Morgan, says 1987 was as bad a year for press responsibility and press freedom as any he could remember. 'At one end, we have falling standards of taste and decency, such as the invasion of privacy and the breaking of embargoes, while the qualities are trying to explore important issues and being prevented by injunctions.'

This year has already got off to a bad start. On Wednesday the *Sun* splashed across its front page a picture of a baby with two heads, with an accompanying story saying one head may laugh as the other cries. It has already prompted complaints to the Press Council and the *Sun* itself.

The paper's editor, Mr Kelvin MacKenzie, refused to comment on his decision to use the picture. It was taken recently in Iran and offered to Fleet Street about 10 days ago. The *Daily Mirror* turned it down immediately on the ground of bad taste. Mr Brian Hitchen, the editor of the *Star*, said it was a tragically revolting picture which should not be used.

The *Sun* is market leader among the tabloids, with sales of about four million. It has been singled out for formal rebuke on many occasions.

The Press Council's annual report, published last month, highlighted the 'lamentable' behaviour of the *Sun* over the case of Mr Terrance McCabe, a lorry driver who refused to cross the picket line at Wapping. The paper had wrongly described him as a 'pervert', using unsubstantiated claims from an old newspaper cutting.

The *Sun* was also condemned last year by the council for its 'Queen's cousin locked in madhouse' story.

The *Sun* broke the embargo on the New Year Honours, naming two George Medal award winners. It led to a rebuke from Downing Street, and then a response from Mr MacKenzie that his paper would not break embargoes again.

But it is not just the *Sun* which erred last year. The Press Council's chairman, Sir Zelman Cowen, is critical of 'the extraordinary two months of the *Star* under the editorship of Mike Gabbert ... 'What concerned me was that the paper was ceasing to be a newspaper.' (Interestingly, however, the *Star* had the same number of adjudicated complaints last year as both the *Guardian* and *Daily Telegraph* although the Press Council would not say how many this was.)

Sir Zelman was pleased that it was self-regulation which finally forced Express Newspapers (owners of the *Star*) to change its mind about the paper. The fall in circulation and the withdrawal of Tesco advertising were factors.

Later this month a private member's Bill by a Conservative MP, Mr William Cash, will attempt to stop papers prying into people's private lives. Next month the Labour MP Ann Clwyd is bringing in a private Bill requiring papers to give prominence to corrections.

On BBC1's 'Question Time' last week, the Scottish Secretary, Mr Malcolm Rifkind, spoke of a plan to force erring papers to cease publication for a day as punishment. He added that this was a personal idea, not government policy.

Mr Morgan says falling standards among the tabloids in particular 'undermines the quality press and their attempts to uncover vital stories. Regrettably, they tend to get tarred with the same brush, and it then becomes harder to get public support for the qualities. The distinction is sometimes not understood by the general public.'

© *The Observer*, 10 January 1988

ESSAYS

1) *Theme* **Public Opinion**

Q? Can the refusal of an elected assembly to reintroduce capital punishment, when the majority of the electorate appear to favour such a measure, be reconciled with democratic principles?

(Oxford and Cambridge, July 1984, P. 1.)

A✓ **Guidance on essay plan**

The introduction should go straight to the key concept of 'democratic principles' – open to diverse interpretations: direct 'people-power' or indirect representation, of people's views or interests – which may not coincide; individual versus minority versus majority versus national views or interests; different interpretations of representative and responsible government.

The next section should be specific and empirical: seek out (in your local library) and give concrete opinion poll figures on the issue of capital punishment; and also give precise details and figures on the periodic debates and votes on the issue in the Commons over the past ten years (see *Hansard*).

Case for elected assembly going against opinion poll findings

- **Note**   Put this case first only if you are going to disagree with it.

1) Opinion poll findings may be wrong, because of poor sampling, [mis]leading wording, etc.
2) If assembly is indeed going against public opinion – case for, in general terms (i.e. regardless of issue):
   - Public opinion may be ill-informed, misinformed, emotional, irrational or fickle.
   - MPs are not meant to be delegates of voters, but 'responsible' representatives using their own judgement in the national interest (Burkean view).
   - Especially on moral issues such as capital punishment, MPs are expected and allowed to obey their own consciences: hence private members' bills and free votes.
   - Liberal democracy stresses the views and rights of individuals and minorities, not just 'tyranny of the majority'.
3) Case for refusal to reintroduce capital punishment, in specific terms:
   - To condemn killing, and punish it by killing, is illogical; and, for Christians and others, immoral.
   - 'Deterrence' argument is unsupported by all available statistics in every country where capital punishment has been abolished or reintroduced (UN studies etc.). Moreover, since most homocides are unpremeditated family/domestic/'passionate' crimes, no scope for deterrence or repetition. Many others committed by mentally sick and deranged; and one-third of all those who murder then commit suicide, so again death seems no deterrence.
   - Selective capital punishment (e.g. for the murder of police officers) produced unworkable anomalies under the old 1957 Homocide Act (e.g. if a robber missed a policeman and shot a passer-by).
   - For the tiny category of terrorist murders, legal definition of terms would be an acute problem; selective capital punishment would punish the motive rather than the act itself, and would give terrorists the special political status which they have long demanded; state execution would make martyrs of them and may provoke widespread sympathetic and/or violent responses.
   - Juries may be unwilling to convict – especially on majority rather than unanimous verdicts – if the death sentence was likely.
   - Judicial errors, e.g. the hanging of Timothy Evans in 1955 cannot be remedied (although he was granted an official pardon in 1966). The more recent cases of the Guildford Four, Birmingham Six and Maguire Seven have added grist to the mill of the anti-hanging lobby.

Case against elected assembly going against opinion poll findings

- **Note**   Put this case last only if you are going to agree with it.

---

3. Write your own 'case against', focusing on the central issue of 'democratic principles'; ensure that it is reasoned, well-evidenced, analytical and unemotional. On arguments for capital punishment, one valuable source is the *Hansard* record of debates on the issue in the

House of Commons. Note that you may offer a 'mixed' conclusion: i.e. that an elected assembly may be right to go against majority opinion, though you personally advocate capital punishment; *or* vice versa. Always put your own case(s) last.

Q?   Discuss the role of opinion polls in British politics.

(JMB, June 1984, P. 1.)

A✓   **Examiners' comments**

'Here weaker candidates tended to *describe* the detailed mechanics of sampling and failed to *discuss* the role of public opinion polls. Many mentioned their influence upon the Prime Minister's choice of election date. The best considered the influence of opinion polls upon voting behaviour, mentioned calls for banning publication in the days immediately before elections and were aware of the use of private polls by political parties. Some even brought in their use by pressure groups.'

2)   *Theme*   **Pressure Groups**

Q?   In what ways can pressure groups both help and hinder the democratic process?

(London, June 1987, P. 1.)

---

4. Find specific and topical examples for each of the points made in the Notes for guidance section below.

A✓   Notes for guidance

Arguments that pressure groups 'help democratic process'
- They enhance pluralism: competing centres of power, representation and choice. Especially true where 'pro' and 'anti' groups co-exist; all shades of opinion represented.
- They 'fill the gaps' in the party system, e.g. by promoting causes which cut across party lines, especially on local or moral issues such as abortion, capital punishment etc.
- They provide channels of collective influence and power for the public where individual action (including voting) may be relatively weak or ineffectual.
- They provide channels of direct participation for the public, going beyond mere indirect representation through Parliament.
- They provide channels of communication between government and electorate.
- They seek to represent deprived or inarticulate sections of society (e.g. NSPCC, RSPCA).
- Protective groups especially are usually internally democratic, in that members elect leaders.
- Trade unions especially are representative of large numbers of people (nine million); and their tactics of direct action may be seen as mass, direct democracy or 'people-power'.
- Pressure groups provide information, education and expertise for public, Parliament and government; therefore are much consulted by MPs and

executive; and may help to enhance open government by exposing events, information and issues.

- They provide a check on parliamentary sovereignty and 'elective dictatorship', especially where the electoral system is unrepresentative and parliamentary opposition is weak; hence checks and balances in liberal democracy.
- They may promote continuity of policy between successive governments.
- They may provide public services, e.g. legal aid and advice.

Arguments that pressure groups 'hinder democratic process'

- They may by-pass or usurp the elected representatives in Parliament and government; MPs may be reduced to 'lobby-fodder'. (Home Secretary Douglas Hurd in 1986 likened pressure groups to sea-serpents, strangling ministers in their coils and distorting the constitutional relationship between government and electorate.)

- Their lobbying tactics may amount to near bribery and corruption of MPs.
- They may be small, sectional or unrepresentative but influential or powerful, at the expense of majority or national views or interests. Thus Lord Hailsham in his 1983 Hamlyn Lecture described single-purpose pressure groups as 'enemies of liberty'.
- They may have a closed, excessively close and secretive relationship with the executive, excluding other views and interests; hence 'the embryo of a corporate state' (**Benn**).

- Their collective power may undermine individual rights and interests, contrary to liberal democratic principles.
- Promotional groups especially may be internally undemocratic – no election of leaders by members, leadership out of touch with membership etc. ('iron law of oligarchy'); or they may claim to speak on behalf of others, but without any consultation or mandate to do so etc.
- Groups with constitutional aims may be internally dominated by people who seek to subvert liberal democracy itself.
- Their methods may be illegal and/or coercive. But note that many pressure groups would defend such tactics in theory and practice (see Chapter 9 and the next essay question).

Q?   How might civil disobedience as a tactic used by pressure groups be justified within a parliamentary democracy? Discuss, with examples, the effectiveness of such tactics.

(JMB, June 1986, P. 2.)

A✓   **Examiners' comments**

'This question was also very popular and generally well done, often also with plenty of examples. Some candidates – generally the weaker ones – had difficulty coping with "parliamentary democracy"; others, including those who produced some quite good answers, dealt at length with whether civil disobedience was justifiable, ignoring or de-emphasising "as a tactic used by pressure groups". The examples were predictable although many candidates failed to mention Wapping – presumably because events there occurred after the subject had been dealt with in class work.'

- **Note**   See Chapter 9 for a discussion of various forms of deliberate law-breaking, including peaceful civil disobedience and political violence.

Lawful excuse for CND protest

By Kevin Buckley

TWO ANTI-NUCLEAR demonstrators who argued that they had a 'lawful excuse' to cause criminal damage at a nuclear air base because they were preventing the greater crime of genocide being committed, were acquitted by magistrates yesterday.

In a legal ruling which could potentially influence politically sensitive civil disobedience cases, Banbury magistrates accepted the defence counsel's argument that the demonstrators – both members of Christian CND – 'had acted honestly and reasonably to avoid a greater crime under the terms of the Criminal Damage Act 1971'.

This permits the defence of 'lawful excuse' against criminal damage charges if the action was to prevent a greater illegality taking place.

Barbara Eggleston, 33, and Brother Richard Finn, 25, a member of a Dominican religious order in Oxford, admitted entering the US Air Force base at Upper Heyford during a demonstration last October, and painting slogans within the base perimeter. But both entered formal pleas of not guilty to charges of trespass and of causing criminal damage. Ms

Eggleston carried out her own legal defence, and Mr Finn was defended by Dr John Finnis, a Reader in Law at University College, Oxford.

Dr Finnis is a trained barrister, but it was the first time he had conducted a case.

During his summing up, he quoted biblical references to justify the action undertaken by the demonstrators. Prosecution counsel are expected to appeal against the ruling.

Both defendants were found guilty of trespass and fined £50 each.

The Independent, 10 January 1989

3)   *Theme*   **Trade Unions**

Q?   The titles below are from the London Board 1981–91; note the changing theme of the questions, from 'the power of the unions' to 'government reform of the unions' and their 'changing role'.

1)   Are there any limits to the political power of trade unions?

(London, June 1981, P.2.)

2)   Comment on the view that the political power of the trade unions is rather less than is commonly supposed.

(London, June 1982, P.2.)

3)   What factors shaped the influence of the trade unions on governments between 1974 and 1984?

(London, June 1981, P.2.)

4)   Has the role and influence of trade unions changed in the 1980s?

(London, June 1985, P.2.)

5)   Why have Conservative Governments since 1979 been more successful than their predecessors in altering the legal position of trade unions?

(London, June 1989, P.2.)

6)   (a)   What steps have Conservative Governments taken since 1979 to alter the legal position of trade unions?
     (b)   Assess their impact on the unions.

(London, Jan. 1991, P.2.)

Q?   Is it more important that individuals should be protected by trade unions or from trade unions?

(Oxford, Summer 1985, P. 0.)

A✓   **Notes for guidance**

Case for protection of individuals by trade unions
- Weakness of individual workers versus employers.
- Historical role of unions in advancing working people's conditions of work, health, safety, pay, living standards and pensions.
- 'Representative' nature of unions: unlike most promotional groups, members elect leaders, who are usually 'delegates' rather than mere 'representatives'; and together they represent a larger population sector than any other pressure groups (nine million).
- Direct action by trade unions (e.g. strikes) may be seen as mass, direct 'people-power'.
- Visible union or workers' power (e.g. strikes) is a negative, uncertain and often self-destructive weapon of last resort, involving loss of pay and job security; it may thus be an indication of relative weakness, i.e. *lack* of alternative sanctions and power.
- Studies, e.g. by the **Glasgow University Media Group**, suggest that media coverage of unions and industrial action is consistently biased and hostile. For example, many forms of industrial dispute, presented as strikes, are in fact 'lock-outs' by management (e.g. the 1988 P. & O. seamens' strike was, in fact, a mass dismissal and lock-out); 95% of all strikes are 'wildcat' or unofficial, but are portrayed as if 'bully-boy' union leaders are calling out unwilling members; employers' figures on the costs of strikes are presented uncritically, omitting company savings in wages, raw materials, fuel etc.

- Thus public hostility to unions and industrial action is greater, the less direct experience people have of them (and people also tend to say 'the unions are too powerful', but *my* union is not strong enough on my behalf').
- Though workers' negative or disruptive power may be significant and inconvenient, their power may be small if measured in terms of results – closures, unemployment, redundancies, growing income inequalities, balance of decision-making power in workplace between workers and employers.
- Contrary to popular myth, Britain was always well down the international league table on strike figures, even in the 1960s and '70s when trade union power was perceived to be at its height.

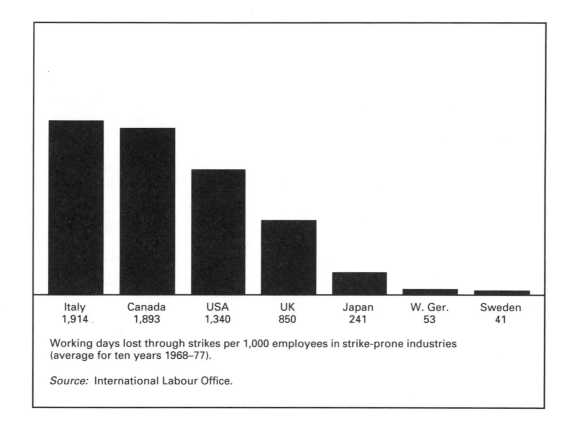

| Italy | Canada | USA | UK | Japan | W. Ger. | Sweden |
| 1,914 | 1,893 | 1,340 | 850 | 241 | 53 | 41 |

Working days lost through strikes per 1,000 employees in strike-prone industries (average for ten years 1968–77).

Source: International Labour Office.

---

5. Write the 'case for protection of individuals from trade unions'; ensure that it is reasoned and well-evidenced.

---

4) *Theme* **Media**

Consider the essay titles and examiners' comments below.

1) 'The vast sums required to finance a modern newspaper mean that inevitably the Press is dominated by moneyed interests and is therefore largely conservative and right-wing.' Is this true, and if true, should it be a matter of concern?

(Oxford and Cambridge, July 1983, P. 0.)

2) Is the freedom of the media a freedom worth defending?

(Oxford, Summer 1990, P. 1.)

Q?   'The mass media shape public opinion on politics.' Discuss.

(London, June 1988, P. 2.)

A✓   **Examiners' comments**

'Candidates needed to address the concept of public opinion: does it exist, and how does one measure it? This is fraught with difficulties but high marks were awarded for pointing out some of the problems and for trying to assess accurately the role of media in relation to public opinion. Too many candidates were determined to discuss the media bias (a different question) and committed the fallacy of thinking that if bias was proven then the role of the media in shaping public opinion is also proven. One good conclusion offered by a candidate read as follows:

"However, the media is only one of several inputs that determine political opinion. Class, race, religion and where you live and work all help to shape your political opinions ... a working class voter in the north is likely to have a Labour view of politics and if his friends and family share the same opinion, the media is unlikely to change it."'

Q?   To what extent do the mass media:
(a)   shape public political awareness   (12 marks)
(b)   set the political agenda?   (13 marks)

(AEB, November 1986, P. 2.)

---

6. Incorporate the points below (which are in no particular order) into an ordered answer to this question.

- Definitions of 'influence' and 'power'.
- Definition of 'political agenda': the issues that people think about and the priorities they give to them.
- This in turn influences public opinion and the views of the policy-makers. Reciprocal?
- The media simply reflect public concerns and interests, e.g. *Sunday Sport*, page 3, royals ... increase circulation. Begs question, how do people develop wants? Socialisation ...
- Diverse roles of media from diverse viewpoints: information, education, communication, entertainment, persuasion, propaganda, social control ...
- Role of advertising: information, persuasion, creating awareness of products and services, creation of wants ...
- Political agenda: derives from pressure and interest groups, politicians and parties, public events, and from what is defined as 'newsworthy', e.g. topic of the moment: child abuse, prison riots, or road accidents involving police cars in high-speed chases.
  Accessible stories, e.g. London versus north.
  Available pictures.
- Use of big news agencies e.g. United Press International (UPI) → uniformity of content.

- Media also influence political institutions and processes, e.g. in election they do not simply cover the campaign, they are the campaign; events and speeches staged and tailored to suit media convenience and accessibility.
- 20 million watch TV news each day.
- Was SDP 'an invention of the media'? (Essay title).
- **Jeremy Isaacs**, 'Media in the Market Place' (Henry Heatherington Lecture, Dec. 1987) in *New Socialist* March/April 1988:

  From which sources do you get the information you need about the world?

	1981	1986
TV	53	65
Newspapers	34	23
Radio	11	10

- 'Agenda-setting' not conscious conspiracy – unconscious consensual assumptions, hidden agenda, creation of consensus, blurring of news and comment e.g. strikes 'bad', etc.
- Negative images: Michael Foot, Scargill, Greenham Common women.
- Stereotypes, e.g. women, muggers.
- Political content/social engineering of soap operas – constant topic of public conversation.
- Events are significant part of political agenda whether media cover them or not, e.g. riots, N. Ireland.
- Sociological approaches: media creation of 'folk devils and moral panics' (**Cohen**), and 'deviancy amplification': e.g. 'hippy' travellers, drug addicts, football hooligans, lager louts …
- Direction of public political awareness.
- Liberal view – pluralist media; 'Fourth Estate', *Sunday Times* Insight team (on deforming drug Thalidomide, Crossman Diaries) – disbanded under Murdoch.
  New technology will enhance range, choice and pluralism.
  Many readers do not recognise political bias in media, e.g. 15% of *Sun* readers think it is a Labour paper.
  Jeremy Isaacs criticises the view of people as passive consumers: 'Human beings are not blotting paper who simply sop up the last impression that is left on them' (in *New Socialist*).
- Counter: Socialists – point to political imbalance of press, unparalleled in western world.
- Not the issue for Marxists – all bourgeois agents, servants of ruling class, opium of the people.
- Other influences on public opinion: family, friends, work, class, education, age, sex, religion, race, region, past experience, etc.

---

7. Write at least one of the following essays.
   Always write a brief plan first.

   1) Should there be limitations on opinion polls during General Elections?
      (London, January 1991, P. 2.)

   2) Assess the effectiveness of:
      (a) opinion polls   (12 marks)
      (b) pressure groups   (13 marks)
      as sources of information for governments on public opinion.
      (AEB, November 1986, P. 2.)

3) 'The problem in Britain today is not that pressure groups are too powerful but that they have too little say in government.' Discuss.

(Oxford, June 1985, P. 1.)

4) What factors have encouraged the development of pressure group activities on the EC level?

(Cambridge, June 1989, P. 1.)

5) 'The trade unions have power – but it is mainly negative power.' Discuss.

(London, January 1980, P. 2.)

6) Is it the function of the media to reflect public opinion or to form it?

(Oxford and Cambridge, July 1984, P. 0.)

—— GUIDE TO EXERCISES

Page 153

2. 1) Block vote: Method of union voting at Labour conferences, where, for example, a majority union vote for an option results in 100% of that union's votes counting towards that option. Being phased out because of unpopularity.

   2) Closed shop: Where an individual must belong to the appropriate union or association in order to work at a particular trade or profession. Largely prohibited by 1980s' legislation.

   3) Corporatism: Tripartite involvement and consultation of workers' and employers' groups with state in economic policy-making. A feature of the era of 'consensus politics'; 'Thatcherism' was anti-corporatist.

   4) Functional representation: Consultation and/or decision-making through occupational or industrial groups (rather than through e.g. parties). Advocated for the second chamber by Winston Churchill in 1930s.

   5) Sequestration: freezing and/or seizure of some or all of a union's assets by the courts, as penalty for contempt of court (introduced in 1984 as alternative to imprisoning union leaders and applied to e.g. NUM and Sogat).

—— REFERENCES

S. Cohen, *Images of Deviance* (Penguin, 1971).

Glasgow University Media Group, *Bad News* (Routledge and Kegan Paul, 1976). (Also *More Bad News* and *Really Bad News*.)

P. Hennessy, in *The Independent* 8.2.88.

R. Miliband, *The State in Capitalist Society* (Quartet, 1969).

J. Tunstall, *The Media in Britain* (Constable, 1983).

11 British Parliamentary Democracy – A Revision Chapter

SOME KEY ISSUES

▶ Majority government in sovereign Parliament with a flexible constitution – elective dictatorship?

▶ How democratic and representative is the British political system?

▶ How pluralist is the British state?

▶ How effective is Parliament in law-making, controlling the executive and representing the people?

▶ Does Britain have Prime Ministerial government?

▶ Is the civil service too powerful or too pliable?

▶ How representative, accountable and effective is local government?

▶ 'The rule of law' – a myth?

▶ Public order and civil liberties: is Britain becoming a 'police state'?

▶ Are pressure groups too weak or too powerful? How do they compare with political parties?

▶ Do the media reflect or shape public opinion and the political agenda?

▶ Does Britain need a written constitution?

—— REVISION EXERCISES

Review Chapters 2–10 before attempting these exercises.

---

1. Give one-sentence definitions of each of the following.

    1) Sovereignty.
    2) Parliamentary government.
    3) A 'safe seat'.
    4) A private bill.
    5) Parliamentary privilege.
    6) The royal prerogative.
    7) Mandate.
    8) Minority government.
    9) Coalition government.
    10) Cabinet government.
    11) *Ultra vires.*
    12) Constitutionalism.
    13) Unconstitutional action.
    14) Anti-constitutional action.
    15) Case law.
    16) Delegated legislation.
    17) Convention.
    18) Civil disobedience.
    19) Civil rights.
    20) Political power.
    21) Political influence.
    22) Pluralism.
    23) Welfare state.
    24) Bureaucracy.
    25) Devolution.

---

2. Quick Quiz. Briefly answer the following questions.

    1) Who coined the phrase 'elective dictatorship'?
    2) Why is the House of Lords not a supreme court in the American sense (i.e. what is the difference between them)?
    3) Who first used the word 'wets', and to describe whom?
    4) Distinguish between the functions of standing and select committees of the House of Commons.
    5) Which one of the following is attached to the EC – the European Court of Human Rights or the European Court of Justice?
    6) Which party operated mandatory re-selection until 1990?
    7) How much is the current deposit for parliamentary candidates; and what percentage of the vote must they win in order not to lose their deposits?
    8) List *five* methods by which Parliament seeks to hold the executive to account.
    9) Who coined the phrase 'the rule of law'?
    10) Which government department is responsible for:
    (a) roads; (b) prisons; (c) food safety?
    11) When was 'one person one vote' established for everyone over 21?
    12) When was the 'Think Tank' abolished?

13) Name three civil servants involved in the Westland controversy.

14) Complete: 'Sarah Tisdall leaked details of _____ to _____; Clive Ponting leaked details of _____ to _____. Only one of them was convicted and imprisoned, namely _____.'

15) Who said: 'Someone must be trusted. Let it be the judges.'? What constitutional reform was he advocating?

---

3. True or False?

1) By convention, ministers must be MPs in the Commons.
2) A 'constitution' is the body of laws by which a state is governed.
3) There are approximately one hundred members of the government.
4) Parliament can abolish the monarchy at will.
5) The two elements in 'parliamentary government' are the House of Commons and the House of Lords.
6) 'Administrative law' is the law which applies to executive and public bodies.
7) Civil servants must be neutral, so cannot vote.
8) Unlike civil servants, political advisers are not required to be politically neutral.
9) 'Parliamentary sovereignty' means that no court can challenge the law of Parliament.
10) The Speaker is an MP of the House of Commons.
11) All government bills must be introduced first in the House of Commons.
12) Backdating a law – i.e. applying it before the date when it was actually made – is illegal.
13) The death penalty still exists in Britain.
14) A 'joint committee' is one comprising both government and opposition MPs.
15) The monarch, in her private capacity, is above the law.
16) The police are forbidden to strike.
17) All Conservative Party members elect the party leader.
18) The 'ten o'clock adjournment' of the House of Commons is when all the MPs go home.
19) Cabinet committees consist only of Cabinet ministers.
20) The Ombudsman is an MP of the House of Commons.

---

4. Give at least *three* specific and topical examples of each of the following.

1) Defeats of government by the House of Lords.
2) 'Expertise' in the House of Lords.
3) Disproportionality of the first-past-the-post electoral system.
4) Other 'defects' of first-past-the-post.
5) Backbench revolts (successful and unsuccessful).
6) Private members' bills (successful and unsuccessful).
7) Sponsored MPs.
8) 'Consensus politics' (party policies).

9) 'Adversary politics' (party policies).
10) Two-party system (e.g. in House of Commons).
11) Multi-party politics in Britain.
12) Role of departmental select committees.
13) Parliamentary privilege (use or abuse).
14) External checks on Parliament.
15) Prime Ministerial government.
16) Cabinet government.
17) Collective Cabinet responsibility.
18) Individual ministerial responsibility.
19) Political advisers to ministers/PM.
20) Civil service influence on policy.
21) Secrecy in British government.
22) Breaches of 'rule of law'.
23) Constitutional law.
24) Alleged judicial 'bias'.
25) Courts' control of executive.
26) Civil disobedience.
27) Police/public order incidents.
28) Promotional and sectional pressure group methods.
29) Media influence on public opinion.
30) Recent changes to British constitution.

Stimulus response question

Study the following passage and then answer questions 1) to 5).

According to writers such as Norton (*The Constitution in Flux*), uncritical acceptance of the British constitution ceased in the 1970s, for a number of reasons: governments' inability to cope with growing economic problems; political pressures such as the rise of nationalism in Scotland and Wales, the troubles in Northern Ireland, the indeterminate results of the two 1974 general elections and, paradoxically, growing fears of 'elective dictatorship' (Hailsham, 1976) in Britain. Suggestions for reform have included a reformed second chamber, electoral reform for the Commons, devolution and a Bill of Rights. None of these, however, has been enacted, nor seems likely to be enacted in the near future.

1) Name the nationalist parties in
   (a) Scotland, and   (1 mark)
   (b) Wales.   (1 mark)

2) Briefly describe the outcome of
   (a) the February 1974 election, and   (2 marks)
   (b) the October 1974 election.   (2 marks)

3) (a) What is meant by the phrase 'elective dictatorship'?   (2 marks)
   (b) Why might fears of elective dictatorship seem paradoxical in
       the light of the 1974 election results?   (2 marks)

4) Select any *one* of the four reforms mentioned in the passage, and give
   arguments for and against it.   (6 marks)

5) Do you agree or disagree with the last sentence of the extract? Give
   reasons for your answer.   (4 marks)

—— ESSAYS

1)   *Theme*   'Elective dictatorship?'

Q?   What control does the government exercise over Parliament?

(Oxford, Summer 1981, P. 1.)

A✓   **Notes for guidance**

- Party discipline (via whips and natural party loyalty), usually over majority in House of Commons.
- Control over timetable (through Leader of House).
- Selection of most legislative proposals, including those on power of Parliament itself (e.g. reduction in Lords' powers 1911 and 1949).
- Guillotine on bills in committee and closure on bills in debate.
- Control of official information, e.g. financial details, defence projects like Zircon, refusal to answer questions on grounds of national security.
- Can ignore select committee recommendations.
- Can prevent civil servants from giving evidence to committees.
- Can ignore Ombudsman's recommendations.
- Can reject Lords' amendments.
- Can reject recommendations of Boundary Commissioners.
- Powers of PM: creation of new peers, appointment of Lords spiritual, appointment of ministers from Parliament, choosing date of general election within five-year term.

2)   *Theme*   **Democracy and representation**

Q?   'Knowledge is power.' Comment, with regard to the extent of secrecy in British government.

(London, January 1985, P. 1.)

A✓   **Notes for guidance**

Link *every* paragraph to the phrase 'knowledge is power' *and* to the issue of secrecy.

- Cases where K → P, or lack of K → lack of P:
  PM and ministers;
  Civil service;
  MPs (lack power to control executive);
  Public (lack 'people-power' – democracy – if lack knowledge for informed choices);
  Constraints on knowledge: e.g. Public Records Act 1958, D-Notice system, Official Secrets Act, Security Services Act, conventions shielding Cabinet committees, policy-making processes, civil service advice to ministers etc.
- But also:
  Power may generate knowledge: PM, ministers and civil servants;
  Knowledge without power: e.g. monarchy; some pressure groups, e.g. Greenpeace – have influence rather than power;
  Power without knowledge: e.g. military, some pressure groups, e.g. strike power of trade unions.
- Therefore the statement 'knowledge is power' is substantially true; means that secrecy is a constraint on democracy or 'people-power', and also on

pluralism. Hence, need for reforms e.g. freedom of information. However, the statement is not always true: despite the degree of secrecy, it is possible to have some forms of power without knowledge, and vice versa.

3) *Theme* **Pluralism**

Q? 'The differences within parties are often just as important as the differences between them.' Discuss.

(London, June 1987, P. 1.)

A✓ **Examiners' comments**

'Although candidates were able to tackle part of this question well, i.e. the differences within parties, very few bothered to address themselves to the question as a whole, i.e. weighing up whether the differences within parties were as important as the differences between them. Candidates must try, even if only briefly, to relate their material to the question as a whole, otherwise the question remains only partially answered. Candidates too often homed in on the Labour Party and Militant Tendency and ignored the Conservative Party, which again made it more difficult to answer the question set and gave the impression of an unbalanced answer.'

Additional essay tips

Also consider the relative significance of the following:
- Differences within parties:
  'Wets' and 'dries' within Conservative Party;
  Splits within Cabinet;
  Backbench revolts;
  Split in Labour Party and formation of SDP 1981;
- Differences between parties:
  Policy differences – essential basis of pluralism and choice in liberal democracy;
  'Consensus politics' and 'adversary politics';
  Organisational differences, e.g. financial resources, internal democracy;
  Splits within and between centre parties in late 1980s.

4) *Theme* **Role of Parliament**

Q? (a) What are considered to be the major functions of Parliament? (10 marks)
(b) How effectively are they performed today? (15 marks)

(AEB, June 1981, P. 1.)

A✓ **Short plan for guidance**

1) Major functions of Parliament:

(a) To make law.
(b) To control the executive.
(c) To represent the people.

These incorporate the subsidiary functions of: debate; controlling the raising and spending of public money; educating and informing the public; redress of grievances; protecting the rights of the individual; training and recruitment ground for ministers.

2) Taking each main function in turn:
   [Point out that enhancing Parliament's effectiveness at one function (e.g. law-making) may limit its effectiveness at another function (e.g. control of the executive).]

   (a) **Law-making**

   Effectiveness enhanced by: greater time and weaker party discipline of Lords versus Commons; committees of Lords and Commons; special standing committees; ten-minute limit to some speeches, introduced in 1985; private members' bills; use of closure and guillotine.

   Effectiveness limited by: lack of authority and power of non-elected Lords; government's control of legislative programme; filibustering; lack of time for private members' bills; delegated legislation; part-time MPs; EC.

   (b) **Control of executive**

   Effectiveness enhanced by: government defeats by Lords; cross-benchers in Lords; backbench revolts; opportunities for Opposition and backbenchers, e.g. Question Time, Opposition Days, ten o'clock adjournment debates; departmental select committees; Ombudsman; Comptroller and Auditor General and Public Accounts Committee.

   Effectiveness limited by: lack of power of Lords; party discipline in Commons and size of government's majority; government control of timetable; use of closure and guillotine; weaknesses of select committees and Ombudsman; MPs' lack of information e.g. on finance and national security, and MPs' lack of office, secretarial and research facilities.

   (c) **Representation of the people**

   Effectiveness enhanced by: universal suffrage and election of MPs; good use of parliamentary privilege; televising of Lords and Commons; use of referenda e.g. 1979.

   Effectiveness limited by: unrepresentative Lords; re-introduction of hereditary peerages by Thatcher 1983; non-proportional electoral system for Commons; lack of devolution; abuse of parliamentary privilege; power and influence of unrepresentative pressure groups; passing of 'bad' law, e.g. constraining civil liberties or freedom of information.

   Conclusion: not very effective, especially in controlling the executive and representing the people. Reforms: elected second chamber, PR for first chamber, devolution, freedom of information.

---

5. Find topical examples to illustrate as many of the above points as possible.

---

5) *Theme* **Role of PM**

Q?   'The present centralisation of power into the hands of one person has gone too far and amounts to a system of personal rule in the very heart of our democracy' (Tony Benn). Discuss this comment on prime ministerial power.

(Oxford, Summer 1984, P. 1.)

A✓   **Student's essay plan**

> <u>Assertion</u> : growth of autocracy with democracy (with ? marks above growth, autocracy, democracy)
>
> Is it 'dem'? 'No' => single elitist/Marxist views ...
>   => 'elect. dict.' (Hailsham) ...
>
> Assuming lib. parlt. democracy ⌐
>
> <u>Cab. govt.</u> : Bagehot, Jones, Stevas, PM 'primus inter pares' ...
>   Coll. resp./indiv. resp. — e.g.s ... buts ...
>   Constraints on PM power: =>
>   Need for authority: Asquith Q^t: '...is able...'
>   Hire/fire (Macmillan 1962 'night of long knives')
>   Party (Parkinson/Britain): Thatcher out 1990
>   Economy, personality, international events ...
>
> <u>PM govt.</u> : Crossman (1960s) changed mind)
>   Mackintosh, Heseltine, Benn ...
>   Cab. committees (Hennessy, 'engine room')
>   Ad hoc bodies (e.g. Economic Seminar)
>   No. 10 office (Pym, 'govt. within govt.')
>   Control of C.S. ... Ingham, Armstrong, Westland...
>   *   Policies : nukes, Falklands, GCHQ, Libyan bombing
>   no S.A. sanctions, Westland, Wright, GLC,
>   poll tax, student grant cuts ...
>
> <u>Conc.</u> : Not pure autocracy — too much for one person.
>   Madgwick : 'central exec. territory' — between
>   PM/Cab...
>   But too PM dominated, + growing* ...
>   Need 'constitutional premiership' (Benn)

6)   *Theme* **Role of Civil Service**

Q?   Are senior civil servants too powerful, or are they too pliable?

(London, June 1984, P. 1.)

A✓   Student's essay

The senior civil servants are the top permanent secretaries and the 600 or so 'mandarins'. A civil servant's duty is to help administer the work of the executive and to advise on policy. The relationship of civil servants to ministers is idealised by Sir Douglas Wass as being 'loyal but not enthusiastic'. The key characteristics of the civil service are its permanence, neutrality (i.e. non-party political) and anonymity. They are not meant to have policy-making power, but in practice the enormous workload of the government means that many decisions are effectively made by civil servants, e.g. the drafting of delegated legislation and compiling the honours list, and it would appear to be more than mere coincidence that 60% of all the honours are awarded to civil servants.

Left-wing Labour ex-ministers such as Tony Benn and Michael Meacher have argued since the 1960s that civil servants are too powerful, and can effectively tie the hands of their ministers. Benn argues that their power comes from their sheer numbers compared with ministers, their permanence (ministers on average last about two years in one post), their expertise (especially in relation to a new government), and their control of information, producing, says Benn, 'misinformation' such as juggling British or NATO troop figures to justify increased expenditure on defence. Meacher lists four specific 'ploys' used by civil servants to manipulate ministers: the 'rules of the game' ploy, 'expert advice' ploy, 'fait accompli' and 'timing of papers' ploys. The excessive secrecy of the British system, and bureaucratic 'red tape', are said to exacerbate this. To counter civil service monopoly of information Meacher says ministers should have more advisers.

It is sometimes argued that civil service power is used to protect civil service interests – hence the Crowther-Hunt accusation of its 'Fulton-mindedness' in 1968, happy to accept reforms beneficial to itself but obstructive of those it disliked – the clash between 'the political will and the administrative won't'. It used to be argued that civil service power was used against left-wing Labour policies such as nationalisation (said Crossman and Barbara Castle), because the senior civil service was inherently right-wing (70% public school and Oxbridge etc.). It is more often argued, however, that the civil service is anti-radical, whether left or right, e.g. Conservative ex-minister Nicholas Ridley accused them of obstructing privatisation through 'procrastination, inactivity and sabotage'; and former Industry Permanent Secretary Sir Anthony Part admitted that the civil service seeks to influence ministers towards 'the common ground'. This may be a perception of the public good, or simply pursuit of administrative convenience.

However, not everyone agrees that civil servants are too powerful. The view that 'Benn achieved nothing precisely because Wilson intended him to achieve nothing' (Heseltine) is not implausible. Recent critics of the civil service have argued that it is 'too pliable' and *too supportive* of the government. Mrs Thatcher was accused of trying to politicise the top ranks of the civil service to the detriment of their traditional neutral status, e.g. the involvement of Armstrong, Ingham and Powell in the Westland affair, and Armstrong's 'batting for the government' (Hennessy) in the Spycatcher trial. Ponting and Hailsham have both argued that civil servants are too deferential and willing to say 'Yes, minister'; and Nevil Johnson questions the integrity of a civil service which can equally serve any government whatever the flavour of its politics.

I would argue in conclusion that the civil service is *both* too pliable – too supportive of government and especially Prime Minister – *and* too powerful, with that power being used to enhance 'elective dictatorship' and PM power. I would advocate more open government and more ministerial, as opposed to Prime Ministerial, control of civil service appointments and powers.

Marker's comments on above essay

'This essay was awarded B+. Structure, relevance and use of evidence were good. However, there was some imbalance between the "powerful" and "pliable" sections of argument; the points made in the essay but not accepted in the conclusion were not explicitly refuted; and there was no consideration of whether the civil service is manipulated by pressure and interest groups. (A survey of 350 organisations in 1988 found that 29% of them considered civil servants to be "the most important channel of influence" – ministers scored 32% and Parliament a mere 8%.)'

7)   *Theme*   **Local government**

Q?   Discuss the view that far from having too much control over local government, central government has too little.

(AEB, June 1987, P. 1.)

A✓   Examiners' comments

'Many candidates knew a great deal about local government and its relationship with central government; unfortunately not everyone used this information to answer the question asked. Some did not even get into the "too much" or "too little" discussion as part of a winding up conclusion. Strong candidates speculated on whether local government would even continue to exist in five years' time. They referred to the erosion of powers since the war; the abolition of various councils, the "norms" imposed by financial control, the privatisation of many services – refuse collection, school meals, cleaning etc. – the "opting out" proposals for schools and the increasing switch of housing activities from local authorities to the private sector and housing corporations. Folk devils such as Ken Livingstone, Derek Hatton and Bernie Grant were often at the heart of arguments which supported the contention in the question. Most answers to this question were balanced, often drawing on experiences from the candidates' own locality and they generally argued a persuasive case for local autonomy.'

8)   *Theme*   **'The rule of law'**

Q?   What are the main threats to the rule of law in contemporary Britain?

(Cambridge, June 1986, P. 1.)

A✓   Short plan for guidance

Principles of rule of law/threats:
- **Clear law:**
  Sheer quantity of law
  Lack of legal guidelines, e.g. phone-tapping (1984 European Court case)
  Uncertain/ambiguous law, e.g. public order laws
  Contradictory law – e.g. legal duties and financial constraints on local authorities;
- **Legal equality:**
  Exemptions, e.g. monarch, MPs, diplomats etc.
  Government 'above law' e.g. GCHQ case law
  'Bias' of judges/police – say Griffith, Hain
  Cost of litigation; limited legal aid;
- **Innocent until proven guilty:**
  Remand
  'Sus' laws
  'Trial by media' e.g. Jeremy Thorpe;
- **No arbitrary law or government:**
  Constitution and executive power based largely on convention rather than on law
  'Elective dictatorship' of majority government in sovereign Parliament with flexible constitution
  Retrospective law, e.g. Financial Services Act 1987
  Flexible public order laws
  'Sus'
  Police 'bias';
- **Trial by fair and independent judges and courts of law:**
  Overlaps between judiciary, legislature and executive
  Judicial 'bias'
  Alleged political interference in cases, e.g. Tisdall, Ponting

Inconsistent granting of bail and sentencing
Jury vetting.

9)   *Theme*   **Public order and civil liberties**

Q?   Some people have claimed that Britain is becoming a police state. What are your reactions to this assertion?

(London, June 1983, P. 1.)

A✓   **Student's essay** (not timed)

✓   The concept of a 'police state' is not easy to define. It implies a situation where the law is dictated arbitrarily 'on the ground' by the police, who are themselves above the law, whose actions are generally rubber-stamped by the courts, and who act in support and with the tacit approval of the government.

✓   An alternative, more detailed definition is suggested by conservative writer Roger Scruton in his *Dictionary of Political Thought*. He defines a police state as one 'dependent on police supervision of the ordinary citizen'. A police state may also have an extended police force which operates secretly, with *de facto* powers to detain for interrogation without charge, to search, to interrupt correspondence and to tap telephone calls, and in general to keep detailed records on citizens accused of no crime, in order to enforce measures designed to extinguish all opposition to government and its institutions.

good✓   Recent controversial events involving the police, e.g. the miners' strike, Stonehenge and Wapping disturbances, riots, the Stalker affair, Guildford Four, Birmingham Six and disbanding of the West Midlands Special Crime Squad, have generated references to a police state in Britain by a wide range of commentators, from miners' leader Arthur Scargill and the Bishop of Durham to CND chairman Bruce Kent, Lord Scarman and Lord Gifford who wrote of 'police state measures which would be condemned as outrageous if they were being imposed on coal miners in Poland' (this last during the 1984–5 miners' strike).

are they new?
✓   Allegations of arbitrary or discriminatory law enforcement are not uncommon. They derive, at least in part, from the very flexible nature of the public order laws themselves – e.g. the 'disorderly conduct' clause in the 1986 Act, and the laws of suspicion ('sus') under which blacks are convicted 13 times more than whites, according to Home Office figures.

link to principles in definition(s) of 'police state' e.g. rule of law
evidence?
link explicitly to 'becoming' in title — i.e. trend   Critics such as Peter Hain and Michael Meacher have also argued that the police may, with relative impunity, use a degree of force not permitted to other citizens. They cite the shootings of innocent citizens such as Stephen Waldorf, Cherry Groce and John Shorthouse, where no disciplinary charges or convictions followed (indeed, the police officer who killed the six-year-old John Shorthouse was promoted). Recent controversy has centred on the (increasing) arming of the police. A fully-equipped TSG transit carries riot shields, visors, truncheons, smoke grenades, pistols, rifles and sub-machine guns. These Territorial Support Groups are specialist 'quasi-military' squads. Many forces (e.g. Manchester), now have permanent mobile armed patrols, and firearms training is now given to all new officers. Michael Meacher MP is critical of the fact that these developments have taken place with little public or parliamentary debate.

✓   With reference to Scruton's definition of 'police state', there is also growing evidence of the extent of secret surveillance of innocent citizens by the British police, Special Branch and MI5. For example, over one in six adult males are now on file in the Police National Computer at Hendon, and many have no criminal charges or convictions. The police themselves have admitted much of the information on file is inaccurate gossip and 'unchecked bunkum' (*Police Review*). There is also evidence (from former MI5 agent Cathy Massiter) of routine surveillance of trade unions, CND, Liberty and other pressure groups. The police have even, on occasion, bugged public telephone kiosks. Patricia Hewitt (Liberty) has said, 'The police and security services operate almost entirely outside the law'. The police raid on the BBC in 1987 over the 'Secret Society' programme about the Zircon spy satellite project caused repeated references to a police state in Britain by MPs such as Tony Benn and Roy Jenkins.

On the other side of the argument, however, the 1984 Police and Criminal Evidence Act (Pace) balanced increased police powers of arrest, stop and search and detention before charge, with new protections for suspects – contemporaneous note-taking, tape-recording and even some video taping during questioning, new guidelines on detention and interrogation and free legal advice. It also established a new, more independent Police Complaints Authority. However, that body says that it lacks the time, training and resources to be effective; the actual investigations are still carried out by the police themselves.

Also contrary to the idea of a police state is the fact that the British police are themselves answerable to the law, both criminal and civil. When pensioner Henry Foley was kicked to death in 1986 while lying handcuffed on the floor of a police cell in Southport, Sergeant Alwyn Sawyer was given seven years for manslaughter. Twenty-four of the Stonehenge 'travellers' eventually won over £25,000 against the police in 1991, six years after the 'battle of the beanfield'. Stephen Waldorf won a record £120,000 after being shot repeatedly by the police (who mistook him for a suspected robber), and the Met. alone now pay out over £500,000 each year in civil cases.

Nevertheless, there is growing evidence of police dishonesty and corruption: planting and fabricating evidence, false confessions, assault and intimidation. Public confidence in the police is falling: opinion polls (e.g. NOP, April 1990) suggest that 25% now have 'little or no confidence' in the police, and that 40% believe that cases like the Guildford Four, Birmingham Six, West Midlands Serious Crime Squad disbandment, and the Wapping 'police riot' are only the 'tip of the iceberg'.

Robert Reiner has suggested that a police state results from five associated trends in policing: centralisation, increasing police powers, militarisation, pervasiveness and de-democratisation. All of these, he says, are occurring in Britain today, but he lays the blame more at the door of the government than the police.

The paradox of a decade of radical right 'Thatcherism' was some 'rolling back of the frontiers of state' in the economic sphere, combined with growing centralisation, control and 'authoritarianism' in the sphere of law and order. As journalist Neal Ascherson put it, 'The trouble about a free market economy is that it requires so many policemen to make it work'. Thus, for example, police numbers rose by 22% between 1974 and 1990, and the cost of policing rose 60% in real terms. Despite this, the 1990 crime figures showed a record 17% rise.

The post-Thatcher government's approach was mixed: on the one hand, it insisted on abolishing defendants' right to silence, but on the other (in the wake of the Birmingham Six case) it set up a Royal Commission to review the whole system of criminal justice in Britain.

Controversy about the nature of policing in Britain is not wholly new: viz. Grosvenor Square (1968), Kevin Gately (1974), Grunwick (1976), Blair Peach

[handwritten marginalia:] but mention Telecomm. Act 1984 · ✓ · ✓ · ✓ · ✓ · ✓ · ✓ · ✓ · ? previous figures? · ✓ · ✓ · (says e.g. John Benyon) · ✓ · good ✓

(A)

(1979) and the controversial Met. Special Patrol Group, etc. However, it is increasing. The safeguards against excessive, arbitrary and illegal policing – through the law, courts, media, politicians and pressure groups – are such that the label 'police state' is not applicable in modern Britain. There are, however, some disturbing trends, the remedies for which lie with Parliament, government and the courts (especially perhaps the Appeal Court) as much as with the police themselves.

10) *Theme* **Pressure groups**

Q? 'Many pressure groups work through political parties, but they can all be clearly distinguished from them.' Discuss.

(London, January 1988, P. 1.)

A✓ **Notes for guidance**

A 'quote – discuss' format requires balanced assessment of every assertion in *every* part of the title. Therefore consider: pressure groups which do and do not work through or with parties; whether links, overlaps and similarities between pressure groups and parties do or do not erase any clear distinctions between them; whether there may be similarities between pressure groups and parties even where they do not work together; and how far generalisations can be made across all pressure groups. Note and stress every little word when reading and re-reading titles: *'Many … work through … but* can *all* be *clearly* distinguished …'.

---

6. Construct an essay around the skeletal plan below.

---

1) Definitions and types of parties and pressure groups; e.g.s …
2) Basic differences between parties and pressure groups.
3) Pressure groups working through parties – e.g.s, methods, links, overlaps and similarities.
4) Pressure groups working independently of parties and vice versa.
5) Differences between pressure groups and parties, with e.g.s.
6) Difficulties of generalising across and among pressure groups and parties – especially large pressure groups and small parties. [Consider: aims, methods, membership, internal organisation, size, resources, power, influence, expertise, links with executive/legislature.]
7) Conclusion: True that many pressure groups work through parties; also vice versa. Often easily distinguished, but title too sweeping; distinctions sometimes very blurred in practice, even where they do not work together as such.

11) *Theme* **Media**

Q? 'The ruling ideas of any age are the ideas of the ruling class' (Marx and Engels). Discuss with reference to the mass media in Britain.

(Cambridge, June 1985, P. 1.)

A✓ **Notes for guidance**

The Marxist argument can be summarised as follows.

Almost all of human history has been a series of class societies, from ancient society (masters and slaves) through feudalism (lords and serfs) to modern capitalism. In all class societies, there are two main classes (as well as many others): a ruling class and a subject class. The ruling class are those who own and control the means of production (i.e. the factories etc.) – in capitalism they are called the bourgeoisie. The subject class are those who own only their labour power (i.e. their ability to work) – in capitalism they are called the proletariat. The bourgeoisie exploit the working class – i.e. they buy their labour and use it to create and extract 'surplus value' in the process of production; this is the source of profit in capitalism. There is therefore an inescapable conflict of interests between the two main classes.

Every class has its own ideology, that is, its own set of ideas which reflect and protect its own class interests. The ideology of the ruling class is by far the dominant ideology in society, because the ruling class own and/or control the means by which ideas are transmitted – the media, education systems, political and legal processes etc. – what Marx called 'the means of mental production'. The personnel of these institutions (politicians, civil servants, etc.) need not be the ruling class as such; but they always and inevitably act as agents of the ruling class, promoting its interests by defending and preserving the existing capitalist system and class hierarchy, by the partial nature and content of the ideas and values which they promote.

Thus 'the ruling ideas of any age are the ideas of the ruling class'. The dominant ideology in capitalism embodies and encourages support for e.g. private property, profit, competition, hierarchy, law and order, patriotism and the national interest, monarchy and parliamentary democracy (which Marx called 'bourgeois dictatorship', because no major party ever seriously threatens the capitalist system).

Marxism predicts the inevitable abolition of all classes through inevitable revolution. Only then will ideology – class-based ideas and values – disappear.

This essay title therefore requires an evaluation of the role of the mass media in Britain – ownership, control and content – in the context of the Marxist class/ideology theory.

Evidence in support of the Marxist argument could include evidence of the exceptionally concentrated nature of media ownership and control in Britain, and a critique of the media's one-sided treatment of issues such as the monarchy, parliamentary democracy, law and order, defence, the Falklands, a national interest, Northern Ireland, property, poverty, trade unions, family, morality, radicalism, socialism and Marxism itself. Good sources are books by the **Glasgow University Media Group**, e.g. *Bad News, More Bad News* and *Really Bad News*; also **Ralph Miliband**, e.g. *The State in Capitalist Society*, *Capitalist Democracy in Britain* and *Marxism and Politics*.

Counter-arguments could be based on the pluralist perspective which stresses the diversity of media in liberal democracies, and denies the existence of any ruling class or 'ruling ideas'. Pluralists would also make a distinction between the party-political bias of the press and the non-party political nature of the broadcasting media. Marxists, however, would not. Interpreting 'the ruling class' as 'the Conservative Party' is much too narrow for Marxist theory, which perceives the Labour Party to be just as much agents of the capitalist system.

12)   *Theme* **A written constitution**

Q?   'The British constitution itself is now an object of political dispute.' Discuss.

(London, January 1985, P. 1.)

A✓   **Short plan for guidance**

1) 'Now' implies used not to be an object of political dispute. Has always been debate about parts of system, e.g. Lords. However, **Philip Norton** says whole constitution only came under critical scrutiny in 1970s when it was no longer seen to be 'delivering the goods' – e.g. economic decline, rise of nationalist sentiment, indeterminate results of 1974 elections.

2) Reforms and changes have been many, but piecemeal: e.g. joining EC, use of referenda, Anglo-Irish agreement, Commons committees, reforms of local government, decline of ministerial responsibility and changing role of civil service, increasing role of pressure groups, and changes within parties e.g. Labour Party rules and procedures. There has not been substantive change: e.g. written constitution, Bill of Rights, devolution, reform of electoral system or Lords.

3) Many (e.g. Norton) see no need for major change because existing arrangements are seen as adequate with minor modifications; governments are unlikely to increase constraints against themselves, and always have higher priorities, e.g. economic policy.

4) However, growing calls for substantive change: e.g. from Hailsham, Scarman, centre parties, nationalist parties, Campaign for Freedom of Information, Charter 88, and sections of Conservative and Labour parties themselves. Norton identifies six distinct approaches to constitutional reform: High Tory (no change), Socialist (party-dominated strong government), Marxist (inevitable revolution), Group or Functionalist (incorporation of interest groups), Liberal (individualist) and Traditionalist (limited reform – pro-strong government).

5) Reasons: perceived 'elective dictatorship', use of royal prerogative, lack of checks and balances within system e.g. weaknesses of Parliament versus executive, Opposition versus government, Cabinet versus PM, local versus central government; perceived politicisation e.g. of judiciary, civil service, church and education; regional inequalities and imbalances, loss of civil liberties, flexibility of constitution.

6) **Conclusion:** Yes.

---

7. Write at least *five* of the following essays.
Always write a brief plan first.

1) How effective are the principal means of rendering the government publicly accountable?

(London, January 1987, P. 1.)

2) 'In theory British government is both representative and responsible; in practice its performance on both counts is lamentable.' Discuss.

(Oxford, Summer 1985, P. 0.)

3) 'The election of a new government has little effect on the leaders of institutions or on the values by which they work.' Assess the accuracy of this statement in relation to the power of social, economic and political elites.

(AEB, June 1987, P. 2.)

4) Since the Second World War the House of Commons has made numerous attempts to improve its capacity to control the executive. How successful have these been?

(JMB, June 1984, P. 1.)

5) What factors determine the nature of the relationship between the Prime Minister and the Cabinet?

(London, January 1991, P. 1.)

6) To what extent have constitutional conventions concerning politicians and civil servants changed over recent years?

(London, June 1989, P. 1.)

7) 'Centralisation, party politics and the power of officials have combined to destroy democracy in local government.' Discuss.

(Oxford, Summer 1984, P. 1.)

8) What is the 'rule of law'? In what conditions does it flourish, and what are the main threats to its existence?

(Oxford and Cambridge, June 1989, P. 0.)

9) 'The fact that British citizens have the right to take complaints against their government to the European Court of Human Rights at Strasbourg removes the need for a British Bill of Rights.' Discuss.

(JMB, June 1986, P. 1.)

10) Assess the effect of pressure group activity on liberal democracy in Britain.

(AEB, November 1986, P. 1.)

11) To what extent are mass party organisations really necessary since the growth of the mass media?

(JMB, June 1986, P. 1.)

12) 'The case for a written constitution has become unanswerable.' Do you agree?

(Oxford, Summer 1990, P. 1.)

—— GUIDE TO EXERCISES

Page 168

1. 1) Sovereignty: Ultimate power.
   2) Parliamentary government: Executive chosen from the legislature and in theory subordinate to it, hence overlap rather than separation of powers.
   3) A 'safe seat': A constituency which one particular party is virtually certain to win.
   4) A private bill: A piece of parliamentary legislation which affects specific individual or group interests rather than the whole general public.
   5) Parliamentary privilege: The exemption of MPs and peers from some ordinary law, under the special laws and customs of Parliament.
   6) The royal prerogative: The powers of the Crown under common law.
   7) Mandate: The right or duty of a government to carry out its manifesto proposals.

8) Minority government: Government with under 50% of the seats in the House of Commons.

9) Coalition government: Government of two or more parties.

10) Cabinet government: Policy-making and responsibility by Cabinet as a collective body.

11) *Ultra vires*: illegal – as when executive bodies are ruled by the courts to have acted beyond their legal powers.

12) Constitutionalism: Advocacy or stance of acting within the limits of a body of accepted political rules and principles.

13) Unconstitutional action: That which breaks the letter or spirit of the constitution, whether in a major or minor way.

14) Anti-constitutional action: That which opposes the whole existing constitution and seeks either to replace or abolish it.

15) Case law: Judge-made law – judicial interpretation of law in a test case, which sets a precedent for future, similar cases.

16) Delegated legislation: Law made by bodies other than Parliament under legislative power passed down by Parliament.

17) Convention: An unwritten, customary rule or practice of the constitution which has no legal force.

18) Civil disobedience: Deliberate, peaceful, public law-breaking as an act of political protest.

19) Civil rights: Entitlements which are granted to members of society by a particular government or state, often by law.

20) Political power: The ability to do, or to make others do something in the public policy-making sphere, by the threat or use of sanctions such as rewards or punishments.

21) Political influence: Persuasive effect on others' ideas or actions by example or authority.

22) Pluralism: Diverse and competing centres of political and economic power.

23) Welfare state: Provision of money, goods and services by the government to those deemed in need.

24) Bureaucracy: Professional administration of any large organisation such as business or government.

25) Devolution: The passing down of legislative, executive or judicial power from central to regional bodies within a state.

Page 168

2. 1) Lord Hailsham.

2) Two possible answers: the Law Lords are not separate from the legislature as supreme court judges are in the USA; and they cannot veto the legislature as they can in the USA.

3) Mrs Thatcher – to describe non-Thatcherite Tories in the Conservative Party such as Pym, Prior and Gilmour.

4) Standing committees scrutinise bills; select committees investigate specific issues of public concern or scrutinise the executive itself.

5) The European Court of Justice in Luxembourg.

6) The Labour Party.

7) £500; 5%.

8) Debates and votes on government bills; Question Time; Opposition Days; departmental select committees; the Ombudsman.

9) A. V. Dicey (1885).

10) (a) Environment; (b) Home office; (c) Agriculture/Health.
11) 1928.
12) 1983.
13) Sir Robert Armstrong (Cabinet Secretary); Charles Powell (PM's Private Secretary); Collette Bowe (Director of Information, Department of Trade and Industry).
14) 'Sarah Tisdall leaked the date of arrival of Cruise missiles in Britain from the USA to *The Guardian* newspaper; Clive Ponting leaked details of the sinking of the Belgrano to Labour MP Tam Dalyell. Only one of them was convicted and imprisoned, namely Sarah Tisdall.'
15) Lord Denning – was advocating the power of judicial veto of parliamentary statutes.

Page 169

3. 1) False – they may be peers in the Lords.
    2) False – a constitution is a body of rules and principles; not just laws, but also conventions etc.
    3) True.
    4) True.
    5) False – the two elements in 'parliamentary government' are the executive and the legislature.
    6) True.
    7) False – they may vote.
    8) True.
    9) False – international courts, such as the European Court of Justice, can challenge the law of Parliament, although no domestic court can do so.
    10) True.
    11) False – all except money bills may be introduced first in the Commons or Lords.
    12) False – Parliament may pass retrospective law.
    13) True – for treason, and arson in Her Majesty's dockyards.
    14) False – a 'joint committee' is one comprising members of both the Commons and the Lords.
    15) True.
    16) True.
    17) False – only Conservative MPs elect the Conservative Party leader.
    18) False – the 'ten o'clock adjournment' is an opportunity for debate on topics chosen by backbenchers.
    19) False – cabinet committees may include civil servants, outside experts etc.
    20) False – the Ombudsman is a permanent, non-elected official attached to Parliament.

Page 169

4. ● **Note**   These examples should be updated wherever more recent and significant examples are available.

    1) The Paving Bill 1984; War Crimes Bill 1990; Statutory Sick Pay Bill 1991.
    2) Ex-PMs e.g. Douglas-Home, Wilson; Law Lords e.g. Scarman; businessmen e.g. Lord Williams of Elvel.
    3) 1987 figures of votes versus seats for all main parties (see Chapter 3).

4) No government since 1935 has had an absolute majority of votes cast; many votes are wasted; independents are disadvantaged.

5) Sunday shopping 1986; three-line whip on Richard Shepherd's secrecy bill 1989; freezing of child benefit 1990.

6) Sidney Silverman's Abolition of Capital Punishment 1965; David Steel's Abortion Act 1967; Shepherd Bill 1989.

7) Neil Kinnock (TGWU); John Prescott (National Union of Seamen); Dennis Skinner (National Union of Mineworkers).

8) During the 1960s and 1970s the two main parties shared similar stances on economic policy, welfare and nuclear weapons.

9) In the early 1980s the two main parties disagreed on economic policy, welfare and nuclear weapons.

10) Over 90% of MPs are Labour or Conservative; the constitution recognises only 'Her Majesty's Government' and 'Her Majesty's Opposition'; parliamentary procedures such as pairing and Opposition Days.

11) Nine parties in Parliament; 23% voted for Alliance in 1987; regional differences in party strengths, e.g. in Scotland.

12) Home Affairs Select Committee report on hard drugs encouraged government action; Foreign Affairs Select Committee won right to see the 'Crown Jewels' – secret documents about the sinking of the Belgrano; Agriculture Committee insisted on questioning Edwina Currie over the salmonella in eggs scare.

13) Brian Sedgemore on Johnson Matthey Bank (1986) helped to produce criminal convictions; Dale Campbell-Savours (1987) on the 'Spycatcher' affair; Geoffrey Dickens (1986) on alleged child abuse by private individuals.

14) EC e.g. on equal retirement ages for men and women; pressure groups e.g. the Bar on reforms of legal profession 1989; media e.g. on football hooliganism.

15) PM policy decisions are said to include: nuclear weapons; Falklands; abolition of GLC; Westland; bombing of Libya; poll tax, etc.

16) Cabinet policy decisions are said to include: refusal to discuss 1982 Think Tank report on NHS reform; refusal to lift rent controls 1986; refusal to sell British Leyland to General Motors 1987; refusal to introduce school vouchers 1987–8.

17) Resignation of Sir Geoffrey Howe over Britain's stance on EC 1990; resignation of government after vote of no confidence in 1979; Heseltine over Westland 1986.

18) Leon Brittan over Westland 1986; Edwina Currie over the salmonella in eggs scare 1988; Nicholas Ridley over remarks in press interview 1990.

19) Advisers to Thatcher: Lord Derek Rayner (Marks and Spencer), Sir Robin Ibbs (ICI); to Major: Sarah Hogg (financial journalist).

20) Westland; poll tax; role in Cabinet committees such as PSIS.

21) Public Records Act 1958 (thirty-year rule); Official Secrets Act 1989; D-Notice system. Plus Tisdall, Ponting, 'Spycatcher'.

22) Cost of litigation; GCHQ ruling and Local Government Act 1987 said to place government above the law; 'sus' laws.

23) Local Government Act 1987, Official Secrets Act 1989, Criminal Justice Act 1991; case law in GLC 'Fares Fair', Ponting and GCHQ cases.

24) Tisdall, Ponting, GCHQ and trade union cases.

25) *Ultra vires* rulings: Okehampton by-pass, board and lodging allowance cuts, Ridley versus GLC, Young versus Lambeth on poll tax capping 1990.

26) Greenham Common women, Committee of a Hundred's refusal to pay poll tax, Greenpeace protests e.g. on Nelson's Column.

27) Miners' strike 1984–5, Stonehenge 1985, Wapping 1986.
28) Animal rights groups – from posters to bombs; CND demos; NFU meeting Agriculture Minister, e.g. 37 times in 1988.
29) Food safety 1988–9; environmental awareness 1988–9; Gulf War.
30) Creation of departmental select committees 1979; Anglo-Irish Agreement 1985; abolition of GLC and Mets; poll tax; Education Act 1988 (gave 366 new powers to Secretary of State for Education); new secrecy and security service laws 1989; EC 'single market' 1992; changing conventions e.g. decline of collective responsibility.

Page 170

Stimulus response question – suggested answer (note form).

1) (a) Scottish Nationalist Party.
   (b) Plaid Cymru.
2) (a) Minority Labour Government under Harold Wilson (with fewer votes than Conservatives).
   (b) Labour Government under Wilson with small majority of three seats (which was lost by 1977).
3) (a) 'Elective dictatorship' (Hailsham, 1976) implies strong majority executive in effective control of sovereign Parliament, with a flexible constitution – usually on minority vote – but virtually unassailable between elections.
   (b) 1974 elections results produced either minority government or one with a very small majority, which would suggest weak executive; nevertheless, Hailsham asserted 'elective dictatorship' against 1976 Labour government.
4) Bill of Rights:
   Case against: Power of interpretation and enforcement would be in the hands of judges who may be unrepresentative, unaccountable and conservative; it would be hard to reconcile individual/collective or minority/majority rights; every Bill of Rights has a 'get-out' clause which may render it worthless.

   Case for: Risk of 'elective dictatorship' of strong government in sovereign Parliament with flexible constitution, and lack of checks and balances in system; constitution and power of government resting largely on conventions – needs legal limits and safeguards; UK already signatory of European Convention – would be more logical and efficient to incorporate it into British law; growing constraints on civil liberties, e.g. police and public order laws, secrecy and constraints on media, Northern Ireland, changes in British criminal justice system, e.g. decline of jury trial, Clause 28 etc. On balance, case for is stronger.
5) Could disagree because: there have been limited reforms of Lords, e.g. 1949, 1958, 1963; devolution only just failed in 1979; and there is growing pressure for various reforms across all parties and from groups such as Charter 88 and the Scottish Convention.
   However, agree because: past reform very limited; neither major party advocates electoral reform or a Bill of Rights; Labour does advocate devolution and reform of Lords, but would need a large swing in the vote to win power at next election; main advocates of constitutional reform (centre parties) have declined in strength since 1988; and when the time comes, no government is keen to increase constraints against itself; and all governments have higher priorities, e.g. economic policy.

12   Countdown to the Exam

```
╭─────────────────────────────────────────────╮
│                                             │
│   KEY POINTS                                │
│                                             │
│   ▶  Before the exam                        │
│      How to revise                          │
│      Just before the exam                   │
│                                             │
│   ▶  In the exam                            │
│                                             │
│   ▶  After the exam                         │
│                                             │
╰─────────────────────────────────────────────╯
```

── BEFORE THE EXAM

How to revise

Revising ('seeing again') means **reviewing** the topics, **reorganising** your information in a relevant and useful way and **rethinking** the issues and arguments as required by the exam. Like all study, it should *not* be passive note-cramming, but active exam preparation and practice. For Politics A Level you should start revising about six weeks before the exam, even if you are still doing new work on the course itself.

● First, check the exact **dates** of your exams.
● If you have not already done so (see Chapter 1), write a list – in logical order – of the **topics** which you must cover for the exam. Use your syllabus for guidance, and ask your teacher to check it. Organise your files according to the topic list, with separate sections or pockets for each topic, clearly labelled.
● Devise a **weekly timetable** for the six weeks leading up to the exam, showing when each topic is to be revised. Do *not* do only as many topics as there are essay questions to be answered! The examiners often cover two or three topics in one question; and your favourite topic may come up in the form of a difficult question, or not at all. If you have four questions to answer on one paper, do at least eight or nine topics in depth, and do not wholly neglect the others. Look very carefully through past exam questions for any topic/theme patterns.
● At the beginning of each new week, devise a **daily timetable** for the rest of that week. This should show everything you plan to do: the different balance of time on different topics, depending on your own preferences and weak areas; methods of revision, e.g. noting/timed essays/stimulus questions/current events; other subjects and exams to be revised; eating, sleeping and leisure. Make it realistic and flexible – do not aim to start revising at 8 a.m. if you are a night person. Plan for short, but frequent and productive sessions of work; the sense of achievement is greater as you tick off more tasks done.

SUBJECT	POLITICS	ENGLISH	F
25.4			
2.5			
9.5			
16.5			
23.5			
30.5			

POLITICS REVISION TIMETABLE

25.4
Marxism
Western socialism
Conservatism
Liberalism
Democracy

2.5
British constitution
House of Lords
Electoral systems
MPs
The parties; the party system; the two-party system
House of Commons

9.5
Monarchy
P.M. and Cabinet
Civil service
Local government

16.5
Autocracy, authoritarianism and absolutism
Totalitarianism
Nationalism
Racialism
Fascism and Nazism

23.5
Pressure groups
Judiciary and law and order
Rights and freedoms

30.5
Anarchism
Feminism
Varieties of communism
Overview

Paper 1: Friday June 10th. a.m.

Paper 3: Thursday June 16th. p.m.

Revising is sometimes tedious, and often requires willpower. When the TV beckons or the telephone tempts you, imagine the day when you will be sitting in front of the exam paper itself, or the day of the results. Remember that the constant choice between success or failure is now yours alone. It is not you versus teachers or parents; it is you versus the exam – so win! It is better to be working and fed-up with it than not working and guilt-ridden or panic-stricken about it.

WEEK 25/4

	MON	TUES	WED	THURS	FRI	SAT	SUN
7.00	Sleep	Sleep	Sleep	Z z	z z z	z z z	zzzz
8.00	Up	→	→	→	→	Sleep	Sleep
9.00	Current events		Current events	Philos.	Eng.	Up	Up
10.00	Marxism Ⓝ	Eng.	Review pol.	Philos.	Eng.	Current events	
11.00	Eng.	Review pol.	Philos.			Dem. Ⓔ	Eng.
12.00	Eng.	W. Soc. Ⓝ/Ⓢ	Philos.	Eng.	Review pol.	Philos.	Eng.
1.00	Lunch						→
2.00	Marxism Ⓢ/Ⓟ	W. Soc. Ⓟ/Ⓔ		Eng.	Dem Ⓝ		Review pol.
3.00	Marxism Ⓔ		Eng.	Eng.	Dem. Ⓝ	Philos.	Review pol.
4.00		Eng.	Cons. Ⓝ/Ⓢ	Review pol.	Dem. Ⓢ/Ⓟ	Philos.	Review pol.
5.00			Cons. Ⓔ/Ⓟ	Lib. Ⓝ			
6.00	Dinner						→
7.00		Philos.	Out	Lib. Ⓢ	Out	Out	Philos.
8.00	Philos.	Philos.		Lib./Cons. Ⓟ/Ⓔ			Philos.
9.00	Philos.						Philos.
10.00							

Ⓝ = Notes Ⓢ = Short answers Ⓟ = Plans Ⓔ = Essays

See Chapter 1 for points on study skills, hints on factual learning, note-taking, essay-writing and exam techniques. Write your own 'do's' and 'don'ts' list for a trouble-free exam programme.

Find a good, quiet, comfortable place to work – *not* in front of the TV! Be honest: is your environment helping you to study or providing welcome distractions? Look after yourself in the weeks leading up to the exam and stay healthy (see Chapter 1), at least until the post-exam celebrations.

PEANUTS®

By Charles M. Schulz

Start each revision session with something easy, routine and confidence-building, such as reviewing a checklist of basic facts, definitions or examples from the previous session. Then:

- Take out the notes on that day's topic and keep them in a separate folder while revising (you will find it is less daunting that way). Sort them into a logical order, and throw away any dross;
- Go thoroughly through a list of all past questions on the topic. Jot down the four or five recurring 'angles' on the topic and keep a constant look-out for points relevant to each angle as you read around the topic. Always read, note, learn and test yourself with an eye to past exam questions, to ensure relevant answers. If you try to learn chunks of material verbatim, you will recite them in the same way, they will be irrelevant to the question, and you will fare badly;

ASK YOUR TEACHER FOR COPIES OF
PAST EXAMINERS' REPORTS

- Try to condense each topic to a one-sheet note summary of key essay angles and related terms, concepts and definitions, facts and dates, names, arguments, quotations and examples. Actively re-organise your material to suit your needs. Skim and dip-read critically; weigh up issues, assertions, opinions and evidence in your own mind;
- Go through your current events diary (see Chapter 1) and rewrite lists of key examples under topic headings.

Most important

Do a comprehensive sample of past questions (of all types in your exam) on each topic: short answers, stimulus questions, essay plans, timed essays. Be ruthless on timed work; do not get into the habit of going even slightly over time. Do not do all the easy titles, or those you have done well before. When you come across a problem title, ask your teacher about it, then try a brief plan and have it checked.

Work hard on the different timing and techniques required by different types of questions. Look critically over your own past work – read it aloud and listen to the wording and style, correct factual errors, write in missing facts and examples, and ask your teacher what you need to do to go up one grade.

Decide your own chosen stance on every key angle of every topic at this stage, not in the exam itself. How should Parliament be improved, and why? Are you going to opt for PR or not? What kind of PR and why? Are you going to say that Britain has Prime Ministerial government or not? What reforms would you suggest and why? Do you advocate a Bill of Rights – why/not? (Review Chapters 2–11 for the key issues and angles on each topic.)

You should occasionally attempt a full mock exam. If not coerced into it, volunteer – your teacher should be ecstatic! Remember that it does not matter how badly you do; with practice, the next effort, and the exam itself, will be better.

Assess your own weaknesses and aim to eliminate them one by one.

?	Factual learning	✓
?	Essay planning	✗
?	Structure	✗
?	Relevance	✓
?	Argument	✓
?	Evidence	✗
?	Timing	✗
?	Handwriting	✓
?	Waffle	✓

When you get very bored, read the paper or a weekly journal such as the *New Statesman* or *Economist*, watch the TV news or *Spitting Image* and brush up on current events!

Just before the exam

- Carefully check the time and place of your exams. If you have never been there, try an advance visit to locate the place and check how long the journey will take at that time of day.
- If you fall ill or have any kind of accident or upset, tell your school or college immediately. Even if you sit the exam, they may think it appropriate to notify the exam board, and special consideration may be given in the marking of your script. <u>Do not wait until after the exam before saying that you were not on top form.</u>
- On the day before the exam, lay out all necessities – clothes (check the weather forecast), good pens, rulers, watch, tissues, sweets etc. NO correcting fluid – it will probably be confiscated anyway. Decide your own exam timetable in advance – timing and order of answers, whether you are going to do a compulsory question first or an easy/difficult essay question first etc. (hence mock exam practice).

—— IN THE EXAM

- Synchronise your watch with the clock in the exam hall.

TIME YOURSELF RUTHLESSLY

- Breathe deeply; aim for cool, calm, concentration. Ignore everything around you: clicking pens, jangling bracelets, hysterics and all.
- Read the rubric, and follow it.
- Pick your titles, but then read them all once more, slowly, word for word – you may have chosen a nasty title on your pet topic, and neglected a much better title. Do not start an essay and then change your mind half-way through: that will waste too much precious time.
- Keep referring back to the title constantly, especially before you write the conclusion.
- If panic or memory-failure threatens, move on to something else.
- Do not try to fool the examiner with invented quotations, half-finished answers, and illegible scrawl when you've forgotten how to spell a name – they know all the tricks!

- Try very hard to balance your timing across all questions. The example below shows that a good first answer cannot compensate for a bad final answer. If you mistime, do the last question in brief, detailed note form with an explicit conclusion. Do not write half an essay.

Student A	Student B
19	15
15	14
9	12
4	12
47%	53%

- If you have spare time at the end, do read over your work and make amendments; even if messy, they will gain marks. Do not stare into space and do *not* walk out, no matter how keen you are to get away – every available moment is precious.
- If you feel ill during the exam, tell the invigilator (supervisor) at the time, even if you stay to complete the exam.

—— AFTER THE EXAM

Most students prefer to avoid detailed post-mortems on the exam and everything they might have said but did not. Instead, now is the time to reflect on how much you have gained from studying politics, besides an A Level: political gumption, critical acumen, sound knowledge of current events and issues, and the satisfaction that you can have topical and philosophical arguments with parents and friends, and win.

This should not arise, but if the exam result is not good, you may want to ask the exam board for a report or re-mark. Usually this must be done through your school or college, according to the board's regulations and procedures; discuss it with your teacher as soon as possible.

If you have worked through this book thoroughly you should not need it, but – good luck!

Recommended Reading

General

David Childs, *Britain Since 1945: A Political History* (Methuen, 1986).
A chronological survey of political events and administrations since the war, up to 1985. A good reference book even for students of purely contemporary politics. (See also Sked and Cook.)

P. G. Cocker, *Government and Politics: Essential Topics for Examinations* (Checkmate/ Arnold, 1986).
A topic-based book for A Level students, concise and well-ordered, with self-assessment questions at the end of each chapter.

Glasgow University Media Group, *Bad News* (Routledge and Kegan Paul, 1976), *More Bad News* (Routledge and Kegan Paul, 1980), and *Really Bad News* (Writers and Readers, 1982).
A series of radical, and readable, critiques of media bias based on empirical data.

Bill Jones (ed.), *Political Issues in Britain Today* (Manchester University Press, 1987).
A concise, balanced and well-ordered outline of key political issues in the fields of policy, economics, institutions, defence and law and order.

Bill Jones and Dennis Kavanagh, *British Politics Today* (Manchester University Press, 1989).
A short book of well-ordered, concise notes under numbered headings on key topics and issues.

L. J. Macfarlane, *Issues in British Politics Since 1945* (Longman, 1986).
A short survey of key political issues with a historical slant, including international events and institutions such as the Falklands and EC.

Ralph Miliband, *The State in Capitalist Society* (Quartet, 1969).
A classic Marxist analysis of the British state and politics.

R. K. Mosley, *British Government and Politics* (published by the author, 1974 onwards).
An annual survey of current political events and issues in booklet form. Strongly recommended.

Philip Norton, *The Constitution in Flux* (Basil Blackwell, 1982).
A classic analysis of key political issues such as reform of Parliament, Prime Ministerial government and a Bill of Rights. Weighty – not introductory reading, but excellent for essays.

Alan Renwick and Ian Swinburn, *Basic Political Concepts* (Hutchinson, 1987).
A well-written and topical book on key political concepts such as power and authority, order and disorder, rights and representation. Good introductory reading; simple without being simplistic.

Alan Sked and Chris Cook, *Post-War Britain: A Political History* (Penguin, 1984).
A survey of post-war administrations since 1945 (to 1983), one chapter per government.

D. Stephenson, *British Government and Politics* (Longman, 1987).
A study guide for A Level students with potted notes on key topics and issues, recent exam questions and outline answers.

Specific issues

Lord Denning, 'Misuse of Power' (Dimbleby Lecture, 1980).
A controversial plea for judicial power over Parliament: 'Someone must be trusted. Let it be the judges'. Discuss!

J. A. G. Griffith, *The Politics of the Judiciary* (Fontana, 1985).
A classic, critical thesis of a 'political' judiciary, with a mass of empirical evidence.

Lord Hailsham, 'Elective Dictatorship' (The Dimbleby Lecture) in *The Listener*, 21.10.76.
A classic thesis of overweening executive power in modern Britain.

H. Young and A. Sloman, *No, Minister: An Inquiry into the Civil Service* (BBC Books, 1982).
An outdated but short, readable and revealing inside look at the relationships between ministers and civil servants in the 60s and 70s.

Journals

Contemporary Record
Journal of the Institute of Contemporary British History; articles combine historical and contemporary perspectives on politics. Published quarterly.

Politics Review
Excellent compilation of articles on key issues by writers such as Drewry, Madgwick, Norton and Zander; summaries of political and parliamentary affairs; examiners' comments on students' essay answers and on exam techniques etc. Readable and well-presented. Five issues each academic year.

Talking Politics
Began Autumn 1988, produced by the Politics Association. Three issues each year. Some useful articles by writers such as Kavanagh and Norton.

Reference books

The Fontana Dictionary of Modern Thought (1987).
The Penguin Dictionary of Politics (1985).
Roger Scruton, *A Dictionary of Political Thought* (Pan, 1983).

Index